LIVING *choices*

Create the home to suit your needs

BBC BOOKS

The Open University Community Education Department

produced in asociation with

**GOOD
HOUSEKEEPING**

with major sponsorship from

I▾I

MERCANTILE CREDIT

This book accompanies the BBC/Open University television series
Living Choices, first broadcast on BBC2 from April 1989.

Published as part of The Open University Community Education pack
P935 *Living Choices*.

Published by BBC Books, a division of BBC Enterprises Ltd, Woodlands,
80 Wood Lane, London W12 0TT

in conjunction with The Open University, Walton Hall, Milton Keynes
MK7 6AA.

First published 1989

Copyright © 1989 The Open University

All rights reserved. No part of this publication may be reproduced,
stored in a retrieval system or transmitted, in any form or by any means,
without written permission from the publisher.

Designed by the Graphic Design Group of The Open University.

Typeset by The Open University. Printed and bound in Great Britain by
Mackays of Chatham PLC , Chatham, Kent. Colour separations by Dot
Gradations Ltd, Chelmsford. Colour printed by Chorley & Pickersgill
Ltd, Leeds. Cover printed by Fletchers of Norwich.

ISBN 0 563 20724 8

CONTENTS

The Open University Course Team

Course chair: Monica Darlington

Course team: Simon Baines, Janice Dale, Mick Jones, Cassandra Kent *(Good Housekeeping)*, Aude Leonetti, Bill Mathieson.

Secretarial and materials development support:

Teresa Adams, Linda Johns, Claire Mahoney *(Good Housekeeping)*, Sandi Millar, Jan Smith

Library support: Joan Carty

Consultants: Maggie Boxer, Tim Stout

BBC producer: Alison Tucker

Editor: Julie Bennett

Designer: Sian Lewis

Cover designer: Lesley Passey

Critical readers: Graham Atherton, Philip Bell, Ann Brechin, Julian Edwards, Pat Hutchinson, Sam Miskelly, Jill Moore, Pat Waring, Helena Wiesner

External assessor: Ann Maree Rees

Director of Community Education: David Howie

Acknowledgements

We wish to thank the following organisations for permission to use their material in this book.

Text

Consumers' Association, publishers of *Which?* 48, 150, 154

The Birmingham Settlement 126

The Research Institute for Consumer Affairs 149, 150

Signs and Labels Ltd: artwork for hazard symbols 148

Photographs

Mike Levers/The Open University Cover (main picture), 5 (left), 6, 7, 8, 10, 2, 20, 26, 31, 33, 35, 36, 38, 39, 40, 43, 44, 45, 46, 49, 50, 51, 52, 53, 54, 55, 56, 58, 68, 69, 70, 71, 76, 79, 81, 82, 83, 85, 88, 90, 92, 93, 94, 95, 103, 104, 106, 107, 108, 109, 111, 112, 114, 116, 118, 119, 123, 124, 126, 129, 130, 131, 132, 133, 134, 135, 136, 137, 139, 144, 154, 156, 157, 160, 163, 165

BBC 51 (top), 56 (top), 135 (top right, bottom left), 78

Consumers' Association 19, 23, 29, 127, 145, 146, 150, 152, 161, 162

Creative Company Cover (small pictures), 9, 14

Helen Darlington 5 (right), 77, 86

Keep Able Ltd 121

Neighbourhood Energy Action 142

Pegler Ltd 140

Photographers' Library 57, 74

RoSPA 147

Scottish Tourist Board 11, 16, 27

This book is about homes. Its aim is to help you to choose the one which will suit you best, to make good use of space in it, to equip it so that you can get necessary jobs done efficiently and to run it as you want. In short, it should help you to make the right living choices.

YOU AND YOUR HOME

The people who read this book will be very different from one another and have different needs. Some of you will be just starting out, setting up a first home of your own, with a lot of ideas and possibly very few resources to realise those ideas. Some of you will be established in your own homes and considering a change — perhaps a major one, such as setting up home with someone else, or having children. Some of you will be on your own; others members of households of several people, probably including children. You might want to change your home because you have too little or too much space. You may be well on in life and have some spare money to devote to improving your home. You might be thinking about moving to a smaller place because you no longer need so much accommodation, or because your lifestyle or resources have changed.

Whatever stage of life you've reached, there should be something in this book to help you make plans to suit you.

WHAT THIS BOOK COVERS

This is a practical book, which will help you to make real decisions about your home. While you will be able to use it to make plans for change, it *doesn't* cover the detail of putting these plans into practice — actually designing a new set of shelves, choosing which colours to paint your kitchen, deciding on furnishings to fit your rooms or working out precisely how to install double glazing. There are plenty of other books and magazines around which will give you guidance on how to carry out these tasks. This book *will* help you to balance all the different demands, find out about the options open to you and come to a reasonable decision with which you can feel happy.

A STUDY PACK

This book, *Living Choices*, is complete and free-standing in itself. It also forms the main part of a pack of learning materials with the same name. This has been produced by the Department of Community Education at The Open University. The other components of the pack are

■ A study guide which has additional study information, further reading and resource listings and suggestions for group use of the study pack.

■ Two C60 audiocassettes which contain further examples of a whole range of choices people have made, including the way they have dealt with problems, such as debt of different kinds.

■ Supplementary booklets on how to study, both on your own and in groups; how to find and use information; lists of useful organisations.

■ Four 25-minute television programmes which are being transmitted regularly on BBC2; these programmes have case studies which show different ways of living and organising your home. The programmes will also be available on a VHS videocassette.

Transmission times for the television programmes can be found in the *Radio Times* or your daily newspaper. These programmes will be broadcast twice yearly with repeats.

For further details and information on ordering the *Living Choices* study pack and other Open University Community Education courses and packs write to Learning Materials Services Office (LMSO), The Open University, P.O. Box 188, Milton Keynes MK7 6DH.

HOW DOES THIS BOOK WORK?

This book is probably different from others that you've read about home-making. Instead of telling you what you should — or shouldn't — do about your home, it suggests ways in which you can look at different possibilities, sort out your priorities and make your own decisions.

ACTIVITIES

There are lots of activities for you to work through, checklists of points for you to use and suggestions as to how you might put things into practice. The activities are picked out from the text with their own special headings, and with the type in blue, like this paragraph. When you see this type of heading you should work through the activity and make notes, or write things down somewhere. We suggest that you keep a notebook, or file of these notes, as you may well want to come back to them later. Besides these specific note- or list-making activities, there are other points in the text where you'll be asked about particular issues, your experiences and your ideas, without necessarily having to write them down.

Taking a fresh look at your home and the way you use it, and planning changes, is a complicated process with far-reaching consequences. You will obviously need to consult with other people in your household if there are any. You can do this either by discussing things with them, or by getting them to do the activities as well, if they wish. The more you can involve the other people who share your home in decisions, the better the solutions will be for everyone. This is particularly important in view of the changes in roles in families in recent years. Particular jobs are no longer reserved for particular members of the household. Men don't necessarily go out to work and come home at six o'clock to sit down to meals which have been prepared by women who have spent most of the day engaged in housework, or even the other way round. Jobs are now shared on a much more equal basis — decisions should be shared in the same way.

MAKING THE BEST USE OF THIS BOOK

At the beginning of this introduction it was acknowledged that the people who read this book will be very different, and have different housing needs. These differences will mean that you use the book in different ways. You will find that you concentrate on one particular section, rather than another, according to what will be most useful and of greatest interest to you just now. Other sections

may be more relevant to your particular situation in the future. Just as an example, you might be wondering whether or not to move to another home. The first chapter of this book, **Choosing Your Home,** will obviously be of prime interest to you; you could then go on to work your way through the other chapters. You might decide that making better use of the space you've got is most important, in which case you should concentrate on chapter two, **Organising Space**. Chapter three, **Equipping Your Home,** looks at a whole range of household tasks and offers suggestions to help you choose how to carry them out. If you are primarily interested in getting housework done efficiently and making wise buys in household equipment, then you should spend most time on this chapter. The last chapter, **Running Your Home,** aims at helping you to decide which jobs need doing most urgently and how you should set

about getting them done. You will probably need to work through this chapter whatever your circumstances, since virtually everyone has to make decisions of this kind about their homes from time to time. At the end of chapter four there is a section entitled **What To Do If Things Go Wrong.** While it may be worthwhile reading this section the first time you work through the book, the advice will be more important to you when problems actually arise and you need to know what your rights are, or are wondering to whom you should complain.

HOW THIS BOOK WAS PRODUCED

This book is the product of collaboration between Community Education at The Open University and *Good Housekeeping* magazine. It has also drawn on the experience of consumer educators from all over the United Kingdom, as well as being read and tested out by a range of individuals, families and groups. The course team would like to thank all those who contributed to the development of this book and the other learning materials with their criticisms, comments and useful suggestions; Marian Lever and the Strathclyde Open Learning Experiment groups were particularly helpful. We would also like to thank the Consumers' Association, publishers of *Which?*, for all their help, and for allowing us to quote from and draw upon their reports.

CHOOSING YOUR HOME

Your home isn't just a place where you sleep and eat. What does 'home' mean to you? People who were asked this question mentioned 'security', 'a safe place', 'a place which shows the world what I'm like', 'a place for me to recharge my batteries', 'an investment', 'somewhere to relax', 'a worrisome burden', 'a place I can call my own'. So homes are not just bricks and mortar. People have strong feelings about the places where they live, their emotions are aroused by them — for example, when their homes are threatened in some way. And moving home is acknowledged by psychologists to be a major life event which can, if you're unlucky, cause a great deal of stress. So choosing 'the right place to live' is a very important decision.

This first chapter of *Living Choices* is about choosing the home that suits you. Perhaps you are planning a move in the near future. You may be perfectly happy with where you live at the moment, but think that a time will come when you will need a change. You might be wondering if it's worth extending your present home or making changes to the layout. You will almost certainly be worried about whether you are making the right decision and be wondering what you can afford.

This chapter is divided into six parts. Each part deals with a different stage in the process of considering how you can make your home fit your needs. Working your way through these six stages will help you to be sure that you've considered the choices available from all possible angles as well as showing you how worthwhile it can be to use a systematic approach to making important decisions.

The home you'd like

You probably dream about your ideal home — but need it only be a dream? And how often do you do some hard thinking about what you really need in a home? Have you considered the importance of your home's location and how much it contributes to how you feel about your home? What sort of area and facilities would best suit you and those you share your home with? The first stage in tackling any change is to take time to consider your needs carefully.

Taking stock

The next step is to review how well your current home fits the bill. You may find that it suits you very well. But if there are a lot of things or even some aspects you'd like to change, then you'll want to consider what choices you have.

Looking at choices

There are broadly three possible ways of making your home fit your needs more effectively. You can

- change the way you use your home
- adapt your current home in some way, by converting or extending it
- move to another home which will suit you better.

So **Looking at choices** encourages you to consider how each of these possibilities might help you in your situation.

Finding out more

By the time you've reached this point you will have some ideas about the sort of change you'd like to make. But what can you afford? You'll need to take a close look at your financial resources and commitments. If you are going to have to borrow money, then you want to be sure that you choose the way of doing it which is best for you. You'll need to make sure you've found out enough about possible places to move to, so that you are able to make a fully informed decision.

Making your choice

This is where you actually compare the different possibilities which are realistic — and affordable — for you. There are ideas here for decision-making techniques you could use which will help you to handle a lot of different bits of information, yet leave you confident that all the needs of all the people involved have been taken into consideration.

Making plans

Now that you've come to some sort of decision about your home and how you might change it, you need to make your ideas happen. To do this in a way which is best for all concerned you will have to plan ahead. So the last part of chapter one suggests ways of making detailed plans and timetables so that the change you want to make is under your control.

THE CASE STUDY FAMILIES

As you work your way through this chapter you'll find references from time to time to some typical people who are all considering a move. Here is some background information about them, to help you to understand why they made some of the decisions they did.

Raj and **Satpal,** who are 22 and 20 respectively, are expecting their first baby. Raj is a fitter with reasonably steady prospects. Satpal does not have a paid job at the moment. They are currently living in a one-bedroomed council flat and are desperate for more space, and they would like to move before the baby comes. They would prefer a house with a garden as both would like to grow vegetables.

Sue is 35, divorced, a college lecturer. Currently living in a privately rented one-bedroomed flat, she would like more space and wants to invest in a home of her own. She can afford to buy and is fed up with paying rent.

Clive and **Toinette** are 30 and 31, with two young sons aged five and three. Their council flat doesn't seem to give them enough space, and there are various things about their neighbourhood they aren't very keen on. But as they are both unemployed they are uncertain what changes they can actually make, since their financial resources are very limited.

Philip and **Molly** are both retired people in their late sixties. Their children are grown up and have left home, and Philip and Molly would like a home which is smaller and easier to run than the rambling five-bedroomed semi they own at the moment. They are particularly worried about Molly's arthritis and her difficulties with stairs and getting about generally.

Rick and **Penny** are in their forties and have two children, Adam (14) and Kate (10). Rick is an administrator and Penny a secretary — both their jobs seem secure. They would like to move to a larger home (four bedrooms instead of three) with a bigger garden.

Working through this chapter

Depending on your circumstances, you may decide not to work in detail through every stage outlined in this chapter. You might, for instance, look carefully at the first couple of stages, come to some initial decisions, read the rest of the chapter and then move on to another chapter in the book. You can always come back to the parts of the chapter that you haven't looked through in detail. The notes and lists you've made when working through the chapter now will be particularly useful when you come back to it in the future. So it's important to make these as full as possible and keep them in a safe place until you need them again.

Most of us have some ideas about the home of our dreams — the place where we'd live if we had enough money ... could move to the country ... could find a job in an area we like. Where do these ideas come from? It might be from someone else's home, a programme we've seen on television, somewhere seen on holiday, a house glimpsed from the top of a bus or something entirely different. But although we may have fantasies about living in some kind of dream home, we don't usually take the time to think through this vision in any great detail. Here is an opportunity to do just that. It won't be a waste of time. Besides being enjoyable, it will get you thinking about different kinds of homes, why you like some and dislike others, why you'd prefer to live in one kind of location rather than another and so on.

CHOOSE YOUR IDEAL HOME

Below is a short list of examples of different ideal homes. On a separate sheet of paper, or in a notebook, describe your own ideal home, its immediate surroundings and location. Add as much detail as you like and make a brief note of the reason for your choice. This could, for example, be something like 'Converted lighthouse, set in wild unspoilt scenery, on a coast in a remote part of the country. This would appeal to me because I would be far from the dirt and noise of the town and always within sight and sound of the sea.' Don't restrict yourself too much — this is your opportunity to write out your dreams. Talk to other people in your household, if there are any, about their dreams and fantasies regarding homes. You could show them your list, and get them to make a similar one.

There are some examples from people who helped to develop these materials listed below.

Dreaming about different kinds of homes and settings shquld have been enjoyable. But is it all fantasy? Would it be possible to achieve some, if not all, aspects of your dream home?

Think a bit more about the images you've conjured up and see if you can summarise your ideal home. What is the building like? What surrounds it? Whereabouts is it?

The building	Its surroundings	The location
Very old listed property	Huge garden with room to grow vegetables, flowers, fruit trees	Quiet village within reach of modern amenities
Labour-saving bungalow with all mod cons	Small low-maintenance garden, secluded, with sheltered space to sit out in	Quiet suburb of town with good shops
Houseboat which could be moved to different moorings whenever I wanted	Quiet mooring with electricity and other amenities	Would vary according to where I want to be
Fantastic, space-age home with latest technology	Must have swimming pool, tennis courts etc.	The top of a hill or mountain with fantastic views in every direction

THE HOME YOU NEED

The other way to start thinking about your home is gradually to build up a picture by working through your needs. Very few of us are able to live in a home which is ideal for all our needs. To do that you'd probably need unlimited resources, and the ideal home would actually have to exist in the place where you wanted to live. But it should be possible to work out something which will do the best possible job, given the limits of your resources. This might be the home you have now, with minor or major changes, or it might be another home. In that case, you can use the list of rooms and features you've decided you need as the basis for the specification for a new home.

Some of the people who helped to prepare these materials were aware that their choice of homes was so restricted as to be virtually non-existent. They were council tenants on low incomes with very few chances to make changes to their buildings. This meant that improving their immediate surroundings and the quality of their lives were the only kinds of change open to them and thus extremely important. They found that by joining a tenants' group, working to clean up their streets, improving childcare facilities and other group activities they were able to make really big changes to their local areas. They emphasised the importance of talking to local decision-makers, such as town counsellors and getting publicity for their ideas and opinions.

Raj and Satpal's ideal is a self-built house by the sea, with an orchard and large garden. This ideal is not possible for them yet. But thinking about it has shown Raj that what he would really like to do is to convert or extend a house to try out various layouts and building techniques. This gives Raj and Satpal the idea of looking for an older house with a large garden which they could convert to their own requirements. This plan will, of course, have to wait a few years.

Making a note of the reasons why certain ideas appeal to you should have got you thinking. What other possibilities are there in the way of housing that you might choose in preference to where you are now? Hold on to your dreams — you may be able to build them into your long-term plans.

Clive and Toinette found that this was a solution which helped them. They were unable to move, because neither had a job and they couldn't afford it. They joined a local community group which was campaigning for a number of community causes. This group eventually succeeded in setting up a social club, which became very popular. It also carried out surveys of rubbish collections, and waiting times at the local doctor's surgery, which led to improvements in both those services.

YOUR SPECIFICATION

The next stage is to think about your needs and what would be right for you, and to work out in detail what the home that would be right for you and your household is actually like. There are five different sections here, headed

- building (the home itself)

- surroundings (garden, grounds)

- general area (town, street, country etc.)

- facilities (shops, schools etc.)

- quality of life (features such as community spirit, climate, crime rate etc.).

Go through each section, considering all the points raised, and then draw up lists of what you need. These five lists should make up a complete specification of the right home for you. Talk to your partner and anyone else who shares your home to make sure that everyone's ideas are considered.

The building you need

The description of the home you need should cover basic things like number of rooms, how many floors there should be, approximate sizes of rooms, bathroom facilities, parking facilities for whatever transport you've got, as well as any special needs that have occurred to you, and final touches which are particularly important to you, such as a fitted kitchen or sunken bath.

Here are some reminders about points you might need to consider.

Your household

Do you have children in your household?

Do you have visitors?

Do they stay overnight?

Are any of your visitors elderly or handicapped?

Do you have a car/motorbike/bicycle/caravan/boat?

Does anybody work at home?

Does your family have home-based hobbies like music, do-it-yourself?

You might need

- ☐ a quiet place for them to do homework
- ☐ a quiet place for you to work
- ☐ a place for hobbies/activities
- ☐ somewhere they can entertain friends
- ☐ storage space for toys, bicycle

- ☐ a good-sized living room
- ☐ a dining-room

- ☐ a separate bathroom and w.c.
- ☐ a spare bedroom(s)

- ☐ a downstairs lavatory
- ☐ a downstairs bedroom

- ☐ a parking space
- ☐ a shed for storage
- ☐ a workshop or workspace

- ☐ a room/quiet place to work
- ☐ storage space for work materials
- ☐ storage space, e.g. for tools
- ☐ a room big enough to hold a meeting

- ☐ a dark room for photography
- ☐ a work area indoors or outdoors

Now draw up the list for the building you need. Keep this by you while you think about the setting for your home.

The surroundings you need

The number of people in your household and their ages and interests, the way you spend your time and how keen you are on gardening are all going to affect your ideas on the size and type of garden and immediate surroundings you need. Several of the points mentioned above for the building should also give you ideas and reminders about aspects of the garden you should be thinking about. If other people's needs are involved, make sure you include them in discussions about the kind of surroundings that will best suit you all.

Now draw up the list for the surroundings you need.

The general area you need

When you are thinking about what kind of area you would like to live in, your decision will be influenced by both practical considerations and your feelings about what is important for you and your family.

First of all, think about which practical points are going to help you to decide on the general area where you would prefer to live. These will probably be to do with

■ your work ('My home must be close to where I work — I don't want to spend valuable time on a long home-to-work journey')

■ your family ('I want to live in the same village as my parents')

■ your children, if you have any ('Our new home must be near enough to the children's school so that they can walk there on their own').

Now think a bit about the area where you would like to live. What does it look like? Did you have a picture in your mind when you were drawing up your list of features? Perhaps you feel that only a town, or only the countryside, could serve as the background for the home you would like. You might have been thinking of a particular place that you know about, maybe even where you're living now. Or you might have constructed an imaginary place which provided everything you need. Are your assumptions necessarily correct? What are the realities of actually living in the town or the country? This is going to vary a great deal depending on the part of the

country, the size of the village, town or city, the popularity of the area — you can almost certainly think of many more points which might give rise to tremendous differences.

What other aspects are involved when you're considering the general area? You might be thinking about whether you'd prefer to live in the town centre, where there is a lot going on, or in a quiet suburb, on the outskirts of a town, in a small village, in a cul-de-sac, on an estate and so on.

Now draw up the list of features of the general area you want in order of their importance to you. You don't have to spend a lot of time on deciding which point is marginally more important than another. What you can do is to say which things you must have, and which things you would like to have. Making up a list in this way should enable you to get a rough idea of the general geographical area where you need to live.

The facilities you need

It is not just the area where you live that makes you feel good about your home. Local facilities may play an important part in determining how much you like living there. Think about those facilities which you consider essential, and those which you'd like to have if you could. This will serve as the basis for a checklist for deciding on whether the facilities you have at the moment are satisfactory, or might be better elsewhere. As an example, here is Philip and Molly's list — yours will probably be quite different, depending on your circumstances. Below is Sue's list, which was a bit different.

Now draw up your own list of the facilities you and your household need.

The quality of life you need

The facilities that are available are not the only things that are important where your choice of area is concerned. There are other factors which could be described as contributing to your quality of life, such as fresh air and low pollution, good local schools, low traffic noise, good shopping and health facilities, the general standard of housing, special facilities for the disabled, sports and leisure facilities, low cost of living, low crime rate, no vandalism, racial harmony, convenient local transport, climate and weather, easy parking, friendly neighbours and so on.

Now draw up your own list of things that determine the quality of life for you, and put them in order of importance. Divide them into two levels of importance in the same way as was suggested above, that is, those which are essential to you, and those which you'd like if possible.

Measuring the quality of life

You've just drawn up lists of things that would make you feel that you were enjoying a good quality of life. Obviously, these won't be the same for everyone. But is there any general agreement on what the most desirable characteristics are? What makes a particular area the most pleasant place to live for most people? Various attempts have been made to work this out. Most recently, a

---

Philip and Molly's list

Facilities we MUST have

Doctors surgery and Chemist within easy walking distance

Shop with newspapers and basic provisions within walking distance

Catholic church

Renault garage

Park

Facilities we'd like to have

Cinema

Social clubs for senior citizens

Betting shop

Railway station

choice of supermarkets

Public library

Sue's list

Facilities I must have

Post office / newsagent

Doctors surgery / health centre

Launderette

Park for jogging

Bus route nearby

Facilities I'd like to have

Fast food — Chinese takeaway

Supermarket

Pub

Bicycle routes and bike lanes on roads

Cinema

Public library

COMPARING QUALITY OF LIFE

national opinion poll carried out in 1987 produced the following list. At the top, in order of importance, came

- low rates of violent and non-violent crime
- good health facilities
- low levels of pollution
- low cost of living
- good shopping facilities
- racial harmony.

Further down the list, still in order of importance, came the climate (which people talk about a lot but don't rate as very significant), the cost of owner-occupied housing, the quality of, and access to, council houses, the cost of private rented accommodation, education facilities, employment prospects, wage levels, levels of unemployment, travel-to-work time, access to areas of scenic beauty and sports and leisure facilities. How does this list compare with yours?

Edinburgh — 'Britain's most desirable city'.

Having decided which 'quality of life' features are important for you, how do you decide which area actually has those features? While some of them you can judge for yourself by looking around — the extent of graffiti and vandalism, for instance, and how much traffic noise there is — other things like the crime rate and the number of patients each doctor has to look after might be harder to assess. The Geography Department at the University of Glasgow recently compared the major British cities in terms of qualities considered to be the most important in choosing where to live, using the list which was the result of the national opinion poll already quoted. On the basis of known facts about the cities, Scotland came out of the comparison best, and the West Midlands worst. Edinburgh was judged to be Britain's most desirable city to live in, with more desirable features than anywhere else. Aberdeen also did well. Plymouth (lowest crime rate) and Cardiff (low cost of living) came next in the league table. Apart from those two, most cities in the South did badly, except for Reading, with London doing particularly badly because of the low quality of its council housing, the high costs of owner-occupied and rented accommodation, its high cost of living and bad record on race relations. Hamilton-Motherwell (best ratio of doctors to patients, low pollution, good shops), Bradford (access to areas of high scenic quality, good

shops, low cost of living and low costs of owner-occupied housing) and Stoke-on-Trent all came near the top of the cities in the survey. It's worth bearing in mind, of course, that not all of London offers its citizens poor quality of life, and not every part of Edinburgh or Plymouth is as good as the best areas.

The encouraging thing about these results is that places like Edinburgh have achieved a high quality of life not necessarily because they have a lot more natural advantages than other cities, but because the people who run them have kept down pollution and crime, provided good shopping facilities and a good range of council housing. In theory, at any rate, those who run the cities which came at the bottom end of the league table could improve the quality of life there in the same way.

If you are trying to assess different cities for the quality of life they might offer, you may have found this league table useful. But although more of us live in cities than don't, much of the United Kingdom won't have been included in this comparison. If you want more information about an area you think might offer you the quality of life you need, you can find out more about it by

- reading the local newspapers
- writing to the information centre, if there is one, or the council offices with specific questions
- paying visits to the area at different times of the year, if you are lucky enough to have plenty of time to come to your decision.

Which area for Philip and Molly?

Philip and Molly have drawn up their list of features for the area they would like to live in. They are thinking about Cornwall as their ideal area, the place where the quality of life would be right for them. They know a little about Cornwall, as they have been there often for summer holidays. But their problem is that they want some quality-of-life features which can only be found in a town and some which can only be provided by the countryside. They cannot make up their minds between the village in Cornwall they know best and the large town where they live now, which is very convenient. With Cornwall and their current home town in mind, they decide to list the advantages and disadvantages of living in town or country, to try to work out which area would really suit them best. You have to do this with particular places in mind, otherwise you will simply be writing down opposites. Not every town has better hospital facilities than the country, for example, and some parts of the country can be very noisy — if you are under an aeroplane flight path, for instance.

Philip and Molly decided on the basis of this comparison that, although they would love to live in the country, it is really more sensible, especially in view of Molly's arthritis, to stay in the town near health facilities, friends and family. If you have to make a choice of this kind, you will find it useful to make a list of advantages and disadvantages of the two different areas in the same way as Philip and Molly did.

OTHER PEOPLE'S MOVES

Now that you have thought about what you are looking for in a home, you may be interested to see some results from a recent (1988) survey in which people from five different towns in the United Kingdom were asked various questions about why they moved, and why they chose to move where they did. The most important reason why people chose to move from one home to another was to get more space (nearly half those who answered). About a quarter had to move for job reasons; other reasons given were 'to make an investment', 'to have a nicer home or location', 'to go to a better area' and 'because the old home was getting too expensive to run'. The things people liked best about the locations of their new homes were that they were near shops, followed by being near work and school. Other factors mentioned included the house not being overlooked, being on a quiet road and near the countryside. The room which influenced people most in deciding on a particular home was the living room — they wanted a large room, with a good view, but a fitted kitchen with enough space for a table and chairs was almost as important. The most important features that people wanted in newly built homes were central heating, a fitted kitchen, a garage and storage space.

LIVING IN THE COUNTRY

Advantages	Disadvantages
Natural beauty	Many visitors in summer
Walks in the fresh air	No mains drainage
Less pollution	Public transport very limited
Insurance rates low for houses and cars	Hospital very far away and has limited resources
Pace of life slow	Shops expensive

LIVING IN THE TOWN

Advantages	Disadvantages
Good choice of houses and flats	Heavy traffic
Reasonably good public transport	Dirty atmosphere
Hospital near with good resources	Parking difficult and expensive
Shops cheaper	
Neighbours and family near at hand in case of emergency	

How does your current home measure up after all your thinking about the house you'd like? What is there about your home that you like, and want to retain? What is there about it that is reasonably acceptable? What aspects would you definitely like to be different?

WHAT NEEDS CHANGING?

On a separate sheet of paper, or in a notebook, draw up a list of the features of your present home like the one here. You should add any extra things about your home that are important to you. Make three columns, using the headings shown. Put a tick in one of the columns for each item on your list, depending on whether it is something you would like to keep, can tolerate or would like to change. Discuss the list with your partner, and anyone else who lives with you who is interested. They could put in their own pattern of ticks, possibly in a different colour. This would help to highlight points of difference, which will need to be discussed.

	Would like to change	Would like to keep	Can tolerate
The building			
Type and size of home			
Number of rooms			
Size of rooms			
Room layout			
Number of storeys			
Costs of rent/mortgage/rates			
Running costs			
Type of heating			
Immediate surroundings			
Garden — size and type			
Distance from neighbours			
General area			
Type of street			
Closeness to city centre			
Closeness to country or sea			
Facilities within reach			
Doctor			
Shops			
Park			
Hospital			
Library			
Schools			
Sports centres			
Quality of life			
Crime rate			
Cost of living			
Race relations			
Climate			
Quality and closeness of schools			
Jobs available			
Wage levels			

If you found that you had a great many ticks under the 'Would like to change' column, then you are going to have to work out what your choices are for improving matters. If most of your ticks come under the 'Can tolerate' column, you need to work out whether these things are going to go on being tolerable or whether they might change, and whether these features just being tolerable is what you really want. If most of your ticks are under the 'Would like to keep' heading that seems to show that the home you have now already satisfies your needs in most ways and you might not want to make any major changes at the moment.

What conclusions did the case study families reach?

Raj and Satpal had no doubts about wanting a change. They already knew that their one-bedroomed flat was not going to be suitable once the baby came. They realised that they were going to have to move into a different home. Sue could manage in the rented flat, but it was not very convenient. There was no room, for instance, for her mother to come to stay. The majority of her ticks were under 'Would like to change' and she concluded that she would like to move to quite a different kind of home. Clive and Toinette liked their present home and couldn't afford to move, although there were aspects of the layout of their home that they'd like to improve. They would also like to reduce their running costs. Rick and Penny liked their area

and the facilities there very much and didn't want to change them. They would, however, like to change nearly everything about their actual house. So their solution would be to look for a different house which met their requirements in the same area or to extend their present home to make it fit their needs better. Philip and Molly had a lot of ticks under 'Would like to change', but they were not at all clear about what they would like instead. They realised that they needed to do a fair amount of work to find out what would really be right for them.

REVISE YOUR LIST

Now that you've made the comparison between what you've got and what you'd like, you may find that your ideas about the home you want have changed a bit. Go back to your specification and check whether you want to change it in some way before going on to look at what choices are open to you.

The choices that you are going to want to consider will depend on the differences between the home you would like and the home you've got at the moment. If, for instance, you found that there are very few differences between what you'd like and what you've got — you are dissatisfied with the layout of the rooms, for instance, and want more space — then you only need to consider how you might reorganise the space you've already got and perhaps create more storage space. You could also consider whether there is something you want to change about the way your home is equipped and run. If you like the area you live in and the facilities that you've got, but your current home is too small for you, then you could think about altering or extending your home or, if this is impossible, moving within the area where you are now. If home, area and facilities are all different from what you really want, then you need to work out whether you could move house to somewhere else which will give you what you want, or at least make some of the changes you need. If you are a tenant with very few options for change, you could consider whether action might be easier if it were carried out by a group, rather than by you individually. There are many examples of tenant community action groups which have had their properties improved and their streets and local areas cleaned up.

CHANGING THE WAY YOU USE YOUR HOME

The next chapter of this book, **Organising Space** considers changes which may not cost a lot — ideas about how you can take a fresh look at the way you organise the space in your home to make it work better for the people who live there. This could be by changing the use of the rooms, by moving things around within them, by changing the way you store things so as to create extra room and by actually making extra space.

You can also alter the way you use your house by choosing different equipment, or by using equipment in a way which will meet your needs better. This is covered in the third chapter of this book, **Equipping Your Home**.

Finally, you can make improvements to your home in the way you run and maintain it to make it more effective. The fourth and final chapter of this book, **Running Your Home** looks at how you can work out new ways of doing things.

If you have decided that these are the kinds of changes that will meet your needs best, then you should concentrate most of your attention on those later chapters. If a major change, like a move or building an extension, becomes possible or necessary later, then you can come back to this chapter and work your way through the choices available.

ALTERING OR EXTENDING YOUR HOME

If you don't want to move, but need more space, or to use the space you've got more efficiently, you can consider altering or extending your home in some way. Tenants will not, of course, want to undertake major works of this kind and may, in any case, not be allowed to, especially if they rent from the council.

In theory, at any rate, you could extend your home upwards, sideways, forwards or backwards. But in practice, there are a limited number of possibilities for most people. If you know you need more space, you've probably been thinking about different possibilities. The next stage is to try out some ideas by drawing rough plans.

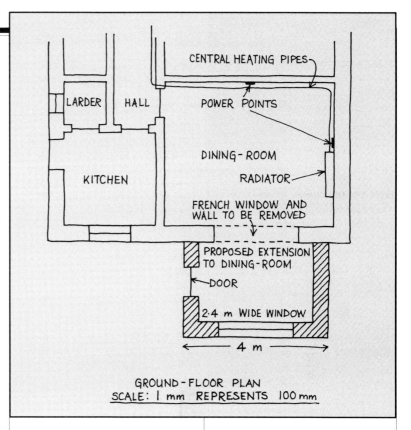

GROUND - FLOOR PLAN
SCALE: 1 mm REPRESENTS 100 mm

DRAW A PLAN

Start by drawing a rough plan of your house, concentrating on the part, or storey, where you think changes might be possible.

Try and do this more or less to scale, with 1 mm on the plan representing 100 mm in your house. It will be easier if you use squared paper. Don't draw the walls as single lines — they are usually something like 300 mm thick outside and 150 mm thick inside, so you should draw them 3 and 1.5 mm thick on a 1:100 sketch plan. Show where the doors and windows will be, and how the proposed extension will link to the house, unless it's already part of it like the roof space.

Show the wall(s) to be removed or changed as a dotted line and make a note of any obstructions, such as electric power points, central heating pipes or radiators. Above is the sketch Rick did for a possible extension to his dining-room.

Make several copies of your plan, so that you can try out different approaches, which you can then discuss with your partner and family or other people who share your home.

Don't limit yourself at this stage to small, low-cost plans because that's all you can afford at present. Do as many plans as you can think of which will improve your home for you in some way.

You might end up with a number of suggestions for alterations and extensions , ranging from, say, a hatch between dining-room and kitchen to a full-scale extension for kitchen and dining-room.

Which of these you actually decide on will depend on

- how great the advantages of the proposed change would be for you

- how much you can afford

- whether it's physically possible to do what you want

- whether you can do what you want without breaking any laws or Building Regulations.

DIFFERENT TYPES OF EXTENSION

	Possible advantages	Possible disadvantages
Large porches, conservatory	■ will cut draughts ■ south-facing structure may heat nearby rooms ■ when sun shines could use to grow seedlings and plants ■ will provide storage for wellingtons, garden furniture, garden tools, bicycles etc. ■ can be done by DIY	■ cold in winter unless heated ■ reduces size of garden ■ might reduce the light reaching rooms nearby
Loft conversion	■ makes use of otherwise unused space ■ relatively cheap — no foundations ■ can be done in winter ■ can improve insulation	■ technical problems and fire regulations may mean this is a trickier problem than originally anticipated ■ stairs may be a problem ■ space you gain may be less than expected ■ often not possible in recently built houses becuse of shallowness of roof ■ building work causes a lot of disturbance in house
Ground-floor extension	■ technically simpler than loft conversion ■ prefabricated type can be DIY ■ no stairs so good for elderly/disabled ■ since it is on the ground floor allows a lot of flexibility — you can replan the whole of your ground-floor accommodation ■ building work doesn't interfere with house as much as loft conversion	■ will lose garden space ■ could be a problem with outside drainpipes and cables — need to locate and protect them from damage ■ design needs special care in order not to make house look odd
First-floor extension — over garage for example	■ usually only suitable for bedroom/bathroom ■ doesn't take up garden or drive space	■ foundations may need reinforcement ■ access may be difficult, e.g. through a bedroom
Garage conversion	■ straightforward, especially with integral garage ■ fewer problems than interior extension	■ cuts parking space
Two-storey extension	■ a lot more space	■ major investment, so need to make sure that doesn't price house beyond what local market will bear ■ may change whole emphasis of house ■ will increase heating costs
Annexe, i.e. granny flat	■ good selling point ■ allows elderly/disabled person independence yet near help if needed ■ could be rented off as source of income	

While only you can work out exactly how useful possible alterations will be for you, there are a number of likely advantages and disadvantages to different kinds of extension, which you may not have considered. Look through the list on the left and think which changes would work in your home. Then check the possible advantages and disadvantages listed (they are based on a *Which?* report) and note those which would be applicable to you. Then you must work out what other pros and cons would apply if you built the kind of extension you want. Make a note of any possible problems and attach it to your rough plan. In general, the larger and more complicated the extension, the greater the number of potential problems with Building Regulations and planning permission.

Is it physically possible?

Once you have decided on a plan or plans, you need to consult an architect and/or a builder. Which you choose will depend on the scale and extent of the change you want. Whichever experts you consult should be able to advise you about what is feasible and what is not. They should also be able to make suggestions on how your original ideas might be improved. Once you get to the stage of asking for quotations, remember that one isn't really enough. Three quotations are usually safer, and if you are borrowing money, your lender will probably require them as well.

Is it legally possible?

You should be able to get advice, and even helpful leaflets, from your local council. Your architect or builder should also advise you on what permissions need to be sought and checks made to ensure that you don't contravene any regulations or restrictions. It is crucial that you don't get too far (and spend too much money) without finding out for sure that your plan is legally possible.

Can you afford it?

There are suggestions later on in this chapter for checking your resources and looking at different ways of raising money. But even if you can't afford to do everything you want in the way of alterations and extensions at the moment, you could think about a long-term plan. This might enable you to make changes in easy stages and would mean that you didn't increase the amount of your debts to an unmanageable level.

Before you carry out alterations, conversions or extensions to your home, you may need planning consent and will probably need Building Regulations approval. You should always check about both before drawing up very detailed plans and starting work. Here are some more details.

Planning permission

Planning permission is required for any change to your home which could be referred to as 'development'. This includes any major change in the use of any building or other land. If your conversion or extension only affects the inside of your property, like a loft conversion, and not the external appearance, then you won't need planning permission. The only exception to this is if you change the interior in such a way that the use is converted from a single-family dwelling to one for multiple occupation — if you turned some of your bedrooms into self-contained bedsitters for students, say. Nor will you need planning permission for small extensions which are not visible from the street. For a terraced or semi-detached house, 'small' means up to 50 cubic metres, or 10% of the existing volume up to a maximum of 115 cubic metres; for a detached house the figures are 70 cubic metres or 15% of the volume. These are the regulations for England, Wales and Northern Ireland. In Scotland the upper limit for a small extension is 50 cubic metres or 20% of the total volume, whichever is the greater. Small porches don't always need planning permission, nor do garden sheds or greenhouses. It is, however, always wise to check as it would be difficult and expensive if you started work and were then told to stop. To get planning permission, you or your architect submit your application to the planning officer at your local authority. He inspects your property, and submits a report to the planning committee, who decide whether to reject or approve your application.

Building Regulations

These are to do with the construction, rather than the appearance of your building. They aim to make sure that you don't build something which will become a health or fire hazard, or injure anyone in any way. It is a good idea to go and see the building inspector at your local council at an early stage of your planning as he can often give useful advice. When you make formal application, you have to pay a plan fee. If your application meets with approval, then there will be a site inspection, for which you also have to pay a fee. Approval will normally only be withheld if the proposed change doesn't comply with Building Regulations in some way. The builder has to notify the local authority when work is due to start, and at certain stages of construction.

Other permissions

In some cases, there are other people whose permission you will have to seek before you go ahead with your improvement project. Here is a list of possibilities. Check through it if you are planning an extension or conversion. The more important and likely possibilities are at the start of the list, less likely ones at the end.

- Owners of adjoining property
- Institutions who have given you a mortgage — the building society, for instance — and who have insured your home
- Your landlord
- Gas, electric or water boards
- Telephone company
- Fire department
- Community groups concerned with preservation and local amenities
- People who lease or rent property from you.

MOVING TO ANOTHER HOME

In the past, this was usually a relatively simple and straightforward process. If you intended to buy a property, the head of the household raised the money and bought a flat or a house. If you didn't buy, then you rented, either privately or from the local council (or Housing Executive in Northern Ireland). Nowadays there are many different ways both of buying and of renting a home. So it's worth taking the opportunity to reconsider your attitudes towards home ownership and non-ownership.

RENT OR OWN

Read through these quotations from different people — some of them from the case study families, others not. They are talking about their attitudes towards renting or buying. Tick those quotations that are close to your views.

Molly 'I'd prefer not to have the responsibility for home repairs and maintenance.' ☐

Rick 'My house is my biggest asset — I wouldn't feel secure if I didn't have that investment.' ☐

Viratch 'I don't like to plan ahead at all. Owning a house would feel like a millstone round my neck.' ☐

Ian 'I wouldn't feel comfortable living in a place which wasn't mine, which I didn't own. I wouldn't feel at home there.' ☐

Jo 'Why should I pay rent to line someone else's pockets?' ☐

Dave 'I would feel very worried about the future if I didn't own my own home.' ☐

Alan 'I don't like the idea of living in my own little box. I want to share jobs and responsibilities with other people.' ☐

Penny 'I like to have my home looking as nice as possible. I don't want to invest my time and money improving someone else's property.' ☐

Louisa 'My ideas about where and how I'd like to live are bound to change a lot over the next few years, so I don't want to tie myself down too soon.' ☐

Nancy 'Wouldn't dream of not buying or owning my own home — it's what every sensible person does.' ☐

Ragi 'I'm only going to be in this area till I finish my course, so there's no point in buying even if I could afford it.' ☐

Who did you agree with?

Many of these people — Nancy, Rick and Dave for example — like the idea of owning their home because it makes them feel really safe. For them, if they can afford it, it makes sense to buy their own home. Penny and Jo were particularly concerned that their investment in their homes benefits them and no one else. If you feel the same way as these people, then you will be happier buying and owning your own home, if you can.

For some of the others, buying wasn't anything like such an attractive idea. Flexibility and the need to be able to make changes easily are important for Louisa, Ragi and Viratch, who are all quite young. Molly, who's getting on in years, is seriously concerned about the burden of responsibility that her house represents. She would rather not be a house owner at all. Alan doesn't like the idea of living quite cut off from the rest of his community. Owning his own place isn't particularly important to him — he's much more interested in renting part of a communal scheme. For all these people, and you, if you agree with them, renting, or not owning, is going to be better. If you are among the 62% of people who currently (1988) own their own home, you may wonder if it's worth changing. But whatever your situation, read through these descriptions of different ways of buying and renting. Think about each one and how possible and desirable it would be both for you personally, and for those who share your home. Make a note of those options which are both possible and desirable and check that you know enough about them to give them further consideration. If in doubt you can always list advantages and disadvantages to see which outweighs the other.

Buying

Single ownership
The most straightforward situation is when one person alone becomes the owner of the property. Only his or her salary will need to be considered when potential lenders assess the size of the mortgage or loan.

Joint ownership

There are various different possibilities here. The first involves sharing the ownership with at least one other person. Each owner will have to supply details of income. Two is the most common number sharing. They can be partners or friends of either sex. Joint owners of this kind often have a trust deed drawn up to define rights and responsibilities. This will cover what happens if one partner wishes to dispose of his or her share.

In a second option, neither owner can sell without the consent of the other. If one should die, the other will automatically inherit the deceased's share. This option is usually favoured by married couples.

A third option has more flexibility than the first two. Each of the joint owners is entitled to dispose of her/his own share as and when she/he chooses. This allows more independence among owners and is favoured by those who are not married.

Shared ownership

This is a relatively new scheme whereby a share in the house is purchased and the remaining share is rented. The percentage of the share purchased can be decided according to your means or what you prefer — it is usually from about 25 to 80%. For many people on low incomes, a shared ownership scheme will be the only way they can get a foothold in the house-buying market. There is the opportunity to increase the share in future years. Shared ownership schemes are very popular amongst first-time buyers and may be difficult to find. If you want to find out whether there is a housing association or other shared ownership scheme in your area, you could enquire from the council, or contact the Housing Corporation in London, which has a network of regional offices throughout the United Kingdom and funds housing associations.

Co-ownership

This is another kind of scheme intended to make it possible for people on low incomes to own property. A co-ownership society is a housing association in which the members have a stake in the value of the homes they occupy, so that they have most of the benefits of owner occupiers. While many of the schemes set up over the last 20 years were dissolved following the 1980 Housing Act, some co-ownership housing is still being developed, in particular for the elderly. These are different variations on the co-ownership idea available, but the intention is usually to combine a sense of community with privacy and the advantages of home ownership.

Renting

Private furnished accommodation

This may be difficult to find. Children are not usually welcomed. Landlords generally say that deposits are necessary. You should seek legal advice before signing any agreement. Such accommodation is often for short leases only (up to a year).

Private unfurnished accommodation

This is usually even more difficult to find. Once again, you should seek legal advice before signing anything.

Local authority rented housing

Local authority (or Housing Executive in Northern Ireland) housing offices can often give advice, even if they cannot supply accommodation! As waiting lists are long, you should enter your name as soon as possible and not wait until you are homeless. Priority is given to those with greatest 'need' (defined according to the council's own criteria). Some authorities insist that you take the first home offered to you (or go to the bottom of the list) while others allow you one or two refusals.

Development corporation rented housing

In new towns and cities there is often a development corporation which builds and looks after public housing. Priority is often given to new people moving into the area to work. You would need to supply proof of being employed in the area.

Housing association rented housing

Housing associations are publicly funded organisations. Their funds come from local authorities or the Housing Corporation which was set up, and is funded by, the government. You can rent either a house or flat from a housing association. Their rents are designated as 'fair rents', but you will need to check your eligibility. Priority is often given to those living in the area or on the council housing list. Some housing associations will buy your property from you, convert it into flats and then rent you one of them for the rest of your life. The feasibility of this depends on many things, including the size and age of your property.

Sheltered housing

Sometimes sheltered housing is run by the council, sometimes by a housing association; in both cases it will be available for rental. Some sheltered housing is available for sale or rent through private organisations. Such housing usually consists of a private flat, with shared facilities such as commonrooms. The flats are independent, but have a bell in each room to ring for help in an emergency. There is a resident warden in a nearby flat. Flats are usually only available to pensioners or disabled people who are not seriously incapacitated and are therefore able to manage independently. Some are for single people and some for couples. Waiting lists are often long. If you have to go into hospital for a long time, you may have to give up a rented flat.

Co-operatives and communes

Two more unusual options, in which a share of a property may be bought or, more usually, rented, are housing co-operatives and communes. In each case, the members of the group own or rent collectively, rather than individually. Housing co-operatives own or rent a number of units or properties, which they manage co-operatively, through a management committee. The members of the co-operative pay a nominal sum to become a member, and then rent. All members are entitled to share in the decision-making and will be expected to carry out various jobs towards the maintenance of the housing co-operative properties and their organisation. Such co-operatives can qualify for government grants and subsidies to buy, build, convert, modernise or renovate property.

Communes are normally run in an even more open and democratic fashion than co-operatives. Members will eat together, sharing the tasks involved, seek to reach complete agreement on all questions which arise concerning the running of the commune and live as an extended family rather than as individuals. Each commune will have its own guidelines for those wishing to enter or leave, but new members will almost certainly have to be accepted by all the existing ones.

Which one for you?

Which of these possibilities are actually available to you will depend on your means, your employment, where you live and your age. Very few people will have the whole range to make their selection from. People who helped to develop these materials found that they weren't familiar with all these options, and some of the suggestions were useful in their plans for change. One of them commented, for example, that knowing about some of these schemes had made him look very much more carefully at jobs in areas where development corporations were operating.

WHAT KIND OF HOME?

Some people know exactly what kind of accommodation they need. But if you are uncertain as to which might fit your needs best, how should you make up your mind between the different kinds? Would a flat or a house suit you better? What about a bungalow?

You will obviously have to consider the pros and the cons of particular flats or houses, or whatever accommodation you have in mind, otherwise the comparison won't be realistic. Philip and Molly have been giving serious consideration to whether they would be better off in a flat or a house. They decided to make the comparison by listing good and bad points of a typical flat (No. 3 The Warren) and a typical house (No. 8 Abbey Road) to see whether either outweighed the other very obviously. This approach had worked well for them when they were comparing town and country life.

This time, the answer wasn't as clear-cut for Philip and Molly. There seemed to be an equal balance between the flat and the house. They decided to take a closer look to see whether some of the advantages and disadvantages were more important to them than others. They decided that their most important concerns were to do with money and running costs and with their furniture and possessions. Although the purchase prices of the flat and house were comparable, there would be a maintenance charge payable for the flat, and no certainty that it would not go up. Molly and Philip felt that the electric central heating would be more expensive to run than the gas central heating in the house. There would be more room for their furniture in the house. Moving into the flat would mean getting rid of cherished possessions and even buying new furniture to fit the space available. In the end, the comparison between flat and house from the point of view of only the most important features meant that Philip and Molly decided in favour of the house.

MAKING YOUR OWN COMPARISION

If you are trying to decide between different types of home, list advantages and disadvantages in the same way. Each kind of home (flat, terraced house, semi-detached house, detached house, bungalow, caravan and so on) will have particular benefits and drawbacks for you. Make up a table listing them. If you don't get a clear answer about the best type of home for you, do as Molly and Philip did and decide which features you feel are the most important. Then you can compare the different types of home according to how well they provide those features. Deciding what kind of home will best suit you and those who share your home with you will mean that you have a clearer idea as to what to look for and won't waste time on the type of property which isn't really what you want.

NO. 3 THE WARREN

Advantages	Disadvantages
Neighbours near at hand	Not much privacy
All maintenance covered by maintenance charge	All electric - no choice of fuel
Porter will take deliveries	No garage, only carport
Lift, so won't have to climb stairs	Not much storage space
Small, compact layout	Furniture won't fit very well
	Maintenance charge may go up

NO. 8 ABBEY ROAD

Advantages	Disadvantages
Garage	Neighbours some distance away
Gas central heating	Cars from pub park outside
Plenty of room for furniture	Garden larger than would like.
Plenty of storage space	North-facing - seems rather cold
	Stairs might prove difficult in a few years

WHAT CAN YOU AFFORD?

If you are planning to change your home in some way, you are almost certainly going to need some money to do it with. How much can you afford? Can you spend money now? Or will you have to wait until some point in the future? When? To get an idea of your financial flexibility, you need to get together the answers to some basic questions about how much money you have to spare. It doesn't have to be a balanced budget, just something to help you to take a realistic look at how much comes into your household and what your financial commitments are. Once you have the answers, you will be able to weigh up the choices open to you from the point of view of just what you can afford. Recording details of your income will also mean that you will have all the evidence you need readily available to prove to a potential lender, or landlord, that you can make the necessary loan or mortgage repayments or rent payments, if this is what you decide to do.

You are bound to need to have details of your earnings ready if you want a mortgage, since mortgage lenders make their offer on the basis of a multiple of your annual income before tax. This may be up to three times your income if you are single; a couple who are both earning would usually be able to borrow up to three times the higher income, plus up to once the lower income.

WORKING OUT YOUR FINANCIAL POSITION

Make some notes in your notebook or on separate sheets of paper. Keep all the details of income on one page, expenditure on another. If you have kept detailed budget records, you should have all the figures easily available. If not, you'll have to look back through pay slips, building society books and other documents. Make all the totals per year rather than per month, if possible. Start with what comes into your household.

Looking at your income

How much do you earn per year now?

Note down your basic salary or wages, that is, what you get paid before tax is deducted.

What are your future prospects?

Will you get annual increments? Is redundancy possible, or even likely?

INCOME

Annual earnings £9,400

Prospects Reasonable – I get an annual increment

Savings £550 in the building society

Investments None, apart from some jewellery we wouldn't want to sell

Home value None as we are still renting

Spare cash Not a great deal, especially round Christmas and holiday time

Possible economies would only have very cheap holidays once we have bought house

Car and Access backlog will be costing us about £500 a year over the next three years

Loan repayments Loan from father for furniture we bought when we got married – £1,000 over the next year.

Other regular financial commitments? None at the moment, but the baby is going to cost quite a lot when it comes.

What realisable resources do you have?

Include all savings and investments unless you don't intend to use them or cash them in to finance a change of home.

How much would you get for your present home?

Obviously, this only applies to home owners.

How much money is there to spare?

Just consider here if you have any money left at the end of the month and how hard you are finding it to make ends meet at the moment.

What other savings could you make?

This could include economies which are coming up anyway, like not having to support one member of your household any more, or some other possible saving like getting a company car.

Looking at your expenditure

What are your general living expenses?

Try to estimate how much you spend each week or month, and work out a total for the last year.

Have you any debts?

Note down anything you have on credit or on bank loans and work out how much you have to pay back each year and over how many years.

Other regular financial commitments?

This would include life insurance, contributions to charities etc.

To sum up

This outline budget should help you to get a feeling for whether you could afford to make a change or a move. If you have a lot of debts and heavy financial responsibilities, this is going to limit your ability to move to a much more expensive home, unless you could make so much profit on your current one that you would be able to wipe out your debts.

When our case study families did this exercise, they found that it helped them in various ways. Raj and Satpal realised that although Raj's prospects are reasonable and they have some savings, they will have to be very careful not to buy a home that will stretch their budget beyond its limit. Rick and Penny have a good income, but they also have heavy outgoings. Their savings and investments, plus the £35,000 they hope to realise by the sale of the house they own now should, however, enable them to move to a larger home, which is what they intend. Philip and Molly are concerned about their financial position. They don't have money to spare, and feel very hard up. While they still intend to move if possible, they mean to try to release some of the profit from selling their current home to invest to give them some more spending money.

RAISING THE MONEY

Ways of getting a mortgage or a loan to make home improvements, extend or convert your home are changing year by year. If you need to borrow large sums, the most important thing — as in virtually everything to do with spending money — is to shop around, to find out which potential lender will give you a good deal. Besides finding the best lender, you also need to decide on the best type of loan or mortgage for your circumstances.

What type of loan or mortgage?

Before following up a list of potential lenders and discussing details with them, you should be clear in your own mind exactly what kind of loan or mortgage would be best for you in your circumstances. Loans for extensions or home improvements are relatively simple. You borrow a certain sum of money which has to be paid back over a fixed period. What you need to do is compare the Annual Percentage Rate (APR) charged, which must (by law) be declared. Generally, the lower the APR, the less interest you pay. Mortgages are normally more complicated, because they are usually for much larger sums of money. You may already have a mortgage, but forget about what type it is for the time being. Try to make an objective assessment of the different mortgage possibilities, so that you have the basic information for a possible choice. As you read through the descriptions of the different types of mortgage, you should assess how suitable each would be for you. Everyone's requirements are slightly different, but you need to have the answers to certain questions before you can decide on the best kind of mortgage for you and start to look at possible lenders. Here is a checklist of questions you could use to assess the different kinds of mortgage.

☐ Would I be eligible for this kind of mortgage?

☐ How flexible is this kind of mortgage and would it be easy to extend the repayments? Is that important for me?

☐ How much risk is involved in taking out this mortgage? How worried am I about that?

☐ If the economic situation were to change (for better, for worse) how would this type of mortgage be affected? How much difference would that make to me?

☐ Is life insurance included or extra? Is that important for me, or am I already covered?

☐ Might I get a lump sum when I finish paying off this mortgage? How vital would this be for me?

☐ Would I be entitled to tax relief?

☐ Would I be penalised if I wanted to pay this mortgage off early?

The final question that you would be asking would, of course, be *'How much will this cost me per month?'* You will only be able to find the answer to that by checking with possible lenders.

The cost of the mortgage may well vary depending on the size and type of loan, as well as other conditions. You need to make careful comparisons!

The case study families you've already met went through this exercise of comparing different types of mortgage. Their conclusions are given at the end of this section.

While there are a lot of new types of mortgage being dreamed up, the main kinds that most people will consider are

■ a repayment mortgage

■ a low-cost endowment mortgage

■ a pension mortgage

■ a maturity mortgage.

How do these different kinds of mortgage work?

Repayment mortgage

Each payment you make is split into two. Part reduces the amount you owe, while the rest is interest on the amount still owing. If you select a level repayments mortgage, the payments you make every month are the same throughout the period of the mortgage, unless there is a change in the interest rate. If you choose an increasing repayment mortgage, you start with lower repayments in the early years (when you are presumably less well off) and pay higher repayments in later years. Most lenders will insist that you have some form of life insurance — usually a special mortgage protection insurance — in case you die before the mortgage is repaid.

So you have to add on the cost of that when working out how much this type of mortgage will cost you. When you start paying back a repayment mortgage you find that virtually all your repayments go towards the interest — which is very frustrating, as you seem to pay out large amounts of money but the debt remains as big as ever. In later years, however, the capital you owe reduces, the proportion of each payment which is interest goes down and by the time you get near the end of the mortgage period only a small amount of what you pay each month is interest. If you move, you pay off the sum borrowed when you sell your home and get another mortgage for the new one.

Endowment mortgage

You do not pay back any of the money borrowed until the end of the mortgage. You pay interest on the full amount of the capital sum you have borrowed for the full length of the loan, plus premiums for an endowment life insurance policy. This policy is taken out for the length of time the mortgage covers. When the policy matures, the lender takes enough money to repay the sum borrowed. If you opted for a non-profits endowment policy that is all you get. If you opted for a with-profits endowment mortgage, as well as paying off the loan you should get a pay-out when your policy matures. However, inflation may reduce the value of the sum paid out by quite a lot. Life insurance is automatically included in the policy. You normally make the same payments every month

unless there is a change in the interest rate. A low-cost endowment mortgage means that, to keep the premiums relatively low, the insurance company only guarantees to pay a certain amount when the policy matures, which is less than the sum borrowed. In theory, this means that you might have to make up the difference, but in practice it is more likely that the profits made by the insurer's investment fund exceed that guaranteed and will pay off the sum borrowed and might even give you some extra. This is the most popular kind of endowment mortgage. You can also buy unit-linked endowment policies, where you buy units in an investment fund. These are slightly more risky than a simple endowment mortgage, as the value of your units goes up if the investment fund performs well, but down if not. Endowment mortgages are not as flexible as the repayment type. If you move your mortgage, the new lender may say you have to take out a different policy, and if you cash in an endowment policy in the early years you may get very little back. If you are lucky, you may be allowed to use the original policy to cover a new loan, extended if necessary. It's not usually very easy to extend the term of the mortgage.

Pension mortgage

You do not pay off any of the money borrowed until the end of the mortgage. You pay interest and premiums to a pension plan. When you retire, you get a pension, part of which is

converted into a lump sum which pays off the mortgage and part of which gives you regular pension payments. At the moment (1988) higher rate tax payers get tax relief on their contribution to the pension plan at their highest rate of tax. A lender might insist you took out life insurance to cover the loan, so you would need to add that to the cost of this type of mortgage. You can't cash pension mortgages in early, which makes them very inflexible.

Maturity mortgage

It may be difficult for anyone over 55 to get a mortgage. There are, however, interest-only maturity mortgages intended for people over pension age. These are for a comparatively small amount, or for a relatively low percentage of the value of the house. No capital needs to be repaid under this mortgage until the house is sold, or the borrower dies.

Which one for you?

If you are over pension age, you might decide on the maturity mortgage. If you don't already make pension contributions of some kind, you might be considering the pension mortgage very seriously. But for most people, the choice will be between a repayment and a low-cost endowment mortgage. How about you?

What people chose

Each of the case study families looked at the information and decided on the type of mortgage they would prefer. Raj and Satpal decided on a low-cost endowment mortgage, as they found that the repayments were slightly lower than for a repayment mortgage and they need to make every saving they can. If interest rates rise in the future, the position might be reversed. They do not have life insurance and are attracted by the idea of having a mortgage and life insurance combined.

Rick and Penny already have a repayment mortgage and they decided that they would stick to the same kind of mortgage, since they don't rule out moving yet again. Philip and Molly were attracted by the idea of the maturity mortgage and have determined to look into it, should they need a mortgage of any kind.

The next stage is to approach potential lenders for more detailed information.

Practical points to check

As soon as you start planning a home improvement or extension, or looking for a house or flat to buy, it's worth going to visit several potential lenders to discuss a loan or mortgage. Besides getting information, visiting different lenders should help to give you an idea of the quality of service they might offer.

Here is a list of points to check. The first half of the list covers both loans and mortgages; the second half applies only to mortgages.

Information you should find out from booklets or a personal visit includes

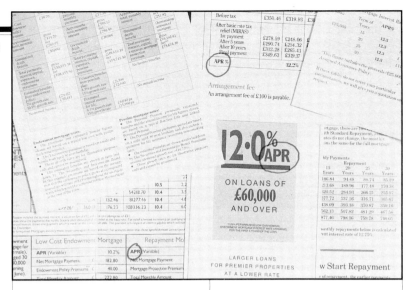

☐ what the monthly payment will be for the amount you want to borrow

☐ the Annual Percentage Rate (APR) — this should help you to make a straight comparison between lenders

☐ what the repayment period is and whether you can change it

☐ when and how payments have to be made
 –in the first month
 –in the rest of the financial year
 –thereafter

☐ what will happen when the interest rate changes

☐ how much more you can borrow with extra security (and what security is acceptable)

☐ whether there will be a redemption charge if you pay off the sum borrowed within a number of (how many?) years

☐ what happens if you have problems with repayments in the future

☐ whether the 'small print' imposes any conditions that might increase the cost of the loan or mortgage in any way, or includes something that makes the mortgage unacceptable to you

☐ the interest rate
 –for different amounts lent (rate may be different for larger loan or mortgage, for example)
 –for different types of mortgage (repayment/endowment/ pension-linked)
 –for first-time buyers (if that's what you are)

☐ how much of the house valuation they are normally prepared to lend

☐ cost of endowment policy (if applicable)

☐ cost of life insurance for pension mortgage (if applicable)

☐ cost of mortgage protection policy (if applicable)

☐ whether you get tax relief

☐ what happens should you decide to sell your home.

CHOOSING THE BEST LENDER FOR YOU

Here are descriptions of potential lenders. If you think that there is any possibility that you might need to borrow money to improve or change your home read through the list and make a note of which lenders would be available to you. Then you can decide which ones you will actually approach when you know how much money you need. When you are checking different potential lenders you will need to make sure what sort of loan you are being offered; check all the costs involved; find out whether life insurance is included or not, or is compulsory — which it may well be for certain kinds of mortgages. Don't take on a big loan just because it is offered to you.

Employers

Some employers are able to make loans or mortgage arrangements for you. This is particularly true if you work in a bank, building society or insurance company who are in the business of lending money. Their interest rates in such cases are usually very low. However, if you change jobs you will probably be required to change your repayments to a higher (standard) rate of interest.

Building societies

Building societies vary as to how much they will lend you. Their interest rates are similar to each other and also similar to those of banks. However, these rates do fluctuate. It is best to consult building societies direct. Arrange

to meet the manager and then you can have the terms and conditions explained to you. Some societies may insist that you invest with them before they will grant you a mortgage. They are helpful in that your local branch will make arrangements for you even if the property which interests you is in a different town. Societies have their own guidelines about how much they will lend to whom on what kind of home, so it's wise to check a number of them. If you already have a mortgage with a building society, it is usually relatively simple to increase your mortgage to pay for home improvements or an extension, or organise a re-mortgage to cover home improvements.

Banks

Many banks now offer first mortgages over a loan period of 25 years. Their rates of interest are similar to those of building societies. Currently all the High Street banks offer mortgages, along with some less well-known names. You should arrange to meet the manager to discuss terms. Banks will also lend money for home extensions or improvements. In the latter case, repayments are usually made over a period of up to a maximum of 10 years.

Finance houses and credit companies

The rates of interest may be higher than building societies, but they may be prepared to lend larger sums. This is especially worth considering if your circumstances are out of the ordinary and you are having difficulty finding a lender

elsewhere. One point you need to check is that the company is registered under the Consumer Credit Act.

Local authorities

Local authorities (or the Housing Executive in Northern Ireland) occasionally offer loans to buy houses direct, but usually only to council tenants buying the property they have been renting, under the 'right to buy' scheme. They will often refer you to a building society who will grant a normal mortgage subject to the usual terms except that they will waive any rule they have about your being an investor with them already. A few authorities may offer mortgages to people prepared to buy and renovate derelict housing.

Builders

Sometimes builders, or developers of new sites, may offer to arrange mortgages, perhaps offering to get 100% mortgages or a lower-than-normal interest rate for the first year as part of a package deal to get people to buy the houses they have built. You will, of course, need to check their offer against other lenders. They won't normally arrange loans for extensions or house improvements.

New schemes

New mortgage schemes are constantly appearing and you should watch out for these. One of them might be just right for you. Just as an example, a building society recently (Spring 1988) advertised what they called a 'Home Hunter Card'. The idea was that you called in to the building society first (before visiting an estate agent) to collect your card, which was a guarantee of a mortgage of up to three and a half times your annual salary. You then started your house-hunting, having sorted out (in theory) the financial worries. Of course, in spite of the headline in the advertisement, you couldn't obtain one of these cards automatically. The card itself was 'subject to status', in other words, you needed to satisfy the society's requirements as to your income and prospects. The actual granting of a mortgage on a particular property was still 'subject to valuation'. But with competition between lenders, new schemes will, no doubt, continue to appear.

LOOKING AT NEW HOMES

By this stage you should be fairly clear in your own mind as to

- the kind of home you would like

- the area which has the facilities you need

- the amount of purchase money you should be able to raise if you are buying

- the amount of rent you could afford if you are renting.

The next step is to look at what is actually available to see how it measures up to your needs and resources. How will you find out what's on the market?

WOULD USING A MORTGAGE BROKER HELP?

Mortgage brokers don't lend money themselves — but can arrange for you to borrow from someone else. They can be particularly useful if you are hoping to buy an unusual home, or one which lenders are not too keen on, if you want a very large loan or mortgages are in short supply. You usually have to pay an arrangement fee if you are offered a repayment mortgage. If you are offered an endowment or pension mortgage, then you shouldn't have to pay a fee, as the broker will get commission from the source of the endowment policy or pension plan. People who helped to develop these materials have found brokers helpful and pleasant. If, however, mortgages are not in short supply and there is not anything particularly unusual about the home you want to buy, there isn't a great deal of point in using a broker.

How to find homes to rent

If you are looking for housing to rent, you will need to contact local authority or development corporation housing departments, the Housing Executive if you live in Northern Ireland, housing associations and estate agents who handle property to let as well as to sell. You can also check in local newspapers — especially for private renting. The development corporations, local authorities and housing associations will almost certainly have long waiting lists, so you need to be prepared to wait. To get on the waiting lists, you may also have to meet certain criteria — you need to check what the priorities are.

How to find homes to buy

The choice of homes to buy is usually greater than those to rent, and there are more ways of finding them. There are estate agents of all types and sizes, property supermarkets, package deals from solicitors, computer networks exchanging details of homes for sale — the list is endless. In Scotland, of course, most houses are still sold through solicitors.

If you really can't manage to go and house- or flat-hunt yourself there are even relocation agents who will do it on your behalf, for a fee. If you have to travel some distance to look at possible properties, you might consider

ESTATE AGENTS' PARTICULARS

How good are you at interpreting the very special language of estate agents' particulars? Besides the many euphemisms like 'suitable for conversion' (= in need of a massive amount of repair), 'bijou' (= can't swing a cat) and 'neat garden' (= minute yard), there are also conventions about the way in which homes are described.

What, for instance, are the particular features of

- a maisonette
- a studio flat
- a garden flat
- a converted flat
- a terraced property
- a townhouse?

A *maisonette* is usually a flat on the first floor reached by its own staircase , or on the ground floor with direct access from outside.

A *studio flat* is usually a very small flat – often one room plus (if you're lucky) a kitchen and bathroom.

A *garden flat* is usually a ground-floor or basement flat with its own garden or access to a garden.

A *converted flat* is a flat or maisonette which has been carved out of a large house. Usually it has a common entrance shared by the other occupiers of the house. You may find it difficult to borrow money to buy a converted flat – some lenders prefer not to advance money on this sort of property

A *terraced property* is a house that has other houses attached to both sides. The end houses in a terraced row will usually be described as end-terrace. A terraced house can be any age.

A *townhouse* is a modern terraced house, often on three floors. It may be large or small and is not necessarily in a town.

Estate agents are being paid to sell the properties on their books – and sellers wouldn't thank them if they didn't do the best possible job by describing the properties in glowing terms. The particulars aren't, however, precise specifications. They are intended to act as inducements for potential buyers to go and take a closer look. By law, the facts should be accurate – the number of floors, for instance, or the size of the rooms. But beware of phrases like 'maximum' measurement – the room might be an odd shape, or have an unusable bow window or alcove. You need to go and measure for yourself how much usable space there is. If no room measurements are given, then you obviously need to be extra careful – a room on the second floor might be described as a bedroom when it only has room for a cot in it, not a full-size bed. Many estate agents include a photograph of the property with the particulars. While this can be useful in giving you a better idea of the style of the house than you get from a written description, it can also be deceptive. Less desirable features may have been painted out, or diminished in some way to make the place look better. There is no substitute for a personal visit.

using a relocation agent, or you could ask an estate agent or solicitor (in Scotland) to set up a series of appointments to view suitable places so that you can make the best use of the time available. You can also advertise yourself, giving your requirements and inviting house sellers to contact you direct. Which method you use to find possible new homes will depend very much on the time, energy and resources you have available for house-hunting. Another important factor which will affect the way you make your search is whether at the time it is a seller's market (few houses or flats available in relation to the number of buyers) or a buyer's market (the reverse). In a seller's market you may need to move very fast to find, view and make your decision about a possible home. In a buyer's market, the buyer has the upper hand and can delay or stall, dictating terms.

TAKING A CLOSER LOOK

No home is perfect, nor can you be sure from the estate agent's particulars that it will meet your needs. When you view possible new homes, you need to have with you a list of what you have decided is important. You could, if you wanted, make an extra note as you go round of particularly good things about the property that weren't on your list, but which would be an added bonus. If you view several houses in the same day, it is very easy to forget or confuse details of this kind ('Was it "Dunroamin" or 40 Acacia Avenue that had the power shower?'). Some people find it useful to take polaroid photos of features they particularly want to record. The other thing you must, of course, check is the condition of the property and whether necessary repairs and replacements would add to the cost of buying it.

You won't be able to check everything – the wiring, for instance, or the condition of the roof. These will be checked in the course of a survey if you get that far in the purchase. But there are some danger signs that you can spot for yourself, such as stained patches on ceilings or walls, loose floorboards and rotting windows. If some improvements have been made, and more are needed, you should check whether an improvement grant was made for the work done. If it was, it is unlikely that a further grant would be made for the rest of the work.

MAKING YOUR RECORD

Keep a notebook or file of papers and list in it the features which are important to you. This could be in two parts — those features which are essential for you and those which are desirable. Take it with you every time you view a possible property and make full notes. If your notebook is big enough, you could paste or clip estate agents' particulars and polaroid photos (if you take them) into the section for each house. As an example, here is the record that Sue made when she was visiting one of the properties on her list.

NO. 2 BROADLANDS

Essential features

At least 2 bedrooms	✓
Garage	✓
Room which will double as workroom	— dining room OK and is at back of house
Reasonable sized garden	— not very big
Central heating	✓

Features I'd like

Quiet road	— pub near - check noise
Fitted kitchen	— don't like colour
Double glazing	✓
Gas central heating	✓
Built-in wardrobes	— very home-made looking

Condition

Paintwork	— windows will need doing
Exterior walls	— look OK — a bit dingy
Garden	— needs a lot of work
Roof	— seems OK
Electricity and wiring	— OK as far as I can tell
Plumbing	— bathroom has nice suite and high-tech shower

DOING IT YOURSELF

Sue's overall impression of No. 2 Broadlands is fairly good. It meets her basic needs, has some drawbacks and one or two particularly good features. As far as she can see, the condition is not too bad, and although some work is required, it shouldn't add too much to the cost of the house. She adds No. 2 Broadlands to her shortlist.

Selling your old home

If you're buying a new home, you'll probably have to sell your old one at the same time (unless you're a first-time buyer or rather rich). You may decide to sell your home through an estate agent or you may decide to do it yourself. If you decide to sell your home yourself, you can put a 'For Sale' board up outside if you wish and you can advertise in the local or national press. Advertising locally will be cheaper; the national papers have more readers but you need to be sure people will be looking for property like yours. You could also consider using specialised advertising papers such as *Dalton's Weekly* (this should be available nationally).

When you're selecting which papers to advertise in check

■ the cost of putting in an ad

■ whether the paper carries plenty of property ads

■ whether the paper carries ads for properties like yours.

The main reason for selling your home yourself is to save money. Most estate agents charge commission if they sell your home. Normally you don't have to pay commission unless the sale goes through — so if the potential buyer withdraws, you don't have to pay. Clearly it's only worth selling your home yourself if it will cost less than selling through an agent. So it's a good idea to set a limit on the amount you're prepared to spend. For example, if the selling price of your house is £50,000 an estate agent may charge you £1000 commission. You could spend £250 on advertising before giving up and handing it over to an agent. You'll need to work out how many times you can advertise your property without exceeding your spending limit.

The no-cost way to sell is to put a 'For Sale' board where everyone can see it. However, remember that if you do this you'll have unexpected callers and many of them will ask to look over your home straight away. If you have access to free advertising space — a notice board at work for instance — use it.

First of all, write an ad for your home. If you include essential information only, like the price and the number of bedrooms (without giving dimensions), you can keep advertising costs down. You can get ideas about how to word your ad by looking in the paper, although you don't need to use extravagant descriptions like some estate agents.

After you've selected which papers you will use you can work out the cost of advertising. The cost will be a major factor in deciding whether or not to advertise in national papers, which are usually more expensive.

When your ad appears you'll have to be available to answer the telephone and to show people around. You can prepare a fact sheet about the property which people can take away .

If you sell within your spending limit, you'll have saved money. If, however, you haven't sold your property you can hand over to an estate agent.

HOW MUCH WOULD IT COST?

Sometimes you have to make a change: your job moves, for instance, and you have to move home. In that case, you just make the best of it, organising your home search and your finances as well as you possibly can. But what about the situation where you have a choice of several changes, including not making any change at all? How would you make your mind up between them? Quite often, you decide for reasons which involve feelings — you want a change, for any number of reasons; you've got embroiled in the moving process and it would be embarassing to withdraw; there are hopes and expectations in your family that you have raised which you can't disappoint. But how about the financial implications of the various options open to you? Weighing them up could be painful, because many of us try to ignore the harsh reality of the extra costs involved if we have really committed ourselves to a major home improvement or a change of home. But it would probably be even more painful (and expensive) if you have to move yet again because you have taken on more than you can afford. You have some idea what your financial resources are, because you've already worked them out. Now you need to work out which choices your resources will cover.

On the following pages are some lists which you can use as the basis for comparison. The first one looks at staying put with no major change, the second at the possible costs for conversion or extension, and the third one should help you to total up all the one-off costs of moving. Some of these costs you'll know, some you can estimate and others you'll have to find out from other people who've recently been through the process of moving.

To make these cost comparisons you need to have got as far as serious consideration of an extension and/or a particular new flat or house, otherwise the comparisons will be too unreal. You may not want to compare all three options. Depending on your circumstances you can choose the two which are most likely for you. If only one option is available to you, then you should still go through the process of costing it and checking your financial resources. ·

The cost of staying put

Not making a major change to your home is probably your cheapest option. But is it entirely cost-free? Is there some major repair or replacement due? Is there anything else you will need to do if you stay in this home rather than move? Have your circumstances changed in some way and made staying in this place more expensive? Here is a checklist of some suggestions as to possible costs of this kind. Work through it, estimating those items which would apply in your case. Add any others that you know about. Add up the total at the end.

- ☐ Increased travel costs due to change or move of job (estimate for one year)
- ☐ Increased travel costs because of change of school (estimate for one year)
- ☐ Cost of re-wiring
- ☐ Cost of new carpets
- ☐ Cost of new windows
- ☐ Cost of double glazing
- ☐ Cost of new roof
- ☐ Cost of cure for rising damp
- ☐ Cost of cure for woodworm
- ☐ Cost of other major repair.

You might be able to get an improvement grant for certain kinds of home improvement. Check with your local council.

If the total cost of staying put is even more than the cost of a home improvement or move, then it is clear that, all things being equal, a change is the best option. If staying put is cheaper in financial terms, then you have to look carefully at the other benefits you hope an improvement or a move will give you.

IS IT WORTH EXTENDING ?

Quite a lot of people make the comparison between the cost of moving to another home and staying in the old one and improving it in some way, probably by extending it. Extensions are an obvious possible solution if you need more space because, although you have to suffer the disruption of having building work done, at least you don't have all the problems associated with moving to a different home, perhaps in a different area. Total up all the costs of a conversion or extension and compare this with the costs of a move. Here are suggestions for the main bills you'd have to pay, but you can add more for your particular circumstances.

One-off costs of conversion/extension

- Architect's fee
- Builder's fee
- Extra insurance for house
- Decoration for converted/ extended areas
- New furniture/carpets.

One-off costs of moving

These include all the costs directly associated with the move. Many of them will have to be paid before you get any money from the sale of your own home, if you have one to sell. You won't have to pay out for all of these (unless you are very unlucky) but some are unavoid-able. You will have to find the deposit on your new home if you are buying, and fees for surveys.

- ☐ Premium for flat if renting
- ☐ Deposit on new home if buying
- ☐ Lender's structural survey
- ☐ Lender's valuation
- ☐ Your own survey if you have one done
- ☐ Fixtures and fittings
- ☐ Solicitor's or conveyancer's fees
- ☐ Search fees
- ☐ Land registry fees
- ☐ Charge for mortgage deed
- ☐ Stamp duty
- ☐ Removal fees
- ☐ Storage fees
- ☐ House-hunting expenses (fares, overnight stays)
- ☐ Costs already paid and lost (due to gazumping, for example, or breakdown of chain)
- ☐ Estate agent's fee if you are selling
- ☐ Essential repairs and decorations to make new home habitable
- ☐ Replacements for fixtures and fittings, carpets, built-in appliances left in old home
- ☐ Extras in a newly built home.

Can you meet this bill?

Maybe you hope to cover all these costs with profit made on selling your previous home, or money from your savings or some other source. Remember, though, that some of these bills will have to be paid before you get the proceeds from the sale of your old home, so you are going to need some reserves to draw on. You might be able to get a bridging loan — but this is not likely to be cost-free. Some bills, or nearly all, may be paid by a new employer or one who has asked you to relocate to another part of the country. If this is the case, you need to check whether all the items in the list will be covered by relocation expenses, or whether there are some that you can't claim for and have to meet yourself.

	Cost per year in present home	Likely cost per year in new or extended home
Mortgage repayments/rent		
Mortgage protection policy		
General rate/community charge		
Water rate		
Ground rent		
Service charges		
Buildings insurance		
Contents insurance if the contents of your home change		
Motor insurance		
Fuel costs:		
■ electricity		
■ gas		
■ oil		
■ solid fuel		
■ other		
Telephone		
Travel-to-work costs		
Travel-to-school costs		
Approximate total annual running costs	£	£

Running costs

But one-off costs aren't the whole story. How about the likely differences in regular, monthly or annual costs? These are more difficult to pin down. It is relatively easy to work out what the difference in rent or mortgage repayments might be if you moved; rates and service charges in flats and insurance can be found out without too much difficulty. Establishing possible fuel costs for the new or extended home might be more difficult. For a new home, you might be able to persuade the present occupants to show you their fuel bills, and check how similar their usage of the house or flat is to yours. For an extended home you could work out a figure based on your current running costs. Fill in the figures in both columns of a table like the one alongside for your own circumstances.

Maybe moving to a new home will give you big savings on running costs, in which case you can move with confidence, knowing that your outgoings will be less. This isn't usually, however, the case, as people often move to larger homes which cost more to run. If you've got the resources to meet those higher costs, fine. If you find that perhaps you haven't, then that choice is not a sensible one for you. You need to work out other options to consider.

The decision as to whether to move or not, and where to move to, is bound to be a fairly complicated, as well as an important one. This is because you have to weigh up many different factors — to do with finance, features you want and feelings about places. An added complication, if more than one person is making the move, is that you have the needs and opinions of a number of different people, often of different ages, to consider. Eventually you are going to get to a point where a decision has to be reached. So how will you deal with all these different possibilities, different people's opinions and different priorities in a way which will do them all justice?

CHOOSING THE BEST OPTION

If you have time, it may well be possible for you to talk everything through to narrow down choices in a way which will be satisfactory to everyone. But you might also like to try following a more systematic decision-making process. Techniques of this kind have proved successful for many people. You can use such techniques for any decision involving a number of different solutions, but they are particularly useful when you are deciding on a change of home.

The simplest method for being more systematic about decision-making is to list all the options open to you and consider advantages and disadvantages for each of them. You can then look more closely at those options which have the fewest disadvantages and the most advantages. A more elaborate method involves weighting and rating.

Weighting and rating

To weight and rate you need a list of your needs and a list of the possible options.

First of all, you take the list of options and give each one a score or rating according to how well it satisfies each need. The scores could be between 0 and 4, in which

4 = very satisfactory, would meet your needs well in every way

3 = satisfactory, would meet your needs quite well

2 = fairly satisfactory

1 = not very satisfactory

0 = not at all satisfactory, wouldn't meet your needs at all.

Then you add up the scores to see which option comes out best.

You might, however, decide that, because some of the needs are more important to you than others, you should score or weight each need on the same scale, 0 to 4, as follows

4 = important/essential

3 = important

2 = fairly important

1 = not very important

0 = not important (although would still like it, if possible).

If you then multiply the ratings you have given the options by the weightings you have given the needs, you should get a score which reflects both the importance to you of the need and how satisfactory the options are. What happened in practice when Sue came to make her decision?

Sue's decision

First of all, you should have a list of the needs you require from a new home. If you remember, Sue had drawn up a list which included those things she felt she had to have, and those things that she would like. She also added one or two items to the list as she looked round several possible houses and realised that some features there would be very useful to her. On the right is her final list.

Next, Sue listed the three main options that she could afford (No. 2 Broadlands, "Hill Cottage" and No. 26 High Street) and gave each a tick or a cross according to whether they would meet her needs or not. As she didn't want to stay in her present flat, she didn't include that among her options, but for some people staying put, and staying put and extending their home, would obviously need to be included. Although this gave her an answer —"Hill Cottage" had more ticks and fewer crosses than the other two options — she was not satisfied with it. The room which was to double as workroom was much smaller than those in the other two houses. There was only part double glazing and there was no garage, only a run-in. She felt that ticking and crossing was too simple, too 'black and white' to give her an answer which took the advantages and disadvantages of the houses into consideration. She decided to *rate* each of the options according to how well they would meet her needs. She rated them on a scale between 0 and 4.

Looking at things this way gave her a slightly different result. Because of the differences in the way that the various houses would meet her needs, No. 2 Broadlands did slightly better (with 30 points) than "Hill Cottage" (29); No. 26 High Street had fewer (22) points. Sue still didn't feel entirely satisfied that she had got a balanced decision. She turned her attention to the list of needs. She had already divided these into two categories — those which she considered essential and those which she would like to have if she could. She now decided to do this in a way which made more

distinction between those needs by *weighting* them on a scale between 0 and 4 according to their importance for her.

The final stage in this weighting and rating decision-making process was to rate the options against Sue's weighted needs. This is the table she drew up. To get the weighted ratings she multiplied each rating by the weighting.

The result of this was that No. 2 Broadlands came out the clear winner. Sue felt that working through this decision-making process had helped her to weigh up the options accurately against her needs — she decided to use this technique when making other buying decisions.

Needs	Importance weighting	No.2 Broadlands Rating	Weighted Rating	Hill Cottage Rating	Weighted Rating	No.26 High Street Rating	Weighted Rating
At least 2 bedrooms	4	4 (×4)	16	3 (×4)	12	4 (×4)	16
Garage	4	4	16	0	0	4	16
Room to double as workroom	3	4	12	2	6	1	3
Reasonable sized garden	3	1	3	4	12	3	9
Central heating -gas	4	2	8	4	16	0	0
Quiet road	3	1	3	4	12	4	12
Fitted kitchen	2	0	0	2	4	4	8
Double glazing	1	4	4	2	2	0	0
Built-in wardrobes	1	2	2	4	4	0	0
Powerful shower	2	4	8	0	0	0	0
South-facing aspect	3	4	12	4	12	2	6
Totals of straight ratings		30		29		22	
Totals of weighted ratings			84		80		70

Making decisions as a group

Sue was fortunate — she was the only person who was involved in the move so she didn't have to allow for other people's needs and other people's opinions. Raj and Satpal made up a list together of what they felt they needed in the way of features in an area, so that they could check them for places to which they were thinking of moving. When they'd drawn up the list, they each gave the features an importance rating.

This was the result.

Drawing up this list helped them to realise that they hadn't discussed the sort of area they wanted at all, and had made assumptions about what was wanted. Although they felt that they would probably have worked out what they both needed in the end, they thought that weighting their needs in this way was a short cut, and determined to use it for more decisions about their move.

	Importance	
Needs	Raj	Satpal
Shops nearby	4	4
Launderette	3	4
Pub	4	0
Sports Centre	4	4
Petrol Station	4	2
Post Office	0	4
Playgroup	0	4
DIY Centre open on Sundays	4	4
Park with ducks and swings	2	4
Library	4	1
Health Centre	2	4
Open market	4	1

NEEDS	OPTIONS				
	Stay at present home	Extend present home	No.6 The Heights	'Dunroamin'	'Uplands House'
Rick					
Larger garden	0	0	2	4	1
Another bedroom	0	4	4	4	4
Penny					
Detached home	0	0	4	4	4
Move nearer parents	0	0	0	2	4
Adam					
More room for bike	0	3	3	0	
Stay near friends	4	4	0	4	
Kate					
A bigger room of own	0	3	4	2	3
Closer to school and sports centre	0	0	2	4	4
Totals	4	14	19	24	23

Rick and Penny decided to try to allow their children to take part in their decision, as they wanted everyone to be happy about the move. They worked out that their options were to stay put, in their present home, to extend it giving more space for the children and an extra bedroom, or to move to one of three houses they had picked out which they thought would be suitable. They would be able to afford (just about) any of these options, although some were more expensive than others. They decided to make a list of their various needs and to give each option a rating according to how well that option met their needs.

Now that you've worked your way through this chapter, deciding on your needs and resources and reaching a decision about which choice is best for you, what should be your next step?

WHAT'S NEXT?

The rest of this book deals with different aspects of making changes in your home. Briefly, chapter two looks at the way you can use the space in your home to make it work better to fit the needs of those who live there. Chapter three looks at the way you equip your home and what will do the job best. The last chapter deals with maintaining and running your home economically to make it a safe and secure place for those in it.

So if you've decided to stay put in your present home and not undertake major improvements or extension, then you can simply carry on and work your way through the other three chapters.

If you've decided on a conversion, extension or major home improvement of some kind, then you will need to look very carefully at the question of how you will get the work done. Decide how much you are able to do yourself and are prepared to take on. Decide on those areas where you will need to employ others. You'll need to go to the part of chapter four which looks at how you make those decisions. You can then go on to work your way through chapters two, three and four for your newly improved or extended home. Incidentally if, in spite of all your work, things go wrong and you encounter a problem of some kind, there is a section at the very end of this book called **What To Do If Things Go Wrong**. Consult this in case of need!

PLANNING YOUR CHANGE

The key to success when you are planning a major change of any kind is to think about things beforehand and work out how best to cope with them. If your decision has been to move to another home, then good timing and planning will be all-important to avoid unnecessary stress, strain and expense.

Timing your move

Moving home has been described by psychologists as possibly one of the most traumatic life experiences. Their advice is to try to avoid combining a home move with other major life events in the family, such as the birth of a baby, or starting school or a new job. This is easier said than done, since it is frequently a major crisis or turning-point such as separation or divorce, the death of a family member or a new job which triggers off a move. Obviously, it makes sense to postpone a move if you know it's going to clash with something important, and not to rush into a move after a family tragedy unless you absolutely have to. If you've no experience of moving, or haven't moved for so long that you've forgotten what it is like, take a few moments to think about and discuss how you, and those who live with you, might face up to possible unknowns. These could be outright disasters, or just general stress and strain.

Possible disasters connected with the house purchase

- Being gazumped — unless you live in Scotland where it's not possible
- Putting up with 'cliffhangers' on house sale and purchase
- Getting caught in a 'chain' of buyers, where one link drops out — again, not possible in Scotland.

The stresses and strains connected with moving

- Travelling around, perhaps over long distances, to view possible new homes
- Finding new schools
- Meeting new neighbours
- Leaving old friends and making new ones
- Planning, purchasing and installing new curtains, carpets, furniture and appliances
- Investigating new shops
- Coping with the physical exertion of the move itself
- Notifying people of your change of address and getting post forwarded
- Going through all your possessions and getting rid of what you don't need or can't use in the new home
- Damage and breakages as a result of the move.

Exhilarating and exciting though many of the changes may be in themselves, the combination of several might prove more burdensome than you realise.

Planning your move in detail

With something as complicated and exhausting as a move, it makes sense to take the trouble to make a detailed plan involving a timetable and checklist. If you can be sure that you haven't forgotten anything vital, you will be more relaxed. Here is an example of a checklist for moving which you could use as the basis for yours, if you need one. Even if you aren't moving yet, you could use the idea of making lists and notes and planning in advance for other major changes.

CHECKLIST FOR MOVING

Three weeks before
- [ ] Get three removal firms' estimates and/or quotes for DIY van hire charges
- [ ] Choose firm: confirm arrangements
- [ ] If necessary arrange extra insurance to cover your belongings for the move
- [ ] DIY: alert friends/family for help on the day (packing, driving, providing meals, cleaning up)

Old address
- [ ] Arrange for meters to be read
- [ ] Arrange for disconnection of cooker and washing-machine
- [ ] Arrange for carpets to be cleaned if required
- [ ] Notify telephone sales office of date account to be closed
- [ ] Contact rating authority

New address
- [ ] Arrange for taking over gas and electricity
- [ ] Arrange for reconnection of cooker and washing-machine
- [ ] Arrange for carpets to be laid
- [ ] Apply to take over telephone or request new telephone to be installed if required
- [ ] Change of address cards — buy, or order printing (after new telephone number known)
- [ ] Arrange insurance of contents at new home from date of move and during removal
- [ ] Arrange buildings insurance for new home from the date of the exchange of contracts
- [ ] Start sorting and throwing out things
- [ ] Arrange extra rubbish disposal
- [ ] Get boxes, packing materials, strong string
- [ ] Buy stick-on labels

	☐ Arrange any hotel booking that may be needed
	☐ Children — arrange to leave with relatives/friends
	☐ Pets — book kennels if necessary
A week before	☐ Prepare outline diagram of new home with location of furniture
	☐ Send off change of address cards
	☐ Bank etc. — arrange for transfer of account
	☐ Notify tax inspector, DVLC, investments etc. of change of address
	☐ Post office — apply for redirection of mail
Old address	☐ Arrange cancellation of deliveries of milk and newspapers and settlement of accounts
	☐ (Rented property) check that there is no damage which has to be repaired, or replacements which have to be organised
	☐ Arrange for leaving keys
New address	☐ Arrange deliveries, e.g. milk
	☐ Check arrangements for collecting keys
	☐ Check arrangements for hiring van/borrowing car
	☐ Get own car serviced so it doesn't break down at crucial moment
	☐ Confirm arrangements and timings for meter readings and disconnection/connection at old/new address for electricity and gas
	☐ Arrange with seller and buyer about leaving off/on electricity, water and heating
	☐ Check that manuals and instructions for appliances are being left
	☐ Finish packing and labelling
Day before	☐ Pack personal overnight case(s)
	☐ Organise meals/drinks for moving day
	☐ Switch freezer to maximum (if moving it with contents
	☐ Check that any work (decoration etc.) which needs to be done at the new address has been completed
	☐ Take children to relatives or friends to stay
	☐ Deliver pets to kennels
	☐ Get supply of cash (e.g. for tips, meals, coins for emergency telephone calls)
	☐ Defrost refrigerator
	☐ Go to bed early.

This checklist has been adapted from one in a useful book called *Which? Way to Buy, Sell and Move House*, published by the Consumers' Association. The *Which?* book ends with a good bit of advice that you might like to take if you can:

'If moving has turned out particularly complicated and strenuous in spite of trying to foresee all the hazards, try to get away; even if only for a couple of days. A break at this point from the physical and mental effort can make all the difference.'

ONE-ROOM LIVING

Since Paul's early retirement, he and Muriel have had a radical change of lifestyle. They have given up their large four-bedroomed detached house in the suburbs in favour of a one-room flat in the middle of town. Paul and Muriel say that this change has produced nothing but advantages for them. Giving up living space has had a liberating effect. They have had to discard much of their furniture and devise storage methods which ensure that there is a place for everything that they really need. Paul and Muriel summed up the advantages of the one-room flat in the town centre as follows

■ few domestic reponsibilities (no need to worry about the fabric of the house, upkeep of garden etc.)

■ less housework and few maintenance jobs

■ central position means easy access to town-centre facilities

■ municipal gardens outside maintained by corporation gardeners mean that they can look out on and walk in lovely grounds

■ everything is to hand — the kitchen is laid out particularly effectively

■ sufficient space to entertain friends and hold meetings for their wine circle

■ no fears as to security — Paul and Muriel can indulge their taste for travel and can leave the flat confident that security is good.

A one-room flat might not be everyone's choice — but scaling down, especially for those whose families have decreased in size, can offer many advantages.

Particular features which attracted Paul and Muriel to their flat included its attractive setting, its central position, the various security devices and good sound insulation.

Moving to the compact one-room flat has meant that Paul and Muriel have had to rethink how much furniture they actually need, and to discard a great deal. They have a fair amount of storage space, but find that they need to be quite disciplined about how they use it.

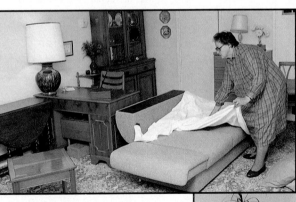

By day Paul and Muriel's pleasant living room provides a background to their daily life and social gatherings. By night, it is easily transformed into a spacious bedroom.

MAKING THE BEST USE OF SPACE

Pamela and Edward live in a houseboat on the River Thames with their three-year-old daughter, Emily. Both Pamela and Edward work freelance so their home is also their work base. Since space is so limited, they have had to put a lot of effort into

■ making use of every scrap of space for storage

■ changing the use of the space they have to make sure that they keep up to date with changing needs

■ extending the space they have by adding an 'extension' — a non-mobile floating structure

■ finding the right equipment to fit into this very limited space.

While not a great many people have the opportunity or even the desire to live on a boat, there are many interesting aspects to the way Pamela and Edward use the space in their home. Because they constantly need to review 'what goes where' they have to find different solutions and ways of fitting people and possessions into the very limited area available.

The houseboat was Pamela and Edward's original home. Edward has now extended their living space with the addition of the extra structure which lies alongside — beyond the houseboat in this picture.

In Edward's words: 'The houseboat is our home. It has been specifically designed to maximise all of the space that is available.'

The addition of Emily to the family meant that the houseboat had to be rebuilt. Her cabin, in the bows of the boat, has toy storage as well as containing the anchor chain locker.

Every bit of space in the boat has been used to the full. Bath, lavatory, shower, wash-basin and storage space are all fitted into the tiny bathroom. The bath is the invalid type which is ideal for Emily to sit in, and also means that showers and baths can be taken safely while the boat is at sea.

Not only does the stove warm the interior of the boat, but washed clothes can be dried and aired around it. The shelving in the boat's main cabin has been designed to fit the television and hi-fi exactly. The space under the two bottom stairs contains a drawer to hold polishes and cleaning materials.

With such a limited amount of space available, Pamela and Edward have had to make careful decisions about how it is allocated. Food preparation, cooking and eating are fitted into the galley area of the houseboat; freelance work is done in the other floating structure.

A LABOUR-SAVING RETIREMENT HOME

Chris and Nancy live in Scotland. Retired from full-time work, they have put a lot of time and energy into creating the home which will be right for their special needs. Although Chris and Nancy were looking for a home to suit them in their retirement, their aims, and the way they set about achieving them, are of more general interest. They summed up their special needs as

- warm, labour-saving home on one level
- minimum-work garden with sunny patio
- space which fits their furniture and possessions
- convenient design to accommodate Nancy's lack of stamina and medical problems.

Chris and Nancy's solution

They took a standard design timber-framed well-insulated bungalow and had a number of modifications made to the original plans.

These modifications were to

- swing the whole building round so that only the narrow double-glazed bedroom end was on the road and the living room and patio faced south
- lower the living room windows to enable Nancy to sit and look out
- give up one of the bedrooms (the original design had four) to give more storage space
- put up a partition wall to divide kitchen and dining-room to give more storage space in the kitchen and to make the two rooms quite separate.

In addition to the changes in the house design, they also introduced labour-saving devices such as

- gravel right through the garden, so there are no lawns to mow
- raised beds in the garden which are very easy to maintain and can be reached without too much bending or kneeling
- rotary dryer in the carport so that Nancy can easily get washing dried.

Chris and Nancy have taken a close personal interest in every stage of the building work on their new timber-framed bungalow.

The original design was meant to face the road broadside on with the front door leading directly to the pavement. Chris and Nancy's changes mean that the front door is at the side and the living room is at the back, well away from the road. Only the bedrooms overlook the road.

Placing the windows lower in the wall than was shown in the original plans means that Nancy can easily sit and look out into the garden.

Re-allocating space and changing the dimensions of the rooms while the house was being built meant that Nancy and Chris were able to have a lot of flexibility. Originally there was no wall dividing kitchen from dining-room. They had one installed which allows just enough space on the dining side for the dining-room table and chairs and other furniture which they had brought from their previous, larger house. It also means, of course, that there is extra storage space on the kitchen side for sink, cooker and fridge.

Another change Chris and Nancy decided on was to move the garage back and put a carport next to the side door. This means that Nancy can get into and out of the car while remaining under cover.
An additional bonus is having the rotary dryer under the carport which means that clothes can be dried outside even when it's raining.

Nancy and Chris find their garden exceptionally easy to maintain, as there is no grass to mow and the central bed is raised so that Nancy can sit in a garden chair to weed.

All in all, Nancy and Chris are very pleased with their new house — the effort has all been worthwhile. As Nancy says: 'It is as we planned it and we're very happy with it .... It's our home and how we have arranged the accommodation is for our benefit and our lifestyle.'

CHAPTER TWO

ORGANISING SPACE

Your home contains a certain amount of space. You and other household members all fit into that space and use it for your daily lives. But how? Are you all satisfied with your space?

This chapter looks at organising space in your home. It asks you to devote some thought to how satisfied you are with that space and to consider whether, and if so how, you'd like to change things.

How you deal with space in your home is affected by its size, how many people live there and what they do in it. Also, of course, it's affected by what resources you have and how you choose to use them. Clearly a fairly well-off single person living in a studio flat will be thinking about different issues from six people living on one income in a semi-detached house.

But whatever your circumstances, organising or reorganising space is something you can do. It can range from reorganising your kitchen to having an extension built; from deciding to sort out the cupboards to having a complete wall unit fitted; from agreeing on what private space is needed for household members to having a granny flat built.

People matter

People differ in the amount of space they require and how they choose to use it. If several people live in your home you may find you all have different views of the space available to you. One person is untidy and sees every surface as fair game for their possessions. Another person is tidy but needs to use space you all share for a very 'big' hobby like model aeroplane building. A third person may know that the dining-room is free all the time, but feels that the room is dark and uninviting, preferring to do their dressmaking all over the living room floor.

So it's not just empty space you need to think about but space as people fill it — people with their personal tastes, preferences and habits. In this chapter you will find frequent suggestions for talking to other people about using the space in your home. And that's not just because people have different requirements but because they'll have different ideas about changes. One thing is certain, you won't be able to bring about change unless you 'take other people with you'. A home is for the people who live in it and any changes need to be based on this fact ... a fact that's often overlooked.

Research matters

It is useful to pin down how you feel about the space in your home. Many people have an area in their home which they like best and where they feel comfortable. Fewer people work out why. If you find out why you like and dislike certain areas of your home you can apply these discoveries — making changes so that you feel comfortable in more of your home than you did before. So there's some detective work to be done in thinking through how you feel about space in your home. And you also need to be clear about what your home's actually like, how much space you have, how it's used, where the wiring is, where the load-bearing walls are, when the 'rush hours' are. All this research helps. Clearly, knowing the current situation is a good start for thinking about change.

Resources matter

However you decide to change things, the alterations need to be within your means. Solutions don't have to involve major changes and expense. There are all sorts of ways of organising space. Changing the way you do something — like arranging things differently for storage — can be effective and costs nothing. And you can always change things back if you don't like the result. Think carefully about big alterations that cost a lot of money. Make sure they're really what you want to do. They will be expensive to change back if you don't like them.

Learn to think of resources as more than just what money can buy. Resources can include your energy and bright ideas. They may be offers of help and hard work from other people which will make an idea work out in practice, or something you already have, but renew or re-use in a different way. We all have some resources at our disposal.

WHAT'S IN THIS CHAPTER

The chapter has five topics in it.

What goes on in your home?

The first topic in this chapter helps you look at the current situation — what goes on in the space in your home, whether you are losing space because you have fixed ideas about how it should be used and which space is being used a lot.

Making a home plan

By working through this topic you should be able to pin down how you feel about the space in your home — what picture of it you have in your mind's eye. It then goes on to help you make accurate plans of your home.

Room for improvement

At this point you will be thinking about what changes you would like to bring about regarding space in your home.

Storage

This topic helps you look at your attitudes to storage — what you have to store, how you can make best use of the space you have and how you can make new storage space.

One home, many needs

This topic is designed to get you thinking about the variety of different activities that take place in your home and what happens when one person's use of space clashes with the needs of other members of the household.

If you live in a flat or house that's like others nearby, how likely do you think it is that your neighbour's home will look and feel like yours inside? The interiors of all homes are unique because the way that people see them and use them is different. People find ways of adapting what the architect planned to make their home 'their own'. They have different values about *how* space should be used and different tasks and routines that make demands on their home space.

MAKING IT YOUR OWN

Architects, of course, have to make assumptions about how a home is going to be used. For example, they include kitchens and bathrooms in all home designs. But they didn't include bathrooms in houses at the turn of the century. The fact that we now see bathrooms as necessary means that many old houses have had them built on or had bedrooms converted into bathrooms. The result is sometimes a bit awkward, perhaps a downstairs extension, out beyond the kitchen and a very long way from bedrooms. Houses grow and change for all sorts of reasons. The fact that the nation's way of life has altered since much of its housing stock was built has brought about all sorts of changes and conversions to old houses as people try and adapt them for current ways of living.

Take, for example, one row of semi-detached houses in a small village in the South East of England. They were built about 1900. The space between adjacent houses is a double footpath — just enough to squeeze one car through. Most of the owners now have garages behind the houses with a shared driveway converted out of the former footpaths. Some people have 'drive on' front gardens. Some people have built front porches because the front door opens directly into the living room. Most people have knocked down the wall between the front living room and the back living room. Some people have converted the third bedroom into a bathroom. Others have had the outhouses converted into bathrooms, and so it goes on.

Just looking at the houses or flats around you will give you lots of ideas for different ways of using space. Even if people live in council property where they're not allowed to knock down walls, they make their houses their own by the way they adapt them to their needs.

Look at the diagrams below. They show the plans of a two-storey house. The left-hand diagram shows what furniture the architect anticipated and how he saw it arranged in the house. The right-hand diagram shows how the house was actually used by one family. Maybe if this family find things in their house crowded it's because they aren't using it as the architect planned.

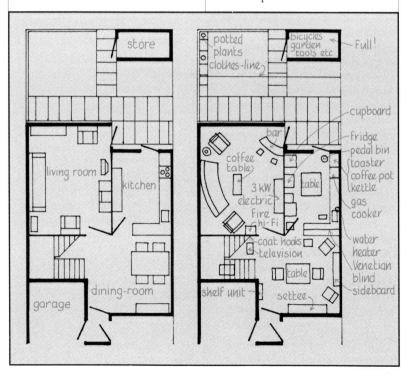

Perhaps the lifestyle and values this architect had in mind do not match those of the people living in the house. He might, for instance, have assumed that the occupants would want to eat in a dining-room and have a standard three-piece suite in the living room. It's worth looking at your own lifestyle and values to see how much they shape what you do in your house. For example, if you have a parlour or best room, is that a room the family don't normally use? Or maybe it's mainly for adults? This will mean less everyday space for the adults or children in the rest of the house The same goes for a dining-room that's rarely used, especially if you all dine in a kitchen that was never intended for eating as well as food preparation.

USING SPACE

Do you find that there are quite large areas in your home that aren't used?

LITTLE-USED SPACE

Make a list of the areas in your home that are not used very often. Of course the main reason you aren't using a particular space may be because it's damp or cold or very inconvenient in some way. It is useful to distinguish between this sort of unused space and somewhere like a parlour which is set aside because of your ideas about how space should be used.

Perhaps you could think about whether the benefits you get from a best room are enough to merit it being out of circulation most of the time? Why is it important to have a best room, or a dining-room that isn't used very often?

Sometimes parlours and dining-rooms and other 'best' areas become damp and cold just because they aren't used. These rooms then smell musty and people want to use them still less, even when it's what they consider to be a suitable occasion.

If you find you do have space in your house that isn't used much, try completing the following sentences about each area of unused space.

We use this room (space) .... times a week/month.

We use this room (space) for ....

The reason we don't use this room (space) much is ....

If we wanted to we could use this room (space) for ....

If we wanted to use this room (space) for some other purpose we'd have to ....

If we changed our use of this room (space) it would relieve pressure on ....

If we changed the way we use this room (space) other people would ....

Ask other members of your household to complete each sentence too and see what ideas you come up with for how well that room or space is currently being used, and what else it could be used for.

While some areas may not get used very much, other space seems to have many demands made on it.

MUCH-USED SPACE

Note down the areas of your home that are used a lot and the variety of activities each area is used for.

You will probably note down something like this:

Kitchen — eating, preparing food, washing, study

Living room — sitting, reading, watching television

Spare bedroom — guests, Linda when she's got a migraine, Michael and his friends when other people are using the living room

Dining-room — occasional dining, Jack for work, Kevin for model aeroplanes, Lizzie for sewing, ironing.

How convenient are these arrangements? Perhaps the various activities fit in easily and there are never too many demands made on a room at one time. People usually expect diverse activities to go on in a room. Living rooms are very public rooms for most people: they share the space to do a variety of things, but activities which take up a large area or which cannot easily be put away can create a strain on public space. Kevin's model aeroplanes and Lizzie's sewing are things from the list on the previous page that seem to demand some space other than that of a living room.

People aren't always clear about the way that space is being used. They only get as far as realising that there are too many demands on certain spaces.

To get a clearer picture you'll probably find it useful to keep a diary of what goes on in your home for a week.

A DIARY

If other members of the household are prepared to co-operate you could try to keep a diary of a week for the whole household. To do this you could stick a piece of paper on each door and ask people to fill it in when they go into a room to do something (not every momentary visit or you'll be up to your eyes in paper). They should note what it is they're going to do and when they go in and come out. You could also ask people to mark down when they would have liked to use a room but it was occupied by someone else.

Your list might look something like the one alongside.

You could do this for every room in the house or flat. This would certainly bring home to everyone the time of the rush hour in the bathroom. Or if you are already quite clear about peak periods and rush hours in your home, you may prefer just to concentrate on the areas you've identified that seem to get used a great deal.

This is a big exercise and you may not get everyone's co-operation. Instead you could try the following approach.

A RANDOM CHECK

Draw a chart for the coming week. Put the seven days down the left-hand side of the chart, and the rooms and areas in your home across the top. To give yourself a general idea of how your home is used, think of, say, a dozen moments in the week. For instance you could choose 1.00 pm Sunday, 8.00 pm Sunday, 9.00 am Monday, 6.00 pm Monday and so on. Jot down the times you have chosen alongside your days of the week. Think about where the members of your household would be in your home at those moments in an average week. Weekday mornings are likely to be similar unless someone is on shift-work, but evenings and weekends will probably vary. You might want to choose one 'rush hour' moment, one quiet moment, and so on.

Then jot down the person and what he or she would be doing in the appropriate box in the chart.

Unless you lead a life with a very regular routine then people may not always be in the same place at the same time each week, but you should get some idea of how the space is used.

Carrying out these exercises should help you to be clearer about those spaces and family activities which need to be looked at more carefully. Either the spaces need changing in some way or people's activities need to be timetabled differently or reorganised.

Spare Bedroom

Day	Time	Use
Monday	6.00pm–7.00pm	Kevin's trumpet practice
	8.30pm–9.00	Michael needs to do homework
Thursday	6.00pm–7.00pm	Kevin's trumpet practice
	6.45pm	Linda – would have liked to read

TASKS AND SPACE

Use of space isn't just about competition with other people. It is also about how you and others actually organise the space you've got to do the things you want to do. A good example of this is the small and simple activity of making a cup of tea.

Tea making will require less effort in the kitchen shown in the top diagram

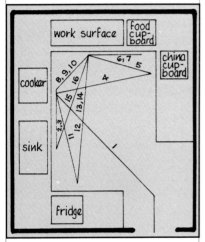

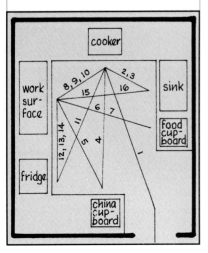

The next time you want to make a cup of tea, take special notice of exactly what you are doing. Better still, get someone else in the house to track you as you do it. Draw, or get them to draw, a simple map of your kitchen and then draw a line for each move you make while you're making the cup of tea. This would be, say, from the door to the tea-caddy, to the teapot, to the cups, to the fridge, to the cooker and so on. The places where the things you need are kept in your kitchen will affect how many little journeys are required to make your cup of tea. The two diagrams show the progress of tea being made in two differently arranged kitchens.

The work triangle

A lot of research has been done to find the most efficient way to plan a kitchen — that is, the way that means the least walking about. A triangle with sides of equal length linking cooker, fridge and sink is thought to be the best way of organising a kitchen. If you can start from scratch you may be able to do this. But even if you can't move fixtures you may be able to rearrange your cups, food and so on to be able to use your kitchen a lot more efficiently. You can plan space to help you move around more easily in your house without going to great expense. Of course there are always people who say it's good for your health to move around a lot!

Where the action is

You may be making life difficult, or at least uncomfortable, for yourself by just accepting the way things are currently arranged in your home. By taking a more careful look at things you may find aspects that can be changed easily to make the space more comfortable.

As you move around your home doing things over the next few days, just notice where and when you seem to be bumping into things, or having to slide past things and think about why this is.

Sarah

'I'd never really put my finger on it, but every time I made our bed I used to get vaguely annoyed. I hadn't really noticed that having it against the wall meant that you had to stand on the blessed thing to make it, and in the night if I got up to go to the loo I was always climbing over John which didn't lead to a great deal of marital harmony.'

Dave

'When we had guests to dinner, if anyone had to get up from the far side of the table during the meal, the person next to them had to get up to let them out.'

Carly

'I'd always used this tiny space at the end of the bed to do the ironing. And every time I did the ironing I'd squeeze past the board in a space about six inches wide. And then one day I stepped on the cord as I was going past and the hot iron fell off the board and

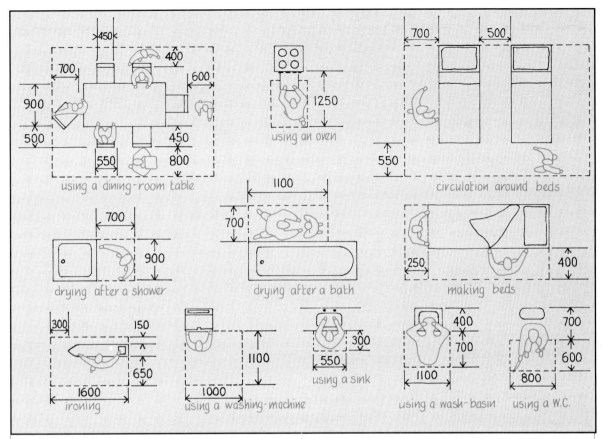

The minimum amount of space needed for common household tasks

missed my foot by a fraction of an inch.'

The government has worked out how much room people need to do various things in the home. The diagram above demonstrates the minimum amounts of space recommended by the Department of the Environment. People don't live in neat little spaces like these, but you could use the diagram to help you work out where you've got space problems in your home. You may find it useful just to measure the areas you're using to do things, where you feel cramped. As you look at the diagram you'll see that the area shown is most often circulating space — the space you need to move around things; elbow space — the space you need to move the top half of your body, particularly your arms; and 'front-loading' space — the space you need to pull things out, drawers, doors and so on. The measurements in the diagram are, of course, based on averages. There is a big difference between the amount of room a person 1.9 metres tall is going to need for using an oven and the room taken up by a person who is 1.5 metres tall. But you could use these dimensions as a guide when you are replanning your use of space.

How you utilise space in your home depends on all sorts of things. Some of these are quite obvious, like not having enough physical space to do certain things. But other aspects of use of space have to do with your values — how you choose to use (or not use) available space. So beginning to think about changing your use of space has got as much to do with what goes on inside your head as inside your home.

MAKING A HOME PLAN

Making a plan of your home is a good way to help you focus on the features of your home as it is now. It is an essential starting-point if you are thinking of making changes.

This topic helps you build up a set of plans that will represent your home in various ways. Some of the plans will help you work out how your home 'feels' to you. Others are accurate practical plans which plot the space and services in your home. Both kinds of plan will be useful in helping you start to assess any changes you might want to make.

MENTAL MAPS

We all have 'mental maps' of the shapes and sizes of our homes. These are 'mind's-eye' views. They may not be accurate, but they can be useful because they help us work out what our impressions of our homes are — what they 'feel' like to us.

YOUR MENTAL MAP

Sketch a map of your home as you think it is. Don't get up and look around: the idea is to draw your home from memory.

- The map should show all the rooms on each floor, looking down from above.
- Include as many major features as possible, like doors and windows, and stairs if you've got them.

When you've completed your mental map, get up and look round your home. How accurate is the map?

How did your map turn out? Were there any surprises?

Sometimes your mental map will be affected by a whole variety of things. You may think a room which doesn't get very much light is small and cramped. You may think alcoves are bigger than they are because you've got a great many ornaments on shelves in them. You may see stairs as poky because six people are always going up and down them and bumping into each other.

DIFFERENT VIEWS

Take the sketch map you've drawn and make some photocopies or trace some extra copies. Use these to record your feelings about your home. Try out the following things using a number of the maps so that they don't get too complicated.

- Put numbers on a map — from 1 for areas you like most down to 5 for areas you like least.
- Put a name on areas you associate with particular people.
- Write the letter 'L' on areas on a map where you think it's nice and light, 'D' on areas where you think it's dark.
- Write 'W' on areas you think are warm and comfortable, 'C' on areas you think are cold.
- Colour areas on a map that are used a lot by the whole household in one colour.
- Using a different colour, colour in areas which you don't think anyone uses very much.

Julie has put numbers on the map of her bungalow to show which areas she likes best

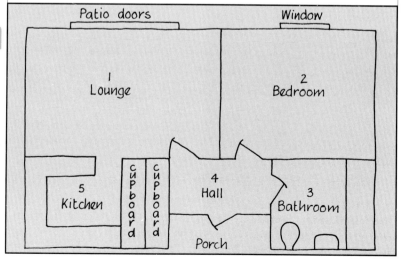

64

■ Draw lines over one map where you think the main routes are that people take to move around the home and in particular rooms. You'll need to think about where the furniture is to do this.

Ask other people in your household to do these exercises too. They may like to start by sketching their own maps. Do you all agree about areas of your home? Look carefully at what you've done. It should help throw some light on the ways that you see your home.

You may have found that you just don't see it in some of the ways suggested. People have different views of how their home is used. For example, if you've got small children you may well have almost a 'child's-eye' view — thinking how steep the stairs are, or being acutely aware of the position of electrical points or doors with glass panels at the bottom.

GETTING THE FACTS STRAIGHT

Now you have a fairly clear idea about how your home feels to you, it's useful to add to it by making an accurate plan of the space available.

Doing this will help you clarify what space, shapes and services you've got in your home. Although it's important to recognise how you feel about the space, its real dimensions and characteristics are also important, especially if you think you might make changes. It is no good having the feeling an alcove is big

and then buying a wardrobe that's too big for it. But it is important to be clear before you start the next exercises that just because you have the space available you don't necessarily have to fill it!

A PLAN OF YOUR HOME

This section shows you how to draw a scale map of your home. If you have never done this before you will find it quite challenging, and you should put aside several hours for doing the exercise.

Taking measurements

Measure each room as accurately as you can. Use a tape-measure or metal tape marked in centimetres, and see if you can get someone to help you. When you measure each room make sure you have got measurements for

☐ the length and width

☐ the position of alcoves in a wall, their width and depth

☐ the position of full-length fitted cupboards, their width and depth

☐ the position of windows and doors and their width

☐ the position of a chimney-breast and its width and depth

☐ the position and size of things which are not normally moved, such as cooker, fridge and bath.

Build up a sketch map as you go, or use the sketch map you've already made for the previous activity, and mark on all the measurements. The sketch map doesn't have to be to scale but it will help you keep your bearings as you gather measurements. Remember to measure hall and

landings if you have them. Mark in the stairs on your ground-floor plan and show where they emerge on your upstairs plan.

When you have taken all these measurements, work out the full length and width of your home by adding up the room lengths (taking into account the thickness of walls) or by taking separate measurements outside if this is possible.

Drawing to scale

When you draw to scale, the aim is to make a drawing which exactly represents the dimensions of the room or the house or flat.

If you do your drawing in such a way that one centimetre on the paper represents one metre in your home, this will produce a scaled drawing of 1:100. If, for example, a room is 3.5 metres by 4.2 metres, your drawing of it would measure 3.5 centimetres by 4.2 centimetres. To do this accurately you will find it very helpful to use graph paper with centimetre squares on it. Then each centimetre square will represent a metre square in your home. If you wanted a larger map, you could use the scale 1:50. A room measuring 3.5 metres by 4.2 metres would then be drawn as 7.0 centimetres by 8.4 centimetres. Each centimetre would equal 0.5 of a metre and your plan would be twice as big as a plan drawn on a scale of 1:100.

Making the plan

Use a large piece of paper. Either buy special squared paper with squares the size you are going to use or, with a ruler, draw squares on a piece of plain paper (perhaps lining paper for walls). Aim to make your plan reasonably large, but keep it small enough that you can work on it on a table or a space on the floor and still see what you are doing.

Before you draw in any lines you may find it useful to work out a scale and convert the measurements you have gathered into scaled measurements, that is the actual length of lines you are going to use on the plan. If you are working on a scale of 1:100 you need to divide all the measurements taken by 100 to give the scaled measurements. If you are working in metres this just means moving the decimal point two places to the right.

Use a pencil to begin with and draw the shape of the whole ground floor, then the shape of the first floor and then the second floor if you have one. Don't start with one room, or you may find your plan goes off the page if you start at the wrong point. Each line you draw should be to scale. Remember that walls vary in thickness – they are usually about 300 and 150 mm thick for outside and inside walls, respectively. Next you can begin to fill in rooms and other areas. When you come to do windows and doors, draw them to show which way they open. You can see how doors can be drawn in the illustration here.

When you are satisfied, fill in your outline with a black pen, preferably not ball-point pen as this often smudges.

You should aim to produce a plan about as detailed as the one here.

Your plan should give you a good idea of floor space — and things that are currently fixed like windows, doors, sinks, baths and so on.

SERVICES

There are also, of course, other important fixed features of your home: electrical fittings (wiring, points and light fittings), pipes and water supplies, and central heating if you have it.

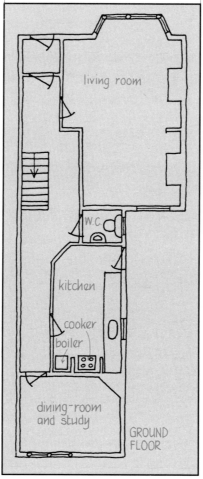

So next on your plan you can draw in the fittings that you know of. Use different coloured pencils to draw in power points, pipes, radiators and boilers. Unless you are familiar with these sorts of services you won't be able to include on your plan the parts that aren't visible. However, the visible portions should give you an idea of places in your home where services are concentrated.

Modern houses contain many services that are generally fitted together to reduce initial costs. The major services include water pipes, electricity cables, gas pipes, telephone wires and television aerial cables. These are expensive, and usually rooms that have similar service requirements are fitted together. For example, bathrooms and lavatories are usually stacked on top of kitchens in modern houses. Older houses have central chimneys serving several fires. If you are planning big changes it's as well to know this because it can be very costly to have a bathroom built on the side of the house away from where services are mainly located.

LOAD-BEARING WALLS

Load-bearing walls are those that, in addition to dividing one room from another, take the weight of the roof and upper floors. Clearly, they must be taken into account if you are considering structural changes. If you knock any of them down you need to make special arrangements to compensate. This is a job for professionals and you should never think about undertaking it yourself unless you have the necessary professional skills. However, in the planning stages of thinking about making changes, it's useful to know where load-bearing walls are. Then you can get some idea about how big various changes are likely to be.

Based on your main plan, draw a simplified plan of your home as viewed from above — a roof plan. You needn't include details of doors, windows, alcoves etc., but all room walls should be shown —

there is an example on the previous page. Show the places where the slope of the roof changes, that is the ridges and valleys.

Draw on to your roof plan double-headed arrows showing the lines of slope of the major roof areas. These arrows show the directions of span of the rafters inside the roof. The walls at the end of these rafters bear the weight of the roof and are therefore load-bearing

walls. Mark these load-bearing walls with thick marker pen so that you can easily see which are the main walls supporting the roof.

If you have a two-storey house, then a major consideration is the support for the upstairs floor. The usual type of floor has wooden floorboards nailed at right angles to wooden joists. These joists are supported at their ends by the walls underneath. Some modern

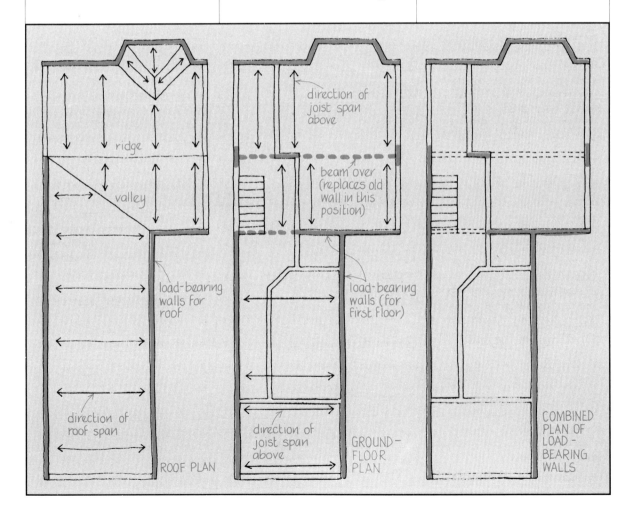

ROOF PLAN

ridge

valley

direction of roof span

load-bearing walls for roof

GROUND-FLOOR PLAN

direction of joist span above

beam over (replaces old wall in this position)

load-bearing walls (for first floor)

direction of joist span above

COMBINED PLAN OF LOAD-BEARING WALLS

dimensions of space in your home. Others will have to do with your beliefs about how the space you have should be used.

All the work you've done should be helpful when you come to think about whether you want to rearrange your home and in what way.

There are all sorts of ways that you can decide to change your use of space. Not all of them by any means cost a lot of money. You may already have new ideas.

WHAT YOU LIKE, WHAT YOU WANT

If you don't know what you want to do, spend some time looking at your plans and see how they can help you. Look at the small plans of your home that helped you take different views.

First, look at which part of your home you labelled as liking least — and then at other things you've noted about that least-liked area in your plans. Jot down all the things you've realised about that area while reading the last two topics. Then do the same thing for the spaces you like best in your home. Try and pin down why it is you like some areas and why you don't like others. Being clear about this should give you a good start in planning changes. After all you want your changes to be improvements, and knowing what you like about various parts of your home can help in working out how to improve what you don't like.

houses have large sheets of chipboard rather than floor-boarding but the direction of the joists can be determined by the lines of nails that pin the board to the joists.

Draw a ground-floor plan of your home with double-headed arrows showing the joists above pointing to the major load-bearing walls which carry the first-floor load. Mark these walls with thick felt-tip pen.

Combine the two plans to show which walls carry the weight of both the roof and the first floor. There are examples on the previous page.

PUTTING IT ALL TOGETHER

Now you have at your disposal a lot of different plans of the space in your home. You have thought about how you feel about this space and you have worked out how people use it . Some of these things are shaped by the real

68

Organising space in your home means adapting the space you have for the things you do. Your home needs to feel comfortable, pleasant and convenient for the life you lead. There are all sorts of ways of achieving this. Not all of them are costly by any means. You can make changes on even a low budget. Just because you can't afford a two-storey extension and a conservatory doesn't mean that you can't make more space for yourself! So bear in mind as you read this topic that resources don't just mean money — they mean imagination, effort and creative thinking, skills which are achievable for everyone.

How satisfied?

Now that you have worked this far through this chapter you should have some idea about how satisfied you are about how space is used in your home.

But even knowing that you aren't satisfied with certain aspects of space in your home doesn't mean that you know what changes you want to bring about.

You can go on for a long time just trying out piecemeal changes and seeing if they work. And they may. But on the other hand they may not. It can be very time-consuming and disappointing (as well as expensive) to keep getting changes wrong.

POSSIBLE CHANGES

Start thinking about possible changes. Jot down as many as you can think of that you would like to make. Write scores down the side of your list — one for the change you think would be easiest, through to five for the change you would find most difficult.

How many scores of one and two did you have? How did you

decide on which would be easy changes and which would be more difficult ?

Easy changes might perhaps include rearranging things, or action which wouldn't require a great outlay of money. Difficult changes might involve spending a lot of money. Changes might also be difficult because they would involve household members altering the way they do things or reaching agreement on sharing space. They might require a long series of negotiations, for example if people are asked to change rooms or mend their bicycles outside instead of in the kitchen.

If you had difficulty with this exercise it could be because you aren't clear about what changes you do want to make; you might be undecided about the level of changes or how committed you are.

PROBLEMS

Write down a list of the problems that you think you have about space in your home. If you already have a list of changes from the last exercise, for each change you've listed write down what the problem is that you want to solve .

Now, for each problem you've listed, try and think of *several* possible solutions and give yourself a range of potential changes. If there are other people in your household ask them to think of solutions too. This sort of activity is called a brainstorm. It doesn't matter if some of the ideas seem silly — it's a matter of tackling the problem from many different angles.

In the case of the example shown it would be possible to put several of the solutions together -– buy a fridge-freezer, have an extra cupboard, do a big turn out and move the dining-table into the living room. On the other hand the single solution of having the kitchen redesigned would cost a lot of money but might well solve the entire problem in one fell swoop.

So now you have the idea of a number of solutions, how do you go about finding the right changes for your home?

Even if you've decided you are able to spend some money on alterations, don't dismiss small-scale changes as well. Very often they will be just as good if not better than large-scale ones.

The next thing to decide is how much change you need to solve your problems.

Problem

The Kitchen is very cramped

Possible Solutions

Ask people to remove possessions which don't strictly belong in the kitchen.

Have some extra cupboards put on the wall.

Do a big 'turn out' of cupboards and work surfaces.

Suggest that people eat at different times if possible and clear up after themselves.

Paint the whole kitchen white instead of yellow and olive.

Have the dining-table out of the kitchen and agree that everyone will eat in the living room.

Bring in a kitchen unit firm and ask them to redesign the whole thing.

Buy a fridge-freezer instead of having the fridge and freezer standing side by side – and use the extra space for a new cupboard

Have an extension built

HOW MUCH WILL YOU CHANGE?

Because you can bring about different sorts and levels of change it's worth looking at your home with a critical eye so that you don't take for granted what you've got and therefore miss out on possible changes. Your brainstorm exercise 'problems' should have given you some nice creative solutions and an open mind about what can be done. Hold on to this attitude — it's a real resource in itself.

There *are* different ways of solving the problem of organising space in your home and they require a variety of resources — for some, skill and effort, and for others, money. Before you assume it all depends on money and go on to lengthy costings, bear in mind that changes come in different sizes and involve different resources.

Resources

'No cost'

At the 'no cost' level, you'll be able to think about how you organise space and rearrange your possessions and furniture, so that, for example, you store things better and people have more space to move about in. You can also think about negotiation with household members about how space is used.

'Low cost'

At the 'low cost' level you can change the effect of space in your house — paint your rooms in colours that make them look

smaller or larger, warmer or cooler, that make ceilings look higher or lower. Or you could change lighting arrangements — a different rating of light bulbs, more lamps, spotlights, less central lighting and so on.

'High cost'

At the 'high cost' level, there are ways of reorganising your space that are undoubtedly expensive — an extension or loft conversion, other extensive alterations, walls knocked through, the house professionally redecorated, a houseful of new furniture or employing professional interior designers both to do your thinking and to oversee your changes.

These various alternative resources mean that whatever your level of income you do have choice. Change isn't just an 'all or nothing' affair. It can take place at the 'no cost', 'low cost' or 'high cost' levels or at all three. And it can happen at different times —

some changes now, some later. So there's plenty of scope.

Given that you do have choices, you can play around with putting together a 'package' of things you can do with problem space in your home.

You will know roughly what sort of budget you have for your changes. If you don't have any spare money then your range of choice comes within the 'no cost' level of change. But you do have choice. In the example earlier in the topic about changes to a cramped kitchen there are four sets of changes that can be brought about at no cost whatsoever and at least one other — painting the kitchen — that would make a big change to the 'feel' of the space for relatively little cost. That isn't to say that some of these changes aren't difficult in some senses. Getting people to change their habits can be very hard work indeed.

PUTTING TOGETHER A PACKAGE

With some ingenuity and flair you can put together your own package for reorganising the space in your home. Read through the following case study to see how one couple went about planning a package for their flat.

'Cheap and cheerful'

Caroline and Des have decided that light is the key to changing the feel of their living room.

It is a ground-floor Victorian room with ceilings 10 feet high and one large sash-window. The room is north-east facing and catches sunlight only for the first couple of hours in the morning. There's some reflected light from the back yard, but on dull days the room is depressing. And because it's dark they think it feels 'poky'. Caroline and Des are both earners but they aren't high earners. They haven't got a lot of money to spend and think that 'cheap and cheerful' is the formula they want to adopt.

They have decided that the question of light breaks down into two major problems

- light in the daytime

- light at night.

So to begin with they brainstorm all the possible things that they think could help. They write a list of everything they can think of and don't at the moment dismiss silly, expensive and fanciful ideas.

After doing their brainstorm Caroline and Des looked through

Have French windows installed

Cover chairs with pale-coloured material

Bring down the height of the ceiling

Raise the floor!

Paint the room pale yellow

Buy a lot more lamps

Put a track of spot lights on the ceiling

Prune the trees in the back yard to give more light

Remove the net curtains from the sash windows

Put mirrors on the back wall to catch the light from the window and from the lights at night.

Knock down the back wall and make one big room with the kitchen/diner to catch the light from the front of the flat

Turn out some of the furniture to make the room seem more spacious

their list and noted down whether they thought each item was 'no cost', 'low cost' or 'high cost'. They decided that 'high cost' changes were out. These were items which were mainly structural changes — installing French windows, lowering the ceiling or knocking down walls. Besides being expensive, one or two of the solutions, such as knocking down the back wall, might have increased heating bills.

Their final decisions about what to do and how to prioritise were as follows.

- The things that could be done at 'no cost' were chosen as first priority — they pruned the tree, removed the net curtains and sold a 1920s chest of drawers that they didn't like anyway.

- Next priority were 'low cost' items. They worked out the amount of money they could afford and from their 'low cost' list they chose to buy things that they were sure were of a size and nature that could be fitted into any other home they might move into. So they decided on lights and new home-made furniture covers. Mirrors were rejected because they might be too big for another flat, whereas lamps and covers would always be suitable. And they decided to paint the room because it was inexpensive and they could do it themselves.

Of course, different people have different budgets and priorities. Doris and Ted, in the first-floor flat above the one belonging to Caroline and Des, opted to turn the two rooms into one and have the ceilings lowered. The whole plan was carried out by professional builders and was definitely 'high cost'. But then they saw the flat as a home they were likely to spend the rest of their lives in. And Doris had just cashed an insurance policy.

MAKING PLANS

Not everyone has the same requirements. And not everyone plans in the same way. Some people are sure of what they want and have the money to go directly from a decision to getting estimates for a job from professional builders.

But if you aren't so sure of what you want, or if you want a 'package' of different changes, the following outline plan may help.

Remember before you begin, that it's a good idea to work through plans with other people in the household if it's going to involve or affect them.

Now that you've read through the plan outlined, with a problem you want to solve in mind, you've probably begun to form your own plan as to what you want to do. You don't have to follow rigidly all the points we've suggested. If you want, you can use the plan just to get some sort of picture in your mind of how things might go.

If you do want to use a plan, you might prefer to build up your own. But do it *before* you start, otherwise you may find later that you wish you had thought things through more carefully.

PLANNED CHANGES

Decide what the problem is.

Brainstorm as many solutions as you can think of to the problem. Get other people to join in and don't reject any ideas at this stage no matter how fanciful.

Remember inconvenience can be as costly in personal terms as a big financial outlay!

Look at your brainstorm list and note whether you see it as a 'no cost','low cost'or 'high cost' idea.

Do a rough costing of 'low cost' and 'high cost' items.

Decide what is a reasonable budget for you.

Draw up three lists, each in order of preference — 'no cost', 'low cost', 'high cost'.

If you choose a high cost item it might be all you can do. Either French windows or everything else.

Put together a package from your lists of things you can do within your budget.

You can always change things back.

Before you spend money try out the 'no cost' list — rearrange possessions, furniture, schedules, routines, negotiate with people.

If you intend to have professional work done get estimates from a number of different firms, check on planning permission.

Get accurate costings for each item in your package.

Check to see you're still within budget. If not, drop items off the bottom of your list until you are.

NOW YOU ARE READY!

People often say they find their homes unsatisfactory because of lack of storage space. Something can be done about this. But you do need to bear in mind that more space often means more things to fill it with. Even people who move into large homes find they soon run out of space!

This topic helps you make the best of storage space in your home. It asks you to think about

- your attitude to storage

- what you and others in your household have to store

- how you and others can make the best of the space you have

- how you can create new storage space.

The way in which you and other people in your household deal with possessions and think about them is important when you are thinking about storage. People have different approaches and styles. Hoarders, for example, obviously have more to store than people who discard possessions when they don't need them. People may be tidy or untidy. Tidy people take a closer interest in storage than those who don't mind a mess.

PEOPLE AND POSSESSIONS

Think first of all about the people who live in *your* home and how they view their possessions. Write a sentence about how each of them stores his or her possessions. You may well not want to sum them up as simply 'tidy' or 'messy'. Your sentences might run more like this: 'Wendy gets things out and doesn't always put them away. She is inclined to hoard things like the Sellotape in her room' or 'Rufus doesn't care if he's up to his knees in his possessions'.

So what implications for storage do the personal styles of people in your household have? You'll almost certainly know whether household members are hoarders, or tidy or messy already. Hoarders think things like: 'It may come in useful', 'It'll be a mistake to throw it out', 'You never know when....' They often have lots of newspapers, cardboard boxes, plastic bags, string and little pots of things all around the house. Hoarders may have their storage well worked out but they can easily get overwhelmed with things. If they are messy as well, they may soon be a problem to other members of the household.

People who don't mind a mess view halfway up the stairs as a suitable place for storage. The seats of easy chairs are also suitable places to store things. Clothes are stored on bedroom floors. People who don't mind a mess may well have storage space to put things away. They don't use it because they know they'll need those things again sometime soon.

You may think these are exaggerations, and for most people they are. However, when you're planning storage in your home you need to acknowledge the styles of the people who live there.

Whatever personal styles there are amongst your household, it's a good idea if everyone can take a fresh look at their storage needs.

It may help you and other people in your home to think about what you need to get at and when. For most people articles to be stored are of three kinds

■ *short-term* — items you're going to need today or tomorrow or next week, things you need to replace often such as foodstuffs and household supplies, rubbish, toys children are going to need at the weekends, dirty clothes

■ *medium-term* — things you won't need to use until next month or the winter, but you do use occasionally, garden equipment, writing paper, best china, winter clothes, books, jumble being saved for the next jumble sale

■ *long-term* — items you don't want to throw away but use rarely if ever, family papers, extra bedding, baby clothes after the baby has grown up, a tennis racket from your school days, a collection of tin soldiers.

What are the implications?

Storage for what you need in the *short term* needs to be at hand, literally. You want to be able to lay your hands on what's kept there immediately, without going up a ladder, turning a drawer upside down or wondering where you've put it.

Storage for things needed in the *medium term* doesn't have to be immediately to hand — a bit of effort reaching up to a high shelf isn't going to be too much of a problem.

Storage for what you are only going to need in the *long term* needs to be out of the way. You have to ask yourself if you're going to need to reach what's stored there more than once in a blue moon. If not, does it matter if it's in the loft or the roof of the garage?

If people feel comfortable with the storage in their home they don't complain. They don't get annoyed because they have to go rooting around after something they actually need quite often. And they don't get cross because it takes them 20 minutes to stuff something into a cupboard already crammed with things. So thinking about how accessible you need the things you store to be is a helpful start.

COMFORTABLE OR NOT?

In this exercise you should spend some time thinking about how comfortable you are with your present storage. Do this with other people in your home if you can.

Spend an hour or so walking around your home checking storage arrangements. Involve all the members of your household if possible and discuss whether the arrangements work.

☐ Open all the cupboard doors. Are they crammed full or lying empty? Is the kitchen devoted only to kitchen goods or is there an overflow from other rooms?

☐ Are the right things stored in the right rooms? Is it very inconvenient to have to go and fetch things from another room?

☐ When you get to each piece of storage space think how you normally feel there when you and others come to look for something — does it feel fine or do you get irritated for some reason?

☐ Are there things around the house you'd like to put away in some kind of store but don't know where?

☐ Are there storage places where people are competing for space?

☐ Is everyone in agreement about which storage space needs to be improved?

Make some notes about each of the problem areas.

This exercise should give you some idea of how things are now. The next stage is to think about how to improve matters. Think through what you found out while you were doing the exercise. Where did most problems occur? They might have been to do with

■ short-term storage only

■ medium-term storage only

■ long-term storage only

■ particular rooms

■ things associated with particular activities

■ things which need particular storage conditions.

This is what some people doing the activity found

Vera: 'I don't make as much use of the airing cupboard as I might because it's in Brian's bedroom and he moans when I go in with clean clothes.'

Dave: 'Every time I go to put something in the cupboard under the stairs I hit my head when I come out. I don't know what the answer is, but I certainly don't use that cupboard because I'm too tall.'

Charles: 'Although it makes sense to keep my tools in the garage as there's plenty of space it's so cold out there in winter that I tend to keep the things I need most often in the house, so they're always lying around cluttering up the place.'

The right thing in the right place

One way of thinking about improving things is to look at what you need to store in each room. What do you need in the bathroom? The kitchen? The bedrooms? Is special equipment required for particular rooms? Then examine what you actually have stored in each room. Can you at least make things more convenient even if you can't make more space?

This can be useful if you have someone in your home who has belongings all over the place. Let them decide for themselves what things they need to get at when in their own space . They can then plan the necessary storage arrangements. If their system makes them cross, at least it won't be your problem.

Perhaps then you can agree that a spare bedroom which is rarely used can become a central storage area for household members. Blocks of space in this room could be allocated to each member.

MAKING THE BEST OF THE SPACE THAT YOU HAVE

You have been looking at what needs to be stored. Now look at the problem from another angle — at how well the storage space you have is being used. Improvements need not mean adding to the space, just using it more efficiently. What this is really about is changing the way you think about your storage.

One simple way to improve matters in regard to storage is to throw things out, so you have less to put in the same storage space. If you are going to try this and you know you do have problems 'throwing things out' it would be useful to think about whether you have more problems parting with short-, medium- or long-term stores. For a lot of people the real problems actually lie with things they rarely if ever use and with the temptation to stock up on too many spares. For example did you really need to buy so many extra bags of sugar when they were on special offer?

A NEW ANGLE

Many people just continue with the unsatisfactory use of space they already have however much additional storage they acquire. So before you start to consider adding new storage take another look at each cupboard and piece of storage space again. How much spare space is there? Could you stack things better? What about under-shelf space? What about a few cardboard boxes? What about special stacking boxes? Arrange each cupboard so that you make some space in it. You could

- throw out even one thing

- use the back of the shelves more efficiently

- pile things of the same shape together so you can use the full height of the shelf space better

- remove things you never use from cupboards which are in frequent use and put them to one side to go somewhere else

- check cupboards for how much inaccessible spare space there is at the moment because there's no way of reaching it

■ check that you haven't got into some sort of fixed idea that certain space can only be used in one way. To help you check this last point, ask other people in the house about how they think it would be useful to arrange cupboard space, what they would use it for. While you are doing this you might ask another person to arrange a cupboard for you to make the best use of the space. People often have very different ideas and solve problems in different ways, so you could get a completely new angle on how to use space.

Space you already have

You may well find that your existing space can hold more than you think. One good example of this is wardrobe space. If you hang clothes so that all short clothes are together you find that you make a space under those clothes. And often the floor space and low-level space in wardrobes isn't very well used. For little expense you could buy large plastic stacking boxes, baskets or shoe racks to put in this space so it can be used for storage. The same goes for the top shelf of wardrobes, especially fitted ones. Often there is space high up and further back that people can't reach. Another shelf and some stackers can provide long-term storage space, although this mightn't work for short or badly disabled people.

Once you've rearranged everything and made use of all your present space, what happens if you've still got storage problems? You could look for new space.

NEW SPACE

Creating new space can be costly, so it's not something to take on unless you're sure you've made the best use of the space you've got.

Starting with cheaper solutions and working up to more expensive ones, you could

■ install new shelving

■ put up new wall storage systems

■ put special drawers under the beds

■ install new free-standing storage cupboards

■ make more use of the space near your ceilings

■ buy a garden shed

■ have more built-in storage space made

■ improve your loft or garage roof

■ improve your cellar

■ make more use of your stair-well.

This final section looks at some of the strengths and drawbacks of different sorts of storage. As you read it bear in mind that one form of storage may be useful in one part of your home and not another. Out-of-the-way space will be more use for long-term storage.

SUITABILITY

As you read this section think about each form of storage. Jot down a few lines about where you'd place it and what you'd then put in it. Think too about where and how other storage space would be released if you, for example, put shelves up in an alcove in the living room. Before you consider the actual cost, you should have some idea of the benefit you'd get. It is easy to launch into a costly operation and then discover that you haven't really got any plan about what you are going to do with your new space.

Shelving

There are three main kinds of shelving.

Framed systems
Shelves are installed within a frame of wood or metal which rests on the floor. These are good for heavy loads. Because they are free-standing you can use them as room dividers.

Wall-hung systems

Columns are fixed to the wall and adjustable brackets are slotted into them to support the shelves. To be stable and safe you need an adequate number of columns secured to a sound wall. They won't take very heavy loads.

Bridging systems

Shelves are supported between two side walls using blocks of wood, brackets or studs to hold them up. They won't span very far if they are not supported but can be useful for spaces up to about three feet wide.

Wall storage

There are two main forms of wall storage.

Simple units

These are individual cupboards, shelves, desks etc. that are just hung directly on the wall. Their advantages are that they are easy to move and the space underneath them can be used for something else.

Sets of units

Here a series of components can be assembled across a whole wall or a large part of it. They usually consist of a range of separate units which can be integrated into a whole that looks like one big piece of furniture. The advantage of these units is that you can add to them as you need more space. A lot of people like the look of them because a wide variety of different types of thing can be stored in them and still look tidy.

Free-standing furniture

Many people like free-standing furniture for storage (cupboards, units etc.). You can move it around and make changes without any great inconvenience. But sometimes it's difficult to find a piece of furniture that fits the space you want to fill.

The ceiling

If you live in a house with high ceilings you can make use of the space high up by hanging either things or containers from the ceiling. To do this safely you need to locate the ceiling joists to take the weight of the hanging items. You can build cupboards which reach right up to the ceiling and some people even build little galleries with stepladders up to them in very high rooms.

Built-in storage

This is built into the fabric of the house and fitted. It is not easy to take with you if you leave but if you plan it carefully it uses space well. It may be very expensive to get exactly what you want. Once it's there, of course, you lose flexibility for using that particular piece of space in another way.

Garden sheds

If you've got a garden with enough space, a garden shed can ease the problem of storing bulky things that you don't need often. It is probably better not to put anything valuable in a shed unless it can be made secure.

Roof space

Many houses have dry roof space that could be well used if access was easier. The entrance to most roof space is through a small trap-door above the landing. You can make safe access to the loft with a folding stepladder which fixes onto one edge of the trap-door and folds away into the roof when not in use. You will, of course, have to make a proper floor and some kind of ceiling and install lighting if you're going up into the roof area frequently. Before you begin transforming your roof space check with your local council on use and access regulations.

Cellars

Cellars are usually easier to get into than lofts. The problems of storing in them are dampness and poor ventilation. If the cellar is damp because the house is built on a wet site it's very expensive to do anything about it. But if it is damp because of poor ventilation, this is usually reasonably cheap to rectify. Sometimes it's just a matter of unblocking a ventilation brick. Cellars usually keep an even temperature and so storing food or wine in them is a good way of using them, if you are not troubled by mice.

The stair-well

One place most people don't think about is the stair-well – the space above your head as you walk up the stairs. In many houses it should be possible to make a lot more storage space here. You'll need to get professional help unless you have particular skills because the structure of a cupboard here will have to be strong and secure, and you'll have to be able to reach it from the landing.

POINTS TO REMEMBER

By now you should have a reasonable idea of what storage systems would be possible for you. However, before you start to make any changes think about the following points. They are easy to overlook at the planning stage but are important and worth checking off as you go through with your plans.

☐ First-aid boxes need to be accessible

☐ Medicine chests need to be kept out of the way and locked

☐ Additional shelves in bathrooms can easily (and dangerously) be used as handrails

☐ Things which get wet — towels, tea-towels, outdoor clothes and so on — need to be stored somewhere warm and well ventilated; for coats a free-standing coat rack is best if you've got the space

☐ Storage fittings in damp places like bathrooms need to be made of a material which will not corrode

☐ Hanging storage for clothes needs to be at least 550 centimetres deep so that clothes don't rest on the bottom of the cupboard

☐ Storage space for shoes needs to be separate from other storage so it can be easily cleaned and dust doesn't spread

☐ Breakables like china need to be stored somewhere you can get at them easily — not on high shelves where you may drop them as you get them down or put them away but preferably between knee- and head-height to avoid awkward reaching

☐ Small individual baskets for dirty clothes are better if there are several people because it's not too difficult to carry them

☐ If you live in a home on more than one floor, cleaning equipment is better stored centrally so that it's not too far to carry it anywhere

☐ Children's toys are best stored in boxes where children can get at them and can put them away easily. They shouldn't be too big, as small toys get lost in very large boxes. You can use plastic baskets for small items

☐ If floor space in a garage is very limited then hanging bicycles and other things on rafters is useful; you need to make sure, of course, that they are securely fixed and there is no risk of them falling

☐ Remember to leave sufficient space for odd-shaped items, such as vacuum cleaners and ironing boards.

If there is only one person living in a home then, in theory at any rate, the only problem as far as the use of space and equipment is concerned is sorting out which job can be done where. But as soon as more people are involved, then they will almost inevitably disagree as to who has first claim on space and equipment in their home. It is not very likely that the home will be so big and so well-resourced that people will never lay claim to the same piece of space or equipment. The larger the group sharing the home, the greater the number of competing demands.

Conflict round the kitchen table

It is Sunday afternoon. Helen needs the kitchen table to spread her papers out because she must finish something urgent to take to work the next morning. Brian is doing the accounts for the local community association, whose AGM is coming up soon; he needs the table to sort out the paperwork to do with the accounts. Doris is trying to make a batch of the special shortbread biscuits that the family particularly likes so that everyone can have a treat for tea. She needs the table to roll out the biscuits. Tracy is doing some home dressmaking to save money and needs the table to cut out the skirt she is making herself for the disco next week. Eddy is preparing a project on volcanoes which has to be ready for school and needs the space to spread out his maps so that he can mark in all the

different parts of the world where the earth's crust is thinnest. Five people, all with reasonable claims and competing for the one available space. How do they decide which one is allowed to use it? Here are two possibilities.

Pecking-order solution

Most families have usually worked out some sort of accepted pecking order, so that some people normally have stronger claims or are more effective at getting their way than others. In this family, for instance, Helen points out that the job she needs to do is part of her work, for which she earns money to support the family, so she feels justified in laying claim to the table for as long as she requires it. Tracy is pretty good at getting what she wants because if she doesn't the whole family suffers from her monumental sulks, so she uses the table when Helen has finished. This solution is a foregone conclusion, based on past history, that is, on behaviour and expectations which have been established over time.

The negotiated solution

Rather harder to put into effect is some sort of solution which involves family discussion and timetabling to make sure that everyone gets a turn at some point. Here the family sits round the disputed table and tries to put the jobs in order of priority, so that as many of them can be fitted in as possible. Everyone makes an attempt to be reasonable and not to make exaggerated claims about

the urgency of their work. They find that the accounts for the community association could wait for another couple of days so Brian agrees to put this job off until Monday. Doris does the biscuits first to get this rather messy job out of the way. Helen's and Eddy's jobs both need to be done for the next day and don't require the whole table, so they agree that they can share the space available, keeping their work separate at either end. Tracy has got other clothes she can wear to the disco, so she can either use the floor for her cutting out or wait until the others have finished. This is a negotiated solution, which is based on this particular situation rather than on things which have happened in the past.

This was a rather extreme case, but clashes like this occur in most groups of any size living together, since space is rarely unlimited. Does this sort of situation ever arise in your home? What kind of solution do you usually reach if it does? How satisfactory is that solution for all the people involved? If it's not satisfactory for everyone, it would be worth discussing what could be done to change matters. To start the discussion you could all try writing out your solutions to the family problem described above and comparing them.

One feature of the kitchen table saga recounted above is that everyone was engaged in some kind of useful activity in their home. Each member of the family felt that their work was worthwhile in one way or another and could claim their right to a turn at the kitchen table.

MANY ACTIVITIES

What kind of activities go on in the home? Here is a list. Go through the example above and identify who was doing what from this list.

- Home maintenance (cooking, cleaning, looking after children)
- Paid work based on the home (self-employed outwork)
- Paid work for an employer (work that is being done out of work hours)
- Homework (for school, college)
- Leisure activities (sport, craftwork, music, dance)
- Unpaid voluntary work (for a charity, the community).

Could you fit the different kinds of activity that go on in your home into this list?

As far as we could tell, Helen was doing paid work for an employer, Brian was doing unpaid voluntary work, Doris was maintaining the well-being of the home, Tracy was doing a leisure activity and Eddy homework.

Would you agree that these different tasks are all different forms of work? Most people would probably agree that they are. But the crunch comes when you are forced to prioritise them, as, for instance, when you are competing for the use of space as the family above was. Must paid work always come first, as Helen thought? If you are earning money from that work, do you

automatically earn the right to claim the space you need in your home? Does unpaid work always count as second-best work? Isn't domestic work which benefits the household as a whole just as valuable as work which is paid for by an outside employer? And what is the status of homework? There is no easy answer to these questions. Each group of people that live together have to work things out for themselves.

One thing you should remember when you are discussing the rival claims of different home activities is that this problem isn't going to go away. If anything, it will increase as more and more people do paid work from home. Also, patterns of work and leisure are changing. The working week is getting shorter: by the year 2000 it is likely to have been reduced to an average of 30 hours a week, with up to eight weeks' annual holiday. There will probably be a

number of different employment opportunities, such as compressed working weeks, flexi-place schemes, job-sharing, multi-job holding and industrial sabbaticals. The likelihood is that more family group members are going to be making more frequent, and more varied demands on the space and resources in their homes. With that in mind, perhaps you should take a closer look at your home and see how well it will meet the extra work and leisure demands which may be made on it in the future. Most people would consider that work which generates income is important and deserves time and effort to make sure that it is being accommodated as well as possible. New technology has been used to break down the division between independent homework and work done at an employer's premises to support a new kind of homeworker. How suitable is your home as a base for paid work?

EARNING MONEY FROM HOME

Traditionally, homeworkers have been self-employed craftsmen doing a specialised job based on their homes, and poorly paid people (mostly women) doing unskilled work with few trade union benefits and without the protection of safety legislation. Things have changed in recent years. While both those types of homeworker are still around, there are now homeworkers who use the new technology. They may be self-employed, or operate as outworkers for an employer.

Here are some descriptions of different kinds of homeworker. They carry out a wide range of businesses, but they do have a few problems. Read through them and make a note of their particular problems and what you would do about them.

Ian

Ian and Anne are self-employed. They own and manage several self-catering properties in a small village in the Lake District. They also serve dinners twice a week in their living room for up to nine paying guests. Ian, a former teacher, acts as waiter and serves the meals that Anne cooks. He relies quite heavily on his personal computer to keep records of clients and bookings for the cottages. Both Anne and Ian enjoy their work, as they particularly like meeting people and are glad to have the chance to use their home in this way. They have a son, Ben, who helps out when necessary. Ian points out that having strangers in their home, and being on call all the time for their clients puts some strain on family life. They are never off duty, as people come to the door at all hours of the day (and sometimes night) for help and advice or supplies for the cottages. Some days the telephone never stops ringing with enquiries about bookings.

Viv has three young children and does hairdressing in her kitchen for friends and neighbours. She is glad of the opportunity to earn some much-needed money, since she isn't able to go out to work, and wants to keep up her hairdressing skills as it is a job she has always enjoyed. But there are a few problems as well. With a baby, a toddler and a four-year-old about the place, the house is never very tidy, and as Viv doesn't find time to do much cleaning some clients have started to look askance at their surroundings. Sometimes clients knock at the door, telephone or come in talking loudly when the baby and toddler are asleep and wake them up before they are ready. This makes things difficult for Viv, as she then has to cope with fretful children and keep the clients happy.

Pamela and Edward both work freelance from their home, which consists of two small houseboats, one mobile and the other not. Despite the limited amount of space, they have set up a home office for both of them to use, which is kept quite separate from their living accommodation. As it is situated in the upper half of the non-mobile houseboat they can even cast off and sail away from it if they want to! Although both of them enjoy the way they work and wouldn't want to take more conventional jobs, storage space is a problem for them. Despite ingenious use of every nook and cranny on the boats, they have to be ruthless about what they keep in the way of equipment, work records and materials. Even so, they still disagree about how much

Pamela

should be kept. They make maximum use of modern technology, with a personal computer and several telephones which can be plugged in at various places.

Mikhail loves working with wood and making broken things usable again, so his job repairing and building furniture suits him admirably. He keeps careful records of his customers on file cards. He also does some dealing in antique furniture and uses part of his home as a permanent showroom where people can come to look at items he has for sale. Sometimes he has quite large sums of cash in the house. The rest of his home is also fairly full with odd items of furniture and various pieces of equipment he needs for his work. Unfortunately there is very little parking space outside and when people come by car they often park in his neighbours' parking places or across their drives, and walk across their front gardens to get to Mikhail's home.

This has annoyed some of his neighbours so much that they are threatening to report him to the local authority for running a business from home in a residential area.

How would you solve these problems?

Here are some very different kinds of homeworkers, all of whom enjoy the way they work, but who find that there are disadvantages as well as advantages. If you are a homeworker, you may already have encountered similar pleasures and problems to the people in our case studies , and have worked out some solutions. Some of the problems, such as encroachment on home life and the discipline needed for deciding what to store and what to discard, have to be accepted and dealt with as well as possible. Other problems, like annoying neighbours or disturbing other people in the home when they need to sleep, might have practical solutions. Mikhail could give his

clients maps showing them where they can park and what route they can take to get to his house without walking over anyone else's garden. He should certainly do something about the money he keeps at home, and about the furniture and equipment cluttering up his hallway, which could be a safety hazard. There are regulations about using a home for business that he ought to find out about. Viv might be able to let her hairdressing clients in by the back door rather than the front or try to keep the baby's cot somewhere soundproof where she won't be disturbed. Although her clients can't fault her hairdressing, they might enjoy their visits more if she could keep the place a bit cleaner.

How well organised are you?

You may already be a homeworker, or be considering doing paid work from home. Could you do it? Working from home may be a very fulfilling and useful way of earning your living, as the people described above have found. Obviously, different kinds of homework make different demands on the home, but here are a number of practical points concerned with the home that nearly all homeworkers have to bear in mind. Some of these will also apply to people who don't do paid work at home full time, but sometimes take work home with them to catch up, as well as to people with other home-based activities such as voluntary work and sport. These points will be useful to most people in one way or another. Go through the following list with your work and leisure activities in mind, make notes on those points which apply to you, and decide on what action you might need to take.

Points to check

A special place

Whatever the work you do at home, you need to have a place to keep it which is reserved just for that purpose. This may only be a small space, but if you have to put things away every time you stop work and then get them out again, you are taking more time and giving yourself extra work which shouldn't be necessary. If you are earning money from what you are doing, you must take responsibility for that work by looking after it properly. One of the well-known problems about working at home is that you can't get away from it, so it's also a good idea if you can shut a door or draw a curtain round your work so that it's not constantly in front of you.

Storage

Storage space is another necessity if the work you do involves bulky supplies or materials which are easily inflammable. If you live in a block of flats, it simply will not be possible to store large quantities of this kind of equipment.

Protecting work

If you have young children, then you will need to protect your work from them, and them from your work if there is anything which could harm them. If you only do paid work at home from time to time you may be reluctant to invest in extra storage capacity, so you need to find something which would/could double as a store for something else as well.

Keeping the record straight

Whatever homework you do, you need to keep records from the start. You will need them for tax purposes if nothing else. How you do this will depend of course on the nature of your work, and could range from a computerised system down to a box of file cards or a notebook. Space needs to be kept for these records, in a place where they are easily accessible.

Visitors

If your paid or voluntary work involves people coming to your home — to bring or collect work for you, for instance, you may need to make changes. This could involve keeping part of your home, however small, completely separate as a place where customers wait and/or are dealt with. Take a look at the part of your home which customers will see — does it give the sort of impression you want them to get? Will they leave thinking how efficient and well organised you are? You should also try not to upset neighbours by asking callers not to park outside their homes, especially if this will block the drives.

Noise

Working antisocial hours, engaging in noisy pastimes and disturbing other people, either in your home or nearby, needs some careful negotiation and planning if it can't be avoided. Extra soundproofing might be necessary, in the form of thicker carpets and curtains or even specially reinforced walls.

Safety

It is simply not safe to keep equipment or supplies in passages or hallways where people could trip over them, especially if there were a fire or other emergency. Insurers, if they come to survey your home, will note this sort of possible hazard straightaway. If you set up in business in your home, on however small a scale, you are, technically speaking, invalidating your normal householder's insurance policy. You need to let your insurer know about the change of use. For some forms of homework — typing or teaching for example — insurers will probably go on covering your home as if it were a private dwelling. But if, for example, you have large numbers of customers coming in and out, you might need extra cover against theft. Depending on what you do, insurers may want to check for extra hazards relating to fire and burglary. They might even ask you to install a burglar alarm system.

Incidentally, if you are a homeworker and your home is damaged or destroyed, this means you may be out of work as well. You could consider taking out loss-of-profit insurance if the cost of the premiums is not out of proportion to your potential loss of earnings. If other people's property is entrusted to you, for repair for example, you might need to take out special all-risks insurance in case of loss or damage. You will also have to pay for a business-use extension on your car insurance if you intend using it as part of your work. If you are providing services such as hairdressing or chiropody you will need special insurance to cover you against complaints. You can get advice on all these points from your insurers.

Permissions

Small-scale business use doesn't normally count as change of use, but if you start a large-scale business, you may have to get planning permission to change the use of your house. Whether permission is required and granted depends on the extent and type of your work, whether you employ others and if your homework is likely to affect your neighbours. If you need and get planning permission for the new use of your premises, you may have the rateable value of the part of your home you are using to work in reassessed from the domestic to the commercial tariff. You should also check that you are not in breach of any covenant on your home, and that your mortgage lender has no objections to its use for business purposes.

Other hazards

Keeping a lot of money at home will obviously need extra precautions, such as a safe. Your insurer will probably check on this. If necessary you can get advice from the police on security. If you do a lot of business on the telephone, you need to consider having a special line installed, or at least an extension to where you work.

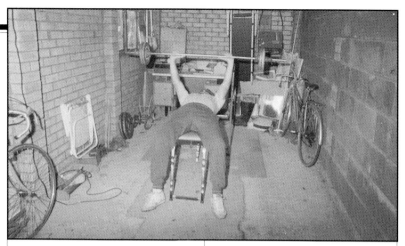

YOUR HOME AS A PLACE FOR LEISURE

Once upon a time there was only a lamp to read by, much of the home was unusable in winter because it was too cold and if people wanted music or entertainment they had to provide it themselves.

The introduction of electricity and gas have meant that the entire home is now potentially usable as a place where leisure-time pursuits can be enjoyed. Music can be enjoyed in every part of the home, lights allow people to read anywhere, television sets can be found in every room.

Recent years have seen a large growth in the number of appliances and amount of equipment available for leisure activities, and people can have entertainment and relaxation within their home, rather than going elsewhere for it. Films are watched at home on video, rather than at the cinema; exercising equipment and weights are used in the home gym, rather than at a sports hall; the picnic in the woods is replaced by a barbecue meal in the back garden.

Another important change is the one already mentioned above. Working hours are getting shorter and more flexible. People have more leisure time to spend on leisure pursuits and it seems likely, from recent trends, that they will want to use their homes for them. Is this going to mean yet more demands on the space and resources available? It is just possible, of course, that trends might reverse. Use of the home as a place for leisure and relaxation has perhaps been a reaction to the idea that you have to go out to work. As work gradually shifts into the home, with the increase in homework, are people going to want to leave the home where they have been working all day to have a break?

The more likely possibility is that the nature and scope of leisure activities which people want to do at home is going to increase. How will you cope in your home?

PLANNING AHEAD FOR LEISURE

Make a list of the leisure activities your household is involved in. Alongside each item on the list make a note as to whether the arrangements are satisfactory and what improvements might be made. Then draw up a list of other leisure activities you might want to take up in the future and check in the same way whether the necessary arrangements can be made in your home.

Below you will see how Helen and Brian's family carried out this activity. They hope that by reviewing their present situation and drawing up plans for future needs they will be able to cut down on possible conflicts later. Helen and Brian found it useful to try to divide their activities up into those which involved noise and those which took up space, either for themselves or because storage was needed.
To make the list of future activities they consulted all the members of the household.

Our Leisure Activities Now:

THE ONES THAT MAKE A NOISE	HOW SATISFACTORY?	POSSIBLE IMPROVEMENTS.
Watching television and video	Usually all right.	Get small portable television to put in bedroom for when we want different programmes
Listening to music on the hi-fi.	All right.	
Talking to friends	Children able to listen and interrupt.	If we were to improve one of the bedrooms, perhaps by putting a small television in there and making it less bedroom-like, would they spend more time in there and leave us alone a bit more?
Practising the	This always going to be noisy - has to be done in bedroom.	If bedroom were better organised, it might make practice easier.
...H NEED SPACE	Not at all satisfactory	Must consider a small greenhouse or shed with a big window.
Yoga	Not enough space in bedroom.	Could reorganise bedroom if bed and chest of drawers moved. Yoga mat also needs storage space

| Family history research | Nowhere to keep files and papers | Need to consider some kind of storage space. |
| Knitting, embroidery and crochet. | All right, but not enough storage space | Need some kind of large (plastic) storage boxes to keep materials in and stop them falling all over the living room. |

ACTIVITIES WE SHOULD LIKE TO DO IN THE FUTURE:

THESE ARE NOISY AND TAKE UP A LOT OF SPACE:

| Tap-dancing | All right as long as she doesn't do it when other people need peace and quiet. | |
| Playing steel drums | Definitely not enough space and too noisy | Will have to be done elsewhere — at school, probably. |

THESE WILL NEED SPACE:

| Wine-making | Those big containers take up a lot of space | As cupboard under stairs already overfull, need to seriously consider creating extra space. |
| Developing own films. | A darkroom will be necessary | Possible to convert cupboard under stairs? Not really, but is the only possibility at the moment, apart from using darkroom at adult education centre, or getting special blinds for kitchen. |

What did Helen and Brian decide?

Drawing up this list helped Helen and Brian to realise just how much noise-generating leisure activity goes on in their home already. They felt that adding to it by letting Eddy practise the steel drums would be impossible, as well as taking up a lot of space. However, tap-dancing would be all right, as it is quieter and the equipment does not take up much storage space. Helen and Brian decided to improve at least one of the family bedrooms by putting a small television set in there, moving the furniture round and clearing more floor space to make it look less bedroom-like. They agreed to think about better storage facilities for their family history research and Doris's handicrafts. A greenhouse looked like a necessity when they could afford it if Helen is to continue growing vegetables. Wine-making and print developing are space-consuming hobbies which they couldn't find room to do in their home at the moment.

All these leisure activities are going to have to run in parallel with the various other activities already going on in this family. If they wanted to, they could draw up a list of work activities, present and planned, in the same way to check how well their home is coping with them now and might be adapted in the future.

CHAPTER THREE

EQUIPPING YOUR HOME

So far in this book you've looked at your home and its surroundings, the space in it and what changes you'd like to make. This chapter takes the process of change a step further by considering equipment and other household buys. It suggests how the same systematic approach to decision-making can be used for equipment as was used for homes. There are some general topics here, related to such matters as paying for the new equipment and planning ahead, but most of the material is concerned with the major household tasks of washing and drying clothes, buying, storing and cooking food and heating your home. You are not likely to have to buy machines to cope with *all* these things at once, unless you are setting up home and don't have any equipment. But most households make these major purchases from time to time.

This chapter contains nine topics

- You and new technology
- Washing and drying
- Cooking
- Buying and storing food
- Choosing the right heating system
- Other household buys
- Choosing aids for living
- Choosing credit
- Planning ahead.

Each of these topics should help you both in developing your decision-making skills and in thinking through different situations to fit your needs.

You and new technology

A major aim of this book is to persuade readers to become more critical of the solutions suggested to them by other people and to rely on their own assessment of their needs and the best choice of solution for them.

This first topic helps you to think about how you feel about modern household appliances and how much you value them. What do they represent to you? A useful helpmate? A bit of the 'space age' right there in your home? A fragment of the glamorous world of the television advertisements? Take this chance to stop and reflect on how your feelings and emotions might be influencing your more rational self when you're buying household appliances.

Washing and drying

In this section you start analysing your household tasks and looking at what equipment would best suit your working method. Washing and drying takes up a lot of time and effort for most families. Not only do we make suggestions about how you might work out your needs, we also give examples from someone who has worked through the exercise outlined, using the weighting and rating method that was suggested in chapter one as a useful device to help you handle a lot of different pieces and types of information and ideas. Following her line of thought should give you insights into the uses you could make of this technique.

Cooking

Cooking is another complex task — how are you going to decide on what fuel and what type of cooker and other cooking appliances might be ideal for you? How will you weigh up different solutions? Once again, it's worth spending time on looking at what you do now and how satisfactory it is, and building on that information about your needs to look at alternatives. Another consumer reveals his needs and solutions — but decides not to take the choice which seems to offer most advantages.

Buying and storing food

You have already taken time to look at your general storage needs. This topic encourages you to take a closer look at how satisfied you are with the way you're buying and storing food, and whether you could adopt a different system.

The right heating system

This topic takes a slightly different approach to the choice of a heating system. Different living patterns require different types of heating system. There is no one standard solution to everyone's heating needs. There is guidance here as to how to work out the best heating system for your family.

Other household buys

By this point you should be well practised in the art of assessing your needs and weighing up solutions. So you will easily be able to suggest how a case study family *should* have set about their carpet purchase. There is some discussion of vacuum cleaners, since different types of vacuum cleaner have specific advantages and disadvantages which might have escaped your notice. Finally, we suggest how you might do some practical comparative testing for yourself on bed buying.

Choosing aids for living

From time to time in this book we mention the particular difficulties experienced by those with special needs in housing and equipment —for example older people and the disabled. This topic looks at the choice of aids for living, and whether there are different criteria involved.

Choosing credit

You need to put just as much effort into choosing credit, if you need it, as into the choice of what you are buying. In recent years there has been an explosion in the availability of credit and there is a huge variety of different possibilities. How can you decide which one will be best? And suppose you take on too much? We consider both these points.

Planning ahead

No one can be sure what will happen in the future, nor can anyone work out exactly what household equipment they will need in the years to come. But it's worth giving some thought to the likely life of your appliances, and considering how long you really want them to last.

This chapter is about choosing equipment for your home and working out how you might do that in a way which will meet your needs and those of your household. Before going on to think in more detail about the different kinds of machine which are available to do jobs of work in the home, stop for a moment and consider what your feelings really are about new technology.

Which of these statements do you feel is closest to the way you think?

'If there's something available that will save me time and trouble I think I should have it.'

'I automatically distrust all the glossy ads I see on television and in the papers – these manufacturers aren't in business for other people's welfare.'

'I'm nervous about having one of those high tech machines — if it goes wrong I haven't the slightest idea how to fix it and it's bound to cost a lot to repair.'

'I don't want to use up precious fossil fuels by having machines gobbling them up in large quantities.'

'I want to take advantage of all the new inventions — I feel I'm part of the space age, benefiting from modern research.'

These are all valid feelings about the range of new appliances available to help with housework. New machines *do* save time and trouble and usually get better results than old methods. However, some of the claims made for them are not justified, and in a lot of cases the advertisements are actually promoting some glossy, unobtainable lifestyle rather than the machines which are supposed to be their subjects. Many people are afraid of what may happen when things go wrong — it's no longer within the amateur's ability to repair much of the modern machinery, and in the case of gas appliances consumers are actively deterred from trying for safety reasons. The world's resources are being used up by modern machines and their operation at a faster rate than they can be replenished. So what can we conclude about machines which can wash, sew, wash up, clean, cook and keep us warm so much more efficiently than the mainly manual methods which were in common use up to 100 years ago?

Benefits

Sociologists such as Caroline Davidson and Christina Hardyment who have looked at the history of the mechanisation of housework point out that when there were virtually no machines in the home, most families spent at least twice as long making themselves less than half as comfortable as would be the case today. The benefits of mass production have meant that the average home is cleaner and healthier now than it would have

been 150 years ago and no one would deny the advantages of that. Very few people would want to return to the days of cooking over open fires and washing by hand with water which had to be carried large distances. When Ann Oakley published her findings from a research study in a book called *The Sociology of Housework* (Pitman, 1974) she stated that 70% of those interviewed described themselves as 'dissatisfied' in an overall assessment of feelings about housework. So, if you agree with this statement, equipping your home with some kind of cooker, fridge, washing-machine and vacuum cleaner can do nothing but good.

Drawbacks

The sociologists mentioned above also point out that mass production requires mass markets, and not everyone who is persuaded to buy the new machines can afford them. 'The darker side of debt and default is carefully concealed behind the slick presentation of the up-to-date lifestyle we all owe ourselves' (Christina Hardyment, *From Mangle to Microwave*, Polity Press, 1988).

When people buy new items of home equipment, are they really buying exactly what they require to do the job that needs doing, and no more? Or are they buying something because it represents the lifestyle they dream of, the unreal images they see on television and in glossy magazine pages? Unfortunately, the

RECYCLING APPLIANCES AND FURNITURE

When you need a new appliance, or piece of furniture, you don't necessarily have to buy it. There are a number of schemes around the country which have been set up to recycle household equipment. The following is one example.

Camden Recycling Ltd is the name of a scheme which provides training and work experience for long-term unemployed people in the repair and renovation of furniture and domestic appliances. The renovated goods are sold cheaply to pensioners, unemployed people and others on low incomes in the community, who are referred to Camden Recycling by the DHSS and social services charities.

Since 1983, it has been run as a Community Programme scheme, guided by a board of voluntary directors composed of local businessmen, residents and representatives from the London Borough of Camden.

possession of a high tech appliance doesn't automatically transform your life — you are still the same person you were before its purchase , except that you've got less money.

THINK BACK

To take a closer look at what has influenced your purchases in the past, think back to the last three items of household equipment you bought. This doesn't mean things like wooden spoons, but some

larger item of equipment. Now note down (you don't have to show this to anyone) *exactly* how you reached the decision to buy in each of the three cases. Would you describe your purchase as

■ an impulse buy — you saw it, you wanted it, you bought it — it was such a bargain!

■ a desire to bring a bit of glamour and excitement into your home by installing the latest technology

■ a sensible buy which you had taken some time and trouble to work out was the right one for you.

How did it work out?

The impulse buy
Did it turn out to be a good buy which did the right job? The problem with spur-of-the-moment decisions is that the results often turn out to be unsuitable for the job you had in mind. A bargain is only good value for money if it suits your needs.

The glamour purchase
You probably really liked it for a while. But how well did it do in the long run? And how soon did you start to worry that perhaps there was something else on the market which was just a bit more up to date? Just because things are available doesn't mean you have to buy them.

The sensible buying decision
With any luck, you should have got something functional which continues to satisfy you because it's doing the job you bought it for.

Decide for yourself

Although many people find it monotonous, housework can't be condemned outright as something that no one could possibly want to do. Some people find many aspects of housework (relaxing at the ironing board, the shine on the bees-waxed table) positively enjoyable. It is up to you (not the manufacturers or creators of television commercials) to decide how much of your housework is unwanted slave labour, which you'd rather have done by machine. It is important to work out for yourself what you and your household need in your particular situation. You are probably unique. You can always get advice from other sources, but in the end the only way to get the right equipment at the price you can afford is to go to some trouble to make an informed choice.

Finally, think about this general principle — that equipment should fit people, rather than that people should have to adapt themselves to equipment.

THE RIGHT MACHINE FOR THE JOB

Read through the following questions and give an honest answer.

Do you have a vacuum cleaner? If so, how many special tools does it have? How many of these special tools do you use regularly?

Do you have a swing-needle sewing-machine? If so, how many attachments came with it, and how many specialised jobs does it do? How many of those attachments

In Sybil's case this very small washing machine was the right choice

do you use regularly, and how often do you do the special jobs?

Have you any multi-function gadgets — an electric coffee grinder which also claims to chop cheese, herbs, chocolate, for instance? If so, how often do you, or anyone else in your household, use it for those other jobs?

How often have you had to accept something that was larger/smaller, more powerful/less powerful than you wanted for a particular job?

If you really think carefully, you will probably find that, in general, you only regularly use a very limited number of features. The rest may get tried once or twice in the first rush of enthusiasm after you've bought the new machine and then be forgotten. But when we are considering buying new appliances, it's very easy to let the existence of special tools or features sway the decision. After all, we *might* use the special embroidery foot on the sewing-

machine, or the delicates/no spin programme on the washing-machine.

Perhaps the lesson here is

Buy the simplest piece of equipment which will do the job you want safely. Extra unwanted features may be more trouble than they're worth.

We've mentioned elsewhere that the equipment that manufacturers make and try to sell to the consumer is not necessarily exactly what the consumer wants. This may be because it's easier, or cheaper, for the manufacturer to make the equipment in a particular way, or because it's simply not possible to produce just what people want at a price they will pay. Most of us have to accept what's on offer because it's just too much trouble to keep trying to find something better.

Don't accept the most obvious solutions. Keep looking for the ideal. You'll get more satisfaction from your purchase if you do.

Just because you haven't been able to find equipment or a fitment in the right size or which will perform exactly as you want doesn't necessarily mean that it doesn't exist. Magazines like *Which?* and *Good Housekeeping* often publish articles on equipment which is out of the ordinary, and you can make your own search by looking at trade directories in the public library, contacting manufacturers direct and keeping your eyes open when you go round shops.

Don't despair! The right size or type of equipment may be available, it's just a question of tracking it down.

Washing is a central household task. In all homes there is always going to be laundry to be washed and dried. This is not a particularly creative job — although there is some satisfaction to be gained from the idea of a job well done (a line of washing flapping in the wind; piles of clean, ironed clothes), but you are not creating anything new, just cleaning and maintaining. That said, does this mean that the best solution for everyone is to automate these processes to reduce human intervention to an absolute minimum? Is a fully automatic washing-machine the right answer for everyone's needs? The answer is probably, but not necessarily.

First of all, everyone's needs and resources are different, so a standard high tech solution will not fit more than some of those needs. If you blindly accept what other people (the media or manufacturers) tell you are the best solutions, then you may well be disappointed. You should always start by working out exactly what your needs are and then look at different solutions before coming to a decision. You'll soon get used to working in this way, but because this is the first topic in this chapter, and because washing takes such a lot of time and effort, we've spelt out the decision process in some detail here.

GETTING THE WASHING DONE

Different ways of getting laundry done include using a commercial laundry, taking washing to a launderette, doing it at home by hand, or using some sort of washing-machine, such as a twin tub or an automatic. Drying washing can be done by hanging it in the open air, or inside the home, simply heating it over a radiator or other heat source or spinning or tumbling it dry. Maybe you've got the whole process worked out to your satisfaction or you may feel that there is some room for improvement.

The logical place to make a start in considering exactly what your laundry washing and drying needs are, is to work out what you're doing now, who is doing it and decide how satisfied you are with that.

You may only do a very small amount of washing in a straightforward way. In that case, working out your needs won't take you very long. But for many people, especially those who organise washing for a large household, washing may be an extensive, complicated task. If you wash more than just a small amount, work through the following list to find out if you would really like to make changes.

A change could, of course, be necessary for a number of reasons. The equipment could be wearing out, your circumstances might be changing or maybe the method you use has never really worked.

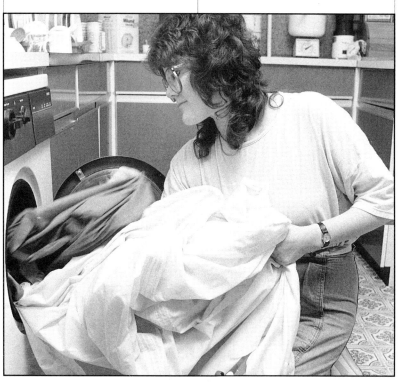

DO YOU NEED TO CHANGE?

Work through this list of different aspects of washing and drying laundry. For each point, consider and make a note as to whether you are satisfied with the way you do things now, or whether you need to change.

☐ Current method of washing laundry (could be by hand, or at a launderette, in a machine, or a combination of different methods)

☐ Current method of drying (hanging it out in the house, on the balcony or in the garden, using a spin-dryer etc.)

☐ Place where washing is done (laundry, launderette, kitchen, bathroom, utility room etc.)

☐ Running costs for washing and drying (laundry or launderette charges, cost of detergent and other supplies, electricity, hire-purchase costs for appliances etc.)

☐ How current method handles your

— *quantity* of washing and drying

— *mixture* of washing (i.e. variety of fibres, different degrees of dirt etc.)

— *frequency* of washing and drying

☐ Reliability of current method.

You should now be able to sum up how you feel about your washing and drying methods in one of three ways.

■ You are satisfied with the present arrangement and see no reason to change it

■ You may be satisfied with the present arrangement, but see that there will be a need to change (because your circumstances are changing or the equipment is going to wear out soon)

■ You are dissatisfed with the present arrangement and want to make a change now, because it doesn't do what you want or is too expensive.

In the case of the first answer, this topic may not be of immediate interest to you, although it is worthwhile going through it for future reference and to practise decision-making. In the case of the second and third answers you should work through the rest of this topic carefully to help you to reach a decision about what to do with your laundry.

LOOK AT YOUR NEEDS

Working through the list of headings about how you wash and dry will have given you many clues about your needs.

If you do very little washing, then it is probably not worth your while investing in a lot of expensive and complicated machinery to do it at home. You could have it done at a laundry (if there is one near you), especially if you are short of time, or in one mixed launderette load. You might also say of your needs: 'I don't want to invest a great deal on equipment' and 'I don't want to spend a lot of time on washing'.

If you do several different kinds of washing (cottons and synthetics, drip-dry fabrics and clothes which need pre-soaking) then you will require a very versatile washing-machine to cope with them all. If the washing you do is mostly of the same kind, then a simpler machine which might be lower on running costs will meet your needs.

Incidentally, it's worth mentioning that getting good results isn't just a matter of having the right equipment to do your washing. Separating your washing properly by fibre and colour will also have a considerable effect on how good the washing looks at the end of the process.

If you have been spending a lot of time and money at the launderette, you could think about having your own machine to use at home — a big advantage for most people would be that they could use the time previously spent at the launderette waiting for a machine to be free and then while the washing was being done, to do something more useful at home. If you have had your washing done at the launderette by the service person you might have found the double journey to take and collect washing too time-consuming. Others might enjoy the regular trip to the launderette as a chance of getting out and meeting people, or having an uninterrupted read.

You might think, as you spend hours hanging clothes out to dry in the garden, that you would prefer a machine to do the drying for you, especially in winter. But other people might just get a lot of satisfaction out of hanging out row after row of washing. If you come to the conclusion that the whole washing process takes up far too much of your valuable time, perhaps you could afford the convenience of having all or part of it done at the laundry?

Most people would agree that they want their washing properly cleaned, that they need reliability both in the quality and the service, whatever system of washing they choose.

SUM UP YOUR NEEDS

Think about the sort of washing you have to do, how much and how often you wash, and any changes you decided you'd like to make when you worked through the last activity. Make a list of your washing and drying needs.

This is what Barbara said about her washing and drying needs. At the moment she has an elderly washing-machine which will soon need replacing, so she is definitely planning a change.

'I do a lot of washing (at least five loads a week at the moment) and need a washing and drying method that will handle large quantities.

'I don't want to spend more than I have to on new equipment —I have some money saved, but not a lot.

'My washing is quite mixed, but I don't usually have to use more than two or three different programmes so I don't need anything too complicated.

'I am spending too much time hanging washing out in the back garden or all round the kitchen —I need to have it dried more quickly.

'I need something which is not too high on running costs.

'I do a large amount of washing and as I go out to work, I can't be forever waiting in for repairmen, so I need something robust and reliable.

'I want something simple so there isn't too much to go wrong.

'I don't want to have to spend a lot of time fiddling around with different settings.'

FINDING OUT MORE

By the time you've looked at the way you do washing and drying now, and made a list of what you need, you will probably have some solutions in mind, although you might well have to find out more about those solutions. If, for instance, you decided that using a launderette would be a good idea for you, you'd need to find out where your nearest launderette was, what services were offered, how much they cost and what your travel costs would be. Incidentally, don't assume that all launderettes are boring, steamy places where the only entertainment is avoiding eye contact with other people. A 'totally new concept in laundry cleaning' which was recently opened offered big-screen television/video, 'attractively styled relaxation/social leisure area' and soft drinks, in addition to self-service washing and computerised drying equipment, an ironing service and professional dry cleaning. You might find that something comparable has opened near you.

If you've decided on a washing-machine and/or a dryer, you'll need to find out what is available to meet your needs. You will also need to look into costs to see whether this is a realistic solution for you. You could check prices and details in your local stores or look up *Which?* reports for this sort of information.

MAKING THE COMPARISON

In addition to the washing method you use now, list the alternatives available to you which you could afford. The most usual methods include using other people's equipment (laundry and launderette); washing by hand; using a machine at home (twin tub, automatic washing-machine, tumble-dryer, spin-dryer). Maybe you have some other method, like having your mother-in-law take it away and do it at her house; this can be included in your comparison.

Now assess each of the washing and drying methods you have listed according to how well it meets each of your needs. If, for instance, one of your needs was low cost, a laundry service will be very good on capital outlay, because you are not buying anything. But it will be very bad on running costs because it is usually the most expensive washing method there is (even if it does include ironing as well). Washing by hand is versatile — it's easy to wash different fibres, but hard if you have a lot to do. Automatic washing-machines

WHY HAVE LAUNDRIES GONE OUT OF STYLE?

A long time ago if people were poor they did their washing themselves, and if they were wealthy they employed servants to do it. In either case, the job was done at home. Then, along with the introduction of equipment which could handle washing, drying and ironing on a large scale, came the heyday of the laundry. Very often our grandmothers, and in some cases our mothers, automatically assumed that virtually all their washing went to the laundry. Who can remember the days of the laundry list and the arrival of the laundry van with the flat parcel of clean washing? Since the benefits from mechanisation of washing facilities can apply equally to large- as well as small-scale equipment, why didn't this lead to cheaper, more efficient laundries for the community to use, rather than moving the work of washing back into the home? Christina Hardyment, who has recorded these trends, attributes this to

■ the bad reputation of early laundries

■ the gap left by the loss of domestic servants being filled by the washing-machine

■ the price of small domestic machines dropping so much that they represented an obvious alternative to hand-washing for the women who had always washed at home because they couldn't afford to send clothes to the laundry.

Are people happy with this situation? Maybe the time has come for washing to be done somewhere else, rather than in the home. Christina Hardyment suggests that for most families it makes more sense to use a launderette, or to share machines between several families.

might score high on versatility and amount of your time taken up, but low on capital cost, unless you bought a second-hand reconditioned machine.

WEIGHTING AND RATING

You can make this sort of assessment simply by looking at each of your needs and making a note as to how well each possible solution meets those needs. You can just put comments like 'good', 'useless' or 'neither good nor bad'. Alternatively, you could use weighting and rating in the same way that you did for choosing homes in the first chapter. Follow these instructions and Barbara's examples to carry out your own weighting and rating activity.

First, list your needs down the side of a sheet of paper, and possible solutions along the top. Give each possible solution a score, or *rating*, between 0 and 4 in which

4 = very satisfactory

3 = satisfactory

2 = average

1 = not very satisfactory

0 = not at all satisfactory

according to how well the solution would fit that particular need. If some of the needs are more important to you than others, then you can give a *weighting* for each need on the same scale 0 to 4, as follows

4 = very important

3 = important

2 = average

1 = not very important

0 = not important.

Each rating is then multiplied by the weighting given to that need, and a final set of totals can be compared.

To show you how this might work out in practice for washing and drying, here is Barbara's list of needs and available solutions with, first of all, her ratings.

NEEDS	POSSIBLE SOLUTIONS			
	Launderette	Carry on with old washing machine	Buy new machine with fast spin	Buy new machine + tumble dryer
Low capital cost	4	2	2	0
Must be able to handle large loads	4	2	4	4
Not too complicated	4	4	3	2
Really good drying	4	1	3	4
Low running costs	0	2	3	2
Must be robust and reliable	2	1	4	4
Must not take up too much time	0	1	4	3
TOTALS	18	13	23	19

Let's look at the *ratings* she gave each different solution. Why were some higher than others?

Launderette

The launderette scored high (4) on low capital cost and ability to handle large quantities — the machines are big and there are usually several available. It is also not at all complicated (especially if you get the service person to do your washing for you) so gets a 4 for that too. Drying is good in the big dryers in a launderette (4), but running costs are very high, so that rates 0. Barbara gave a score of 2 for robust and reliable — several of the machines had broken down recently — and 0 for the amount of time taken: although the actual washing and drying is quick and can be done for you, at a cost, it takes a lot of time and effort to take the washing to a launderette in the first place.

Old machine

Carrying on with the old machine scored 4 for Barbara on 'Not too complicated', as it only has a few basic programmes. The capacity isn't very large (2), and spin speed is low so it doesn't do well on this (1). The machine costs quite a lot to run as it is cold fill, so heats its own water at a higher cost than if it simply took in hot water from the central heating system (2). It doesn't rate well on being robust (1) as the main bearing seems to be going —it gets 2 for low capital cost as it will soon need an expensive repair. It takes a lot of time as the washing needs a long time to dry (1).

New machine

The two solutions which Barbara prefers are to buy a new washing-machine with a high spin speed and a new washer plus tumble-dryer. Both these score 4 for quantity, but 0 for low capital cost, especially if two new machines were to be bought. Both were rather complicated. Barbara hasn't seen any washing-machines as simple as her old one (so gives this solution 3) and the tumble-dryer she has seen in the shop looks rather high tech to her (scores 2). Both get 4 for being robust and reliable, as they would be brand new, and both score well on drying, although the separate tumble-dryer would obviously give better results (gets 4) than the washing-machine with the high spin speed (3). Finally, Barbara gives the new washing-machine 4, as she hopes it will cut down washing time, and the washer plus dryer 3, as she would have to transfer the washing from one to the other.

Your situation is probably quite different from Barbara's, and you might not have assigned scores in the way she did. But working through the solutions and comparing them according to the features you think are important should have given you plenty of things to think about, and made you realise that there is no standard solution to washing problems.

What happens next? Barbara decided to weight her features, as some are much more important to her than others. The needs which she decided were most important were *low capital cost* and that the washing process *must be able to handle large quantities* — so they get a weighting of 4. *Really good drying* is important, although not absolutely top priority — if the worst comes to the worst, washing can always be hung out for a while and it is quite a good thing to dry it in the fresh air in the summer, anyway — it gets a 3. *Low running costs* are pretty crucial, and so is *reliability* — they both get 3 as, although important, they aren't quite as important as the high capacity. *Not too complicated* gets a score of 2 — Barbara doesn't want anything with a lot of complications since she only uses two or three basic programmes on the machine she has and as a general principle she prefers simple machines. Must not take *up too much time* gets a 2 as well, as she is always trying to cut down time spent on housework, although this isn't the top priority.

When Barbara added up the weighted ratings, her list looked like the one on the right.

So her order of preference was

1 Buy new washing-machine with good spin speed (**68**)

2 Go to launderette (**58**)

3 Buying new washing-machine plus dryer (**56**)

4 Carry on with old washing-machine (**38**).

Barbara felt happy with this, and her next step, as yours will be if you've come to the same sort of decision, was to start looking at different brands of machine and ways of buying to make sure she chose something she could afford.

NEEDS	IMPORTANCE	POSSIBLE SOLUTIONS			
		Launderette	Carry on with old washing course	Buy new machine with fast spin	Buy new machine + tumble dryer
Low capital cost	4	4(×4) = 16	2(×4) = 8	2(×4) = 8	0(×4) = 0
Must be able to handle large loads	4	4 = 16	2 = 8	4 = 16	4 = 16
Not too complicated	2	4 = 8	4 = 8	3 = 6	2 = 4
Really good drying	3	4 = 12	1 = 3	3 = 9	4 = 12
Low running costs	3	0 = 0	2 = 6	3 = 9	2 = 6
Must be robust and reliable	3	2 = 6	1 = 3	4 = 12	4 = 12
Must not take up too much time	2	0 = 0	1 = 2	4 = 8	3 = 6
WEIGHTED TOTALS		58	39	68	56

As the launderette scored quite high for Barbara she decided that she could use it if the old machine broke down, and didn't have to rush to get a new machine. She also thought that she would go on using it for very large things like blankets and synthetic-filled duvets as these are really too big to wash in a domestic machine.

What solution has the highest score for you? You might find that you have given the method you have now the highest marks, as it is the one which is most familiar to you, and has the added advantage of no change. The result may confirm what you already felt was the best solution. If the alternative which scores highest is not what you expected, check your weightings to make sure that they really reflect what you want.

Getting more information about models

How would you set about finding out enough about washing-machines to decide which price and type of machine are suitable for you? You need this sort of information to rule out those machines which are out of your price range and unsuitable for your needs.

Walk around the nearest washing-machine retailer and look at what the machines are like — how much space do the pipes at the back actually take up, for example? Are the controls easy to set?

If you have limited hot water, or it is available only from a water heater, then you may choose a machine which has cold fill (heats its own water); if you have lots of cheap hot water, then you can select a machine with hot/cold fill (can run off hot water as well as cold).

Another basic difference in machines is that some are front loaders, some top loaders. If your machine has to fit under a work surface then don't bother considering top loaders. (Twin tubs are always top loaders.) If space is limited check the size of the machine. Some automatic washing-machines wash and tumble dry in the same drum, although drying performance isn't usually as good as in a separate dryer. A machine like this might suit you if you were short of space, or you could consider compact (i.e. smaller) machines or stacking the dryer on the washing-machine. If you choose a machine which tumble dries as well as washing, it will need to be vented in some way.

Once you know what basic characteristics your appliance must have you need to make a long list of all those that 'fit the bill'. To do this, use a publication that lists washing-machines and their specifications in a way that makes it easy to scan — such as *Which?*

You can then collect information from as many sources as possible about the machines on your long list. To cut the list down to a manageable shortlist of machines, you will need to find out different kinds of information.This falls into three categories

Technical — describes physical and measurable features; it is usually provided by the manufacturer

In service — describes how well appliances perform in use over a period of time; it is usually based on the experience of experts or owners

Personal — concerns features that are matters of personal opinion.

GETTING INFORMATION

On the right is a list of possible sources of information. Go through the list with the sorts of choices you're comparing in mind and make a note of the sources you intend to use.

WHERE TO GO FOR INFORMATION

Print

Manufacturers' leaflets	Usually give only good features: will have technical information
Advertisements on television and in the press	As above but without technical information
Which? (available on subscription or in public libraries and Consumer Advice Centres)	Comprehensive comparative information
Magazines like *Good Housekeeping, Practical Householder*	Some physical information; articles on new machines on the market; advertisements with prices
Articles in the press, local papers	Give some physical, but little comparative, information; advertisements with prices for machines in shops near you

People

Sales people in specialist shops, gas or electricity boards	May have good general knowledge. Might be prejudiced in favour of certain makes or types of fuel
Manufacturer's service agent	May have good knowledge but probably of only one brand
Retailer's service agent or independent servicing personnel	May know about several different brands and have strong views on differences in them
Other owners	Useful source of in-service information
Your own preferences	May be an important influence on what you choose
Your own experience	May be very limited if you haven't bought one of these before
Your direct inspection of appliances	Vital for checking some features not described in printed sources and for convenience

If you are planning to choose a tumble- or spin-dryer to help dry your laundry, you could work your way through a similar process to the one we've just described for washing-machines. This should be simpler to do because dryers don't have as many different programmes and features as automatic washing-machines.

Spin-dryers

Here you would choose between the two basic types of spin-dryer –– those which empty by gravity and those which are pumped empty.

Gravity-emptied dryers are usually cheapest, but you have to collect the spun-out water in a bucket placed under a spout at the bottom of the machine. Pump-action models pump the water through a hose into the sink. In theory at any rate, you can get clothes very dry in spin-dryers by simply running them for a long time. In practice, however, this would damage them and put in permanent creases.

Tumble-dryers

There are two kinds of tumble-dryer — vented (cheaper) and air condenser

(much more expensive). While ordinary tumble-dryers simply blow out the damp air, usually through a vent hose, condenser dryers use cool air to condense the steam, which collects in a container that then has to be emptied. The advantage of condenser dryers is, of course, that you can use them anywhere and don't have to vent them out of the window or through an external wall. You do, however, generally have to plumb them into a cold-water supply.

Making the final decision

While you were drawing up a list of washing-machines which met your basic requirements, you probably found several that particularly appealed to you. This may have been because they were very cheap, or available in a shop you prefer to use, because they did well in a *Which?* report , because you've always liked that particular brand or because that machine seemed to offer most of the features you wanted. Armed with information from all the different sources you've consulted, you could draw up a shortlist of features you particularly want and compare that with a list of the machines that you like for one reason or another. If you still aren't certain which to choose, you could carry out another weighting and rating exercise to see which machines really will do what you want them to. Barbara produced a shortlist of four washing-machines and the features she wanted, decided on weightings for the features and started to investigate the machines.

FEATURES I WANT	IMPORTANCE	SUITABLE MACHINES			
		Super Washy	Wash 'n Spin	Klene Wash	Wash master
Price not more than £300	4				
must take 5kg. load	4				
must have economy programme	4				
must have pre-wash for very dirty clothes	3				
Should have spin-only programme for hand-washed clothes	2				
Must have a spin speed of at least 1000 revs/min.	4				
Should have wheels to make it easy to move the machine	2				
WEIGHTED TOTALS					

When the sociologist, Ann Oakley, asked 40 housewives what their order of preference was for household jobs, the most popular one was cooking. This may be because it has more creative aspects to it than cleaning the house or washing clothes or dishes, all of which are primarily concerned with maintenance — keeping things as they are. At least you are making something new when you cook, even if it is consumed at the next meal. Another reason why cooking is not perceived as such hard work as some of the other jobs is that nowadays there are many alternatives to cooking at home, which are available to most people. Not only is there a wide range of take-away foods, or foods which are brought to the home by fish and chip vans or from fast pizza parlours, but shops are selling more and more ready-prepared dishes, either fresh or frozen, which means that it is no longer necessary to go through the often very complex planning and preparation necessary to serve up a meal. Many people now see cooking as being of two kinds — basic day-to-day cookery which is done as quickly as possible, involving ready-made dishes, quick-to-prepare ingredients, frozen foods and the microwave oven, and special-occasion cookery, when time and care can be lavished on the preparation of a meal, often for a large number of people, and usually starting from raw ingredients.

The march of progress

It is perhaps with cooking that we have seen the greatest changes in the mechanisation of housework over the last 150 years. In Victorian times the larger part of the population cooked food over an open fire in some kind of pan. The better-off installed an open range, which offered a more complex arrangement of fire, water-boiler and oven, but someone — usually a maidservant — had to get up very early in the morning to light the fire. The next stage was the closed range, which meant that the fire could be kept alight more easily.

Gas and electric cookers, which concentrated on just cooking rather than heating space and water as well, gradually became more and more easily available during the course of this century. The Aga was invented in 1929, and versions of it are still available today. The microwave oven is the latest development in this line, and represents a whole new approach to cooking food.

You may be thinking about renewing or changing your cooker or possibly supplementing your present cooking arrangements with something extra, such as a microwave or an electrically operated slow cooker. As usual, we would recommend you to take a close look at the way you are cooking now, work out what your needs are and whether the possible solutions would make it worthwhile to change and, if so, to what. Take a look at how satisfied you are with the way you get your cooking done using the same steps that you did when considering your system of washing.

GETTING THE COOKING DONE

Work through the following list of different aspects of cooking. Under each heading consider, and make a note as to whether you are satisfied with, the way you do your cooking or whether you want to change for some reason. Make sure you check your notes with everyone in your home who cooks.

☐ Current type of cooker (oven, hob, slow cooker, electric deep-fat frier, microwave etc.)

☐ Running costs (consider both fuel costs and hire purchase if you have them)

☐ Ease of cooking (how convenient and easy it is to cook using your current method)

☐ Way in which current method copes with

—*quantity* you cook (and whether you sometimes have larger numbers of people than usual)

—*type* of food you cook (fresh, frozen, tinned, dried etc.)

—*timing* of cooking (do you ever want to have meals ready when you come in?)

—*processes* you use when cooking (baking, grilling, frying, heating from frozen etc.)

—*different cooks* and other different requirements

☐ Fuel currently used (electricity, bottled or piped gas, solid fuel, wood)

☐ Layout for cooking (height, space taken up by cooker etc.)

Changes in view?

Can you sum up how you feel about the way you cook and whether you should change?

Are you

- completely satisfied with the present arrangements and see no reason to change

- satisfied for the moment, but will need to change soon — because your circumstances are changing, the equipment is wearing out, you want to have your kitchen rebuilt or some different fuel will be available to you

- dissatisfied with the present cooking arrangements and want to make a change — perhaps because they don't do what you want, are too much trouble or are too expensive?

If you see no reason to change, then you may not have an immediate interest in this topic, but you should work through it to make sure that you have thought of every aspect where cooking is concerned. If you decide you want to make changes, then you can use the topic as the basis for change, either now or in the future.

SUM UP YOUR NEEDS

If you usually cook for only a small number of people, you are not going to need a very large oven or ovens, unless you also entertain large numbers of visitors from time to time. If you have found that you normally use only a few cooking processes, then you need only a simple cooker with a small range of features. You could ask yourself whether you actually need a cooker at all. For example, if all you do is boil water for tea and grill toast, you only need an electric kettle and a toaster or electric grill or sandwich-maker. And if all you make is stews, then it would be more economical to manage with just a slow cooker, or a simple burner. However, most people will be making a choice between different kinds of more conventional cookers or a combination of a conventional cooker with other cooking appliances to cater for all the cooking processes used. If you found that cooking frequently needs to be done while you are out, then you will need an autotimer to turn on the oven before you come in.

How about fuel?

Your choice may be limited by where you live. If not, your basic choice is between gas, electricity and solid fuel.

Solid-fuel ranges (Aga, Rayburn etc.) are relatively big and expensive, but also heat the room they are in and heat water (plus some radiators). The choice between gas and electricity is usually difficult. Running costs with gas are cheaper than electricity, but gas cookers cost more to buy. You may be able to get a reconditioned second-hand cooker which will be cheaper.

Capacity and layout

Maybe you are finding that you haven't enough ovens or rings to cope with the amount and type of cooking you are doing, and need to work out a more satisfactory combination. If you don't like the layout of oven and hob, then you might be considering rebuilding your kitchen and changing the position of oven(s) and hob.

Brian's needs

Brian wants to change his cooking arrangements. He has had a simple gas cooker for about 15 years, which still works fairly well, but he wants to reconsider his cooking arrangements. He says

'Although I cook regularly only for myself, I often have four or six guests at weekends, and I need to have quite a lot of cooking capacity to handle that volume of cooking.

'I am a keen cook and use a lot of different processes. I often cook dishes and freeze them so as to save time during the week.

'I often think I would like to have an autotimer so that my suppers would be cooked and ready when I come in at night.

'I have both gas and electricity available, but am used to using gas.

'I need to have the oven at a reasonable height as I have a bad back and don't like bending to get heavy dishes out of the oven.

'I don't particularly want to spend a lot of money on a new cooker.'

Solutions

The choice is usually going to be between those appliances that use gas and those that use electricity. It is possible to buy two-fuel cookers which offer a gas hob and an electric oven or even a combination of gas and electric heat areas on the hob.

Another big choice to be made is between a slot-in cooker (slides in between units), a free-standing cooker and a built-in oven and hob — all these can be gas or electric.

You may decide to extend your cooking choices by adding a microwave oven to other cooking appliances — or it is possible to have a combination microwave/conventional-heat oven, powered, of course, by electricity. You could choose to add various appliances like those already mentioned — a slow cooker, an electric deep-fat fryer or a sandwich toaster, for instance. You need to find out more about all these cookers before you can decide which to concentrate on, and you can do this using weighting and rating in the same way as for automatic washing-machines. Brian did this, and drew up a list (shown opposite) in the same way that Barbara did for washing options. He has already excluded some solutions — those involving an all-electric cooker, for instance.

My cooking needs	Importance weighting	Possible Solutions Keep current old gas cooker	Electric double oven plus gas hob	Current old gas cooker plus microwave	New gas cooker with big oven
Low capital cost	3	4 × 3 = 12	0 × 3 = 0	2 × 3 = 6	1 × 3 = 3
Wide range of cooking processes	4	1 × 4 = 4	3 × 4 = 12	4 × 4 = 16	2 × 4 = 8
Timer	2	0 × 2 = 0	4 × 2 = 8	0 × 2 = 0	4 × 2 = 8
Oven at right height for me – high up	4	0 × 4 = 0	4 × 4 = 16	2 × 4 = 8	0 × 4 = 0
Totals		5	11	8	7
		16	36	30	19

Brian's rating scores are shown in black. On straight totals, the new electric double oven plus gas hob is the best solution for him. He added the weightings shown in blue and worked out the weighted totals.

Looking at the weighted totals makes Brian stop and think. The weighted total for adding a microwave oven to his present gas oven isn't a lot less than the weighted total for buying an electric double oven with gas hob. He looks at the individual scores a bit more closely. Capital cost is actually a lot lower if he is just going to buy a microwave oven, and there will be no rebuilding necessary, as it will stand on the work surface, where it will be at a good height for him. He will actually get a bigger range of cooking processes, since the microwave will defrost frozen food and warm other things up quickly. There is no timer, but as the microwave cooks very quickly, perhaps he could manage without. On balance, Brian decides that he will be better off simply adding the microwave. Changing the gas cooker can wait for a year or two, when he hopes to be able to replan and rebuild his kitchen anyway.

Brian's next step was to find out as much information as possible about microwave ovens. He drew up a list of things to check, as follows.

■ **Price** — and whether the store offers free or low-cost credit

■ **Dimension and capacity** — to see how it would fit on his work surface. Microwaves come in small (compact), medium (standard) and large (more sophisticated) models

■ **Power output** — whether low power means slower cooking

■ **Power settings** — fewer power settings may be limiting

■ **Turntable and other features** — most microwaves have these plus other gadgets which may *or* may not be useful to him.

Besides checking all these technical features, Brian planned to build up information from other owners, *Which?* and *Good Housekeeping* reports, and combine this with his personal opinion — what he thinks of the different microwave ovens available and the way they look.

In the previous topic you took a close look at the way you do a major household task —cooking — and what equipment would make things easier for you. But before you can actually start cooking, you have to get food — usually by buying it — and store it. It makes sense to take the same sort of approach to the way you buy and store food as to the means of cooking it. For one thing, you will have more information to base your decision on when you come to choose, for example, the type of fridge or freezer you might require. For another, it should help you to take a look at how much storage space you need in your kitchen and whether you're making the best use of what you have now.

STORAGE OF FOOD

You could start by looking at the way your present storage arrangements meet your needs, to see how happy you are with them. Go and look in your larder, cupboard, fridge or freezer, and anywhere else you store food. Are they empty? Just filled to capacity? Overflowing so you can't find anything in there? This may, of course, depend on what day of the week or month it is, or the season of the year — you may just have stocked up, or be about to. But generally speaking, how do you feel about the way food is stored in your home?

1 Just right — neither too much nor too little space available

2 Very short of space all round

3 Some storage places (freezer, for instance) have spare capacity, whereas others (fridge or store cupboard for instance) are full up

4 Too much storage capacity – food is rattling around in the store cupboard and the freezer is half empty

5 There seem to be too many things which you do not use very often, or at all, and not enough things which you really need.

What did you find?

1 Fine — you have obviously planned things really well. But are there any changes possible in the near future? Work through the rest of this topic to make sure that you can cope with any change when

you get to it and to ensure that you really are managing space as well as you possibly can.

2   Sounds as though you might need to find ways of extending food storage, either by building or buying more storage facilities or by getting a bigger fridge and/or freezer (see the section in this topic on choosing a new fridge or freezer). Another alternative might be to shop more frequently and buy smaller amounts so that you wouldn't be storing so much at one time.

3   You could change the type of food you are storing (more frozen food to take up the space in the freezer) and buy less fresh food or canned food to relieve the pressure on space in fridge or store cupboard. Look at the sections in this topic on what kind of food you are buying, when and how often. Alternatively, you could adjust the kind of storage you have to accommodate the type of food you like to store, that is, cut down on the proportion of frozen food storage and increase the proportion of storage for fresh or canned food.

The section in this topic on choosing a new fridge or freezer could help you here.

4   Perhaps your lifestyle has changed recently, you have less money to spend on food than you had hoped or maybe you have overestimated the amount of food you have to store. It is wasteful to run appliances which are much larger than you need. Had you thought of selling them off for smaller or different versions?

5   Most of us fail to clear out items which are hardly used. You need to take a close look at those packets or tins which have been gathering dust for some time and perhaps throw them away to clear more space. If you were to get rid of them, you could build up stores of things which would be of more use to you. The section in this topic on 'Turnover' should help you.

Shopping and food storage

Think about shopping for food. Now that you've got an idea of how satisfied you are with storage, which of these points do you think is going to influence the way you store food?

- How often you buy food
- How much food you buy
- What kinds of shops you use
- How you travel to the shops
- What kinds of food you buy.

The answer is, all of them. It maybe hadn't occurred to you that all these things are going to have an effect on the type and size of storage capacity in your home.

YOUR SHOPPING PATTERN

Do you have a regular pattern for the way you shop? Most people tend to do things in much the same sort of way, even if there are minor variations. For each of the following questions, choose the answer which is most like your shopping pattern.

1 How often do you shop for food?

Every day

Every two to three days

Every four, five or six days

Once a week

Once a fortnight

Once a month

It varies

2 What sort of quantities do you buy?

Little and often

Much the same quantity once a week

A huge shop once a month or less often

It varies

3 Where do you shop?

In small specialist shops

In supermarkets

In hypermarkets

In food sections of department stores

In freezer-food centres

In markets

In bulk-buy stores

Food is delivered

It varies

4 How do you travel to shops?

Walk

Cycle

Car

Bus

It varies

5 What kinds of food do you buy in large quantities?

Fresh

Frozen

Canned

Bottled

Dried

It varies

1, 2 and 3 Research on people's shopping habits has shown that most people have one day each week when they do the main bulk of their shopping (Friday is the most popular, Monday, Tuesday and Wednesday the least popular). The increase in recent years in the number of hypermarkets and superstores with huge car parks outside towns means that car owners can now do a large shop at (usually) monthly intervals, with top-ups of fresh food in between. Many people are taking advantage of this opportunity, although a weekly shopping pattern is still the norm. If you are following the general trend of change from buying little and often to buying large quantities at infrequent intervals, has the way you store food kept up with this change in shopping habits?

4 While walking to the shops was the most common way of getting there 15 years ago, the car, either private car or taxi, is now a more popular way of getting to shops. If you are obliged to walk, cycle or use the bus to go shopping then there is obviously a limitation on what and how much you can buy. Is this difficult for you or are you happy with your method of travel? If you sometimes find yourself short of basic foodstuffs, might it be possible to reorganise your shopping days so that once a month, say, you were regularly able to take a taxi home with a bulk buy to keep stocks at a reasonable level? You could also consider sharing transport with friends to a hypermarket or cash-and-carry store. Another possibility would be to have groceries delivered — this practice is now coming back into fashion.

5 Most of us buy a combination of fresh and preserved food. If food has been preserved in some way — by being frozen, canned, bottled or dried — what assumptions do you make about how long it will last? Does this vary according to the method by which it has been preserved? Fresh food is now labelled with a 'sell-by' or 'best-before' date. Frozen food is usually coded with stars according to how long it can be kept.

Food	Always	Sometimes	Never
Fresh			
Frozen			
Canned			
Bottled			
Dried			
UHT			

DO YOU CHECK DATES?

Think about each of the types of food listed on the right and tick one of the columns according to how carefully you check 'best-before' or 'sell-by' dates.

If you found that you are not checking the date for anything but fresh or fresh and frozen food, you should make a point of looking at the packets, tins and jars in your store cupboard to see whether there is a limit on their storage time. Since 1985 there has been a food labelling regulation that states that pre-packaged food with a storage life of 18 months or less must have a 'best-before' date on it. So products marked in this way will have a relatively short storage life. However, most canned food will last longer than 18 months. It may be, of course, that you have some pre-1985 tins in your cupboard. What else is out of date and should be thrown out or used up very soon?

Turnover

Make a check of all the food you have in your cupboards, on your shelves and in the fridge and the freezer. Don't forget dry goods such as beans and cereals, tinned and packet foods and such things as condiments, herbs and flavourings. Ask yourself these questions. Be ruthless about the answers.

■ *Do you know how old all your stores are?* Dry goods and tinned and packet goods do have a reasonable shelf life, but apart from the high probability that they have deteriorated in quality, things you've had for years and years aren't likely to be a central part of your diet. *Throw out everything that's more than five years old or looks stale, and don't buy replacements.*

■ *Why did you buy those things?* Perhaps you've changed the way you eat to have a healthier diet and these are leftovers from the past. Many of them might be things that you bought for a recipe and then never used the recipe again. Or was buying them just good intention? You'll probably be able to look at some of them and say 'I bought that because I read in the Sunday paper it would be good for me. But I've never tried it.' *Think twice in the future about buying things that you aren't actually likely to use..*

What are the foods which would be really useful to you now and in the future? Before you buy an item for your store cupboard, think how you are going to use it. Are you going to have time to prepare it — soaking beans, for instance? Do you have the right recipes? Once you have created space, expand your stores slowly. Maybe you could buy small sizes to begin with until you're sure that each item is really going to be of use to you. Turnover is, of course, important for other reasons besides storage space. Eating food which has deteriorated too far can have serious health consequences. So for all sorts of reasons, you should *plan before you buy.*

You may already have a heating system which suits you very well and have no intention of changing. You might, on the other hand, be planning a new system, perhaps for a new home, and be wondering what would suit you best. A third possibility might be that you have some form of heating that you're not very satisfied with, and are wondering whether to make a change. If you're in one of the two latter categories, then work through this topic to help you make a decision.

WHICH SYSTEM FOR YOU?

It isn't possible to give overall recommendations since there isn't a single system which is right for everyone. The best heating strategy for you will depend upon such factors as

- what fuels are available to you
- how much money you can afford to spend
- when you're at home
- the size and layout of your home
- the way you use your home.

The two most important considerations for most people are running costs and flexibility of operation.

CAPITAL COST VERSUS RUNNING COSTS

If you are thinking about installing a new heating system, particularly in a new house, running costs are only half the story. Some heating systems are relatively cheap to buy and install, but then have high fuel costs; others are much more expensive to buy and install, but are then much cheaper to run. The commonest example of this trade-off is that between electric and gas central heating.

Since an electric heating system is generally cheaper to buy and install, you could spend the difference in price on additional insulation. The electric system may then be as cheap to run as the gas system would have been in a less well-insulated home. The alternative strategy, and a better one, is to consider insulation first. Then you can compare heating systems on an equal basis. With a well-insulated house you can install a smaller system and so reduce both the running cost and the capital cost of any heating system you are planning to install.

There is another reason why you should consider insulation before deciding upon a new heating system. Insulating a house with an existing heating system could leave you with an oversized heating system. Since an oversized system may be less efficient than a correctly sized one, the fuel savings that you get as a result of installing insulation may be

somewhat lower than you'd hoped. There are topics entitled 'Insulation — what do you need?' and 'Save energy and cut fuel bills' in chapter four.

Recommending one fuel as better value than another is virtually impossible. Looking back over the last 25 years, each of the main fuels used for heating systems — solid fuel, oil, off-peak electricity and gas — have had their turn as cheaper fuel. At the moment (1988) oil has staged a come-back, and off-peak electricity has become less attractive. There are too many variables around for anyone to say what will be cheapest over the next few years.

FLEXIBLE CONTROL

A flexible system can provide you with heat rapidly when you need it, can be shut off when you don't need it, and can provide different levels of heating in different rooms as required. The importance of flexibility to you will depend largely upon how you use your home. The most flexible systems are electric panel heaters or portable electric heaters, and gas heaters, although separate heaters may be more expensive to run. The least flexible are electric storage radiators and underfloor heating. For conventional radiator systems, gas and oil are more flexible than coal. Controls, such as a time switch, room thermostat and thermostatic radiator valves, can improve the flexibility of any radiator system that does not already have them. So how important will flexibility be to you?

HOW DO YOU USE YOUR HOME ?

To help you think about how you use your home, work out what your 'living pattern' is at the moment.

Although the details may vary a little, it is quite likely that one or other of these typical patterns will be more or less the same as yours. Read through these descriptions and tick the one which most closely resembles your own.

Home used all day (most rooms used, or potentially usable; an example would be a household with at least one adult and one or more children at home).

Home with only living rooms used all day (bedrooms hardly used except at night; this occupancy pattern might apply to retired people).

Home empty during the working day (most rooms used in later afternoon or evening; an example would be a household with children at school and with no adults at home during the day).

Home empty most working days and empty irregularly at weekends and in the evenings (single people or other households without children would fit this pattern).

Now read through the following comments on the different living patterns, concentrating on the section which deals with the pattern which is most like your own.

Homes with most rooms used all day

This is the living pattern for which a full central heating system is used at its best: all rooms warm all day. Thus, flexibility is probably less important here than in any of the other patterns.

With this living pattern your heating system will be on more than with any of the others, and so you need to look at how convenient the different systems would be for you. Remember that with solid fuel, you will have to manage the inconvenience of handling, storing, and loading the fuel, plus clearing out the ashes. Also, although the relative inflexibility of solid fuel may not be much of a disadvantage in this living pattern your pattern may change (your children could go to school, for instance), and you would then want more flexibility.

Gas warm-air systems tend to be more efficient than conventional gas boilers for radiator systems. If you cannot afford full central heating, a partial system consisting of several linked gas convector heaters is probably both the cheapest and most convenient method.

You could consider installing a radiant-convector room heater in your main living room. If you put it on during the later part of the evening you can switch off your central heating early. This may even be worthwhile if the room heater has high running costs (as with an electric fire or an inefficient solid-fuel fire), if the savings in heating the rest of the house are sufficient.

Homes with only living rooms used all day

For people with this living pattern, cost may be even more important than in the first pattern. Full central heating is not likely to have much advantage over partial central heating. In either case, it would be a good thing to have separate control over the heating in the bedrooms and in the living rooms.

Even if you are installing a full central heating system try to have a radiant-convector heater in your living room. Make sure the sizing of the system takes this into account, as well as the level of insulation you put in. The living room heater would be likely to provide sufficient heat during milder parts of the cold season, and you wouldn't have to use the central heating system at all. From the point of view of costs, gas or one of the more efficient solid-fuel heaters are preferable.

For partial central heating, you could combine either a gas radiant-convector heater in the main room with some gas convector heaters, or a solid-fuel fire with a back-boiler heating a few radiators. Consider using room heaters with a fast warm-up time to heat your bedrooms in the evening and morning only and run your central heating for a shorter period. Since the room heaters will be on for only a short time, running costs are not too important. Electric fan heaters are likely to be very convenient, but you could consider a gas convector, although installation would cost more. This strategy

will save you money, but with some loss of comfort. An alternative you might consider, if you have a radiator system, is a separate room thermostat for the bedrooms. The best solution, if you can afford it, is to zone central heating using a motorised valve and separate controller so that bedroom radiators can have different timing applied to them from radiators in living rooms.

Homes empty during working days, but used at other times

In this situation, you are likely to need a flexible central heating system with a fast warm-up time. The running costs are probably less important than in the previous two cases as you will be using your heating system for a shorter time.

A fast warm-up time is more important than in the previous two living patterns. If you are looking for a new house, gas warm-air central heating would be an

advantage. For any central heating system, a good control system, including a time switch with two settings, is worth having. Otherwise, be your own control system and adjust your thermostat according to your needs at any time of day.

For partial central heating, considering both running costs and controllability, you could rank possible systems in this order: gas convectors, oil or a small solid-fuel enclosed fire with a back-boiler, electric (day-rate) radiant or convector heaters.

Homes used irregularly

For this living pattern full central heating is not likely to be the best choice, unless you have a very modern, sophisticated system. Flexibility and fast warm-up are the most important considerations. This is probably the living pattern for which a partial heating system is most appropriate. The systems with the most flexibility and fastest warm-up time are gas convectors and electric (on-peak) panel heaters, combined with a radiant-convector heater in the main living room. If you are using separate direct heating electrical appliances, you need to be sure that you are not keeping them on too long, otherwise bills will be very high.

If you do want full central heating, a warm-air system has the advantage of fast warm-up times. And if you were to change your living pattern at a later date — to the first one, for example — then you could do that easily.

CHOOSING A CENTRAL HEATING SYSTEM

If you have decided that what you need is a full or partial central heating system, then you will be looking closely at the different fuels. Each fuel — gas, off-peak electricity, oil used in central heating systems, solid fuel — has different characteristics. What will be the basis for your choice? Think about each of these headings in turn and consider what your needs will be.

☐ Cost (installation and running costs)

☐ Convenience

☐ Flexibility of use

☐ Type of heater, i.e. radiator, open fire, storage heater

☐ Special requirements (i.e. chimney)

☐ Ease of installation

☐ Fuel storage needed.

To show how this might work out in practice, read through Mette's example. She has decided that she needs a full central heating system, as she will soon be at home most of the day with a new baby and her living pattern will be changing. She considers the different kinds of central heating system available to her under the headings above.

	Gas	Off-peak electricity	Solid fuel	Oil
Cost	Fairly expensive to install / running costs steady and fairly cheap	Cheapish to install / running costs have risen lately	Cheapish to install / running costs steady and fairly cheap	Medium cost to install / running costs fairly cheap
Convenience	Very convenient	Very convenient	Not very convenient - have to clean out and fill	Very convenient - but no space for tank to store oil
Flexibility of use	Very flexible	Not very flexible if weather or your plans change at short notice	Fairly flexible	Very flexible
Type of heater	Radiators	Rather bulky compared with radiators	Open fire plus radiators	Radiators
Special requirements	may need flue, though this isn't major rebuilding problem	Straightforward	Chimney — already got one but nowhere to store fuel	no space for storage tank. may need flue.
Ease of installation	Easy apart from flue / gas already in house	Easy	Easy	Easy apart from flue

Drawing up this table enabled Mette to see that solid fuel would not suit her very well, and she was rather worried by the bulky storage heaters and uncertainty about the price for off-peak electricity. She might also have to fall back on full-price electricity in a cold spell to get more heat from the heaters during the day. The prices she had been given for the oil system were higher than for gas, and she wasn't sure where she might put the storage tank, but she decided to do some more price research on the purchase costs of gas and oil systems, as she felt there wasn't a lot to choose between them. She does, however, worry about how steady oil prices are likely to be.

Could you make up a table like this if you were choosing a new central heating system? As further help, here are some tips from *Which?* and elsewhere on how to get a good deal and find a reliable installer.

■ *Check* with the local fuel board for their lists of approved installers.

■ *Be wary* of firms that concentrate on one particular product and offer you standard package deals. They have an interest in selling their system; make sure you're satisfied it's right for you.

■ *Make sure* that the installer you choose is a member of a trade association.

■ *Include* at least one independent firm in your shortlist of installers.

■ *Insist* on a detailed specification which tells you

–what regulations and standards the installer will work to

–size and make of boiler, where it will go, what flue is needed

–what temperatures will be used (normally 21°C inside when it's –1°C outside)

–what assumptions about insulation have been made and what the installer's advice is if you haven't any

–position and type (at least) of all radiators.

■ *Get three estimates* as outlined above so you can make an informed comparison of what they're offering. Bargaining on prices may well be possible.

By this point in the chapter you've had a fair amount of practice at using the decision-making process we recommend.

- What are my needs?
- What possible choices are there?
- How do the choices rate against my needs?

You should now be able to go through that process for any change you're thinking of making in your home. In this topic we take a look at decisions about some other common household items which most people need, to see whether they pose any particular problems. Those items are carpets, vacuum cleaners and beds.

CARPETS

Here is a cautionary tale, to demonstrate what could happen if you don't go about things in a logical fashion.

Anyone who has anything to do with consumer complaints (consumer advisers, trading standards officers) will tell you that complaints about carpets are only too common. Carpets can be a good example of a short-term saving (buying the cheapest) which could lead to a long-term disaster (carpet looks awful and wears out quickly). As you read this account, consider how you would manage things better.

Mr and Mrs Dickinson's carpet disaster

Mr and Mrs Dickinson have bought a three-bedroomed house with an open fire in the living room. The only floor coverings already there are in the kitchen and the bathroom. They can carpet two of the bedrooms with carpeting they've brought from their old house. But they need something for the rest of the house.

This advertisement is circulated to houses in their area.

From £5 per sq yd

C A R P E T S !

C A R P E T S !

C A R P E T S !

Free home estimates
without obligation

The following day a salesman calls, loaded down with heavy sample books. Mrs Dickinson chooses a carpet she likes the colour of — turquoise. The label says 'viscose' and the salesman tells her that viscose is a product of modern science incorporating some of the stronger material found in plants; he says viscose carpets are popular in the latest Mediterranean hotels.

Mrs Dickinson wants the same carpet all through the house (in the hall, up the stairs, on the landing, in the living room and in the third bedroom) as she thinks this would

look smart. So she asks how much it will cost to have the turquoise viscose carpet in all the areas that need covering. The salesman assures her she needn't worry about price as she can pay in easy instalments over several years. He fills out an order form for her to sign, with the payments spread over three years. He points out that her only expense for all this carpet is the £150 deposit, and that fitting is free, including underlay. To cut the cost even further he could give her an extra-special price for carpet without underlay — the deposit would then only be £120.

You can probably guess the results. The turquoise faded — it fades faster than other colours. The carpet wore through on the stairs very quickly and is already looking pretty threadbare in the hall and living room — viscose is suitable only for lightweight use, and no underlay means quicker wear. Besides, it's always worth having underlay for the extra warmth and comfort. There are nasty burn marks in the living room — viscose burns easily. Mr and Mrs Dickinson have already spent far more in their monthly payments than friends who bought better carpets for cash — and they still have to make payments for another nine months.

If you'd been the Dickinsons, how would you have set about making the choice? And how would you decide for yourself? Your recommendations might be something along the following lines.

Needs

Floor covering suitable for three different parts of the Dickinsons' new home

- Living room (must be burn-proof)
- Hall, landing, stairs
- Daughter's bedroom.

Solutions

It would be useful to consider different ways of covering the floors, apart from using carpet, according to how much the family could realistically afford. They might decide that they didn't, in fact, need a carpet of any kind for the living room, the hall, the landing and the bedroom, but that vinyl, quarry tiles, sanded floors or some other solution would be better.

If carpet was what the Dickinsons preferred, then they would need more information about the advantages and disadvantages of different kinds of carpet, such as

- price

- fibre (wool, Acrilan, nylon etc.) and how durable and soft each would be

- colour — and whether some colours fade more quickly than others

- whether underlay is incorporated into the carpet or not and how robust the backing is

- length of pile and what difference this makes to wear

- construction of carpet (Axminster, Wilton etc.) and what this means in use.

Once they had worked out which kind of carpet suited their needs best, they could go on to look at subjective features, such as

- do I like the pattern?

- do I like the feel of the carpet when I walk on it with bare feet?

and so on.

Even if they had decided that they wanted vinyl or quarry tiles, they would still have to look at the different kinds available and work out which features they wanted.

Weighting and rating

Is it useful to use weighting and rating at one or more stages of the decision process when choosing carpets? It could be useful if you were considering different solutions to the problem of how to cover your floors. You would have to list your needs, whatever they were (low price, easy to clean, non-slip, should look luxurious etc.) down the left-hand side of the page, and the various solutions (sanded floors, vinyl, carpet tiles etc.) across the top of the page. You might also weight and rate when comparing different carpets and different shops and/or suppliers. This would depend on how much choice you were left with after drawing up lists of carpets and shops that met your main requirements.

VACUUM CLEANERS

Ownership of vacuum cleaners of one sort or another is so widespread (about 98% of households) that it is fairly safe to assume that most people working their way through this book will own a vacuum cleaner or have access to one. If you are thinking of a change, which kind of vacuum cleaner will be best for your needs? Do you need to supplement it with some other appliance, such as a floor-polisher, or carpet-shampooer, or some extra variant of the vacuum cleaner, such as a small hand-held version for special needs? What are the virtues of different types of vacuum cleaners? Let's take a closer look at the decision about which vacuum cleaner to buy.

Different cleaners for different needs

Different kinds of cleaner (cylinder, upright, wet/dry cleaner) work in rather different ways. The result is that no one type does *all* the possible household cleaning tasks well. So you should look at your needs in relation to the different kinds of cleaner, to see whether one kind or another is best for you.

Which? have summarised what each of the different kinds of vacuum cleaner does best — go through the cleaning jobs listed, and note which ones you do often and which you sometimes do. Then look across at which cleaner performs which jobs well, and which performs less well.

HOUSEHOLD CLEANING TASKS

	Performs well	Performs less well
Stairs	Cylinder/canister; hand-held mains-powered	Upright poor for carrying up and down stairs; wet/dry poor for standing on stairs
Round and under furniture; corners; low, awkward spots	Cylinder/canister; hand-held battery-powered	Upright
Cleaning up after small DIY jobs	Cylinder/canister	
Cleaning out the fire when cold	Cylinder/canister	
Cleaning up after large DIY jobs	Wet/dry cleaner	
Getting out deeply embedded dirt	Upright	Wet/dry difficult to use on some carpets; hand-held mains-/battery-powered
Cleaning large areas of carpet	Upright	
Picking up animal hairs	Upright	
Picking up shavings, sawdust, other workshop debris	Wet/dry	
Car interior	Hand-held battery-powered particularly convenient	
	Wet/dry	
Sucking up water after, say, radiator leak	Wet/dry	Non-wet/dry machines won't do this
Unblocking drains	Wet/dry	Non-wet/dry machines won't do this
Overhead work — walls and pelmets	Cylinder/canister; hand-held mains-powered	Upright poor for upholstery and curtains

What some other people decided

You might find that there is a kind of cleaner which does well all the jobs you most commonly do. Jan, for instance, found that her most common household tasks were picking up animal hairs (because of her large dog) and cleaning large areas of carpet (her bungalow has fitted carpets). So an upright vacuum cleaner was the answer, since it does those jobs best. Bill, on the other hand, found it hard to choose between types of cleaner, as he had both stairs and large areas of floor to clean, and he did both these jobs often. Another task he sometimes did was cleaning out his car, and he would also have liked to have a machine that unblocked his drains on the odd occasion when they were blocked. Since the wet/dry machine is awkward on stairs, and stairs are something he cleans frequently rather than just occasionally, he gave up the idea of being able to use the vacuum cleaner to unblock drains and compared the cylinder/canister type of cleaner with the upright. He eventually decided on the cylinder/canister type, thinking that it would do the carpets, while the upright is not so good on stairs. He thought he would be able to use a cylinder/canister type cleaner for the car as well.

BEDS

Finally, this topic takes a look at choosing beds. How satisfied are you with your bed? Is it time for a replacement, or does some member of your household need a new bed? Choosing a bed is a bit different from choosing a washing-machine or a central heating system. With that sort of equipment, there is a lot you have to take on trust. But with beds, you can actually test for yourself, by lying on the bed in the shop (take your shoes off first!), bouncing up and down, feeling the firmness of the edge and so on. Since beds cost so much and you spend such a large part of your life lying on them, you should not let yourself be rushed into a decision. Before you visit shops, you will have to

do some preliminary work on what you need, and what choices there are.

What do you need?

In recent years people have become aware of the importance of the right kind of mattress, especially for those with bad backs. There is now a much greater range to choose from and you need to try them out since there is no standard grading system for firmness yet. Just because a bed is described as 'orthopaedic', this is no guarantee that it will be the right length and width for you. You must try it out for yourself. There is a greater range of sizes available now, you no longer have to decide between standard single or double.

Choices

What type of bed will you have? You can choose between an interior-sprung mattress, a foam mattress, a solid or sprung base, a wooden-slatted base, even a water bed. You might also consider the advantages and disadvantages of zip-linked beds with different types of mattresses — particularly suitable when a couple's weights vary by 30 kg or more. Or a bed which will tilt so that you can sit up with no effort — especially useful for the disabled and elderly. You can consider the virtues of different types of springing and weights of foam — these are much more important factors than the colour of the mattress covering, which often plays a large part in people's choice of beds.

Making sure you get the bed you need

The bedding industry has recently been working on new standards for beds. These are based on practical, punishing tests and involve the measurement, under controlled laboratory conditions, of induced hollowing, lumping, structural strength of the divan base and other factors. A 'pass' on each will be compulsory for all beds bearing the new label.

In addition, there are further tests on what have sometimes been vulnerable points —mattress handles, for example — and optional tests on the variables, such as firmness.

But whatever the industry may do to help the consumer it is, ultimately, up to the shopper to use his or her own judgement and good sense.

In the shop

☐ Find a retailer who can answer your questions confidently. If you think the seller doesn't know his or her job, go elsewhere — your comfort and money is at stake.

☐ Read the label to check what it says about flammability and what different materials were used to make up the bed.

☐ Lie on the bed (both of you if it's a double) — not just on your back but on both sides. Lie for long enough to get a feel of the mattress — a couple of seconds isn't going to tell you anything.

☐ Check the guarantee, usually five years. The longer it is, the better.

At home

☐ When you get your bed home remember that it will take a few days to get used to it, especially if your old bed had become a

WATER BEDS

Incidentally, water beds are more practical than they used to be. They are made up of water-filled cylinders packed tightly together in a high-density foam casing on a specially formed base. Even if one of the cylinders is punctured the bed doesn't leak. They have a heating system, which keeps the temperature at body heat. Water beds support the body naturally and are good for back sufferers as there are no pressure points.

sagging hammock or sack of potatoes.

☐ Go back to the retailer if you're really unhappy about your bed after a month or so. If you have made a major mistake they should be as sympathetic as is possible.

☐ If you're buying bunk beds for children, check whether the beds rock or can overbalance, the strength and ease of use of the ladder, and whether there is a safety rail on the top bunk.

It is important to check the construction of the mattress you're interested in

New technology and moves in recent years towards helping elderly and disabled people to keep their independence have meant that there has been a great increase in the number and type of special aids available. But, in general, these aids have had rather restricted availability — and the selection of the most suitable for each particular person has often been in the hands of the professional rather than the user.

Even when aids are available for purchase instead of 'on prescription', objective information about different brands and details of their various features is not widely available to those who want to buy. Yet everyone — able-bodied or not — uses aids of one kind or another in their daily life. Why should you have less choice about the aids you want to use just because you are disabled or elderly?

WHO'S DECISION?

Look at this list and think which items need to be 'prescribed' by an expert. How much say should the eventual user have in the decision-making process? Think about each 'aid' and decide on the basis of past experience which category you think it belongs in.

What was your conclusion? As far as we can see, none of these aids needs to be chosen entirely by experts, although in the past the choice of things like hearing-aids, bath-hoists and wheelchairs has usually been dictated by professionals. Some products, such

as spectacles, would need input from both sides — from the expert as to what strength and type of lenses is needed and from the spectacle wearer as to what they can see and the style and cost of the frames. The potential wheelchair user would need to try various sizes and types of wheelchair to see how comfortable, convenient and suitable for his or her needs they were; the user or a helper would compare weights and ease of collapse to check on how convenient the wheelchair would be to move about when not in use; an expert might give an opinion from the experience of a wide number of wheelchair users as to the suitability of the chairs available for the user's particular disability; other wheelchair users, perhaps with a similar disability, would have opinions to offer based on their experience. The efficiency and suitability of a food processor could be judged entirely by the would-be user. There shouldn't really be any difference between the way in which you set about choosing *any* of these different products. You need to analyse

your needs, draw up a list of features that should meet those needs, survey what is available to you and decide how far those products meet your criteria, and make your choice.

Because of their situation, many disabled or elderly people might need some help and assistance when choosing aids. They might need help with tracking down information, they might welcome advice and the chance to discuss the decision to make sure they have considered all the different aspects. But overall, the more say the user has in the decision, the more successful the choice is likely to be. Are there any general principles you would bear in mind if you were choosing aids to help yourself overcome some kind of disability?

Guidelines for choice

People who have had a lot of experience with aids have suggested that the following points are important when aids are being selected from the range available.

Aids	User completely responsible for choice	Expert completely responsible for choice	Decision split between user and expert
Food processor			
Spectacles			
Non-slip bath mat			
Electric typewriter			
Bath-hoist			
Wheelchair			

- The simpler the aid necessary for the task, the better.

- Aids which can be used in several situations (although still relatively simple) are better than those which do only one thing.

- Aids should be as portable as possible.

- Aids should be robust and reliable, especially when part of a life-support system.

- It may be very important that an aid looks good and doesn't draw attention to any disability. You will have to weigh up the balance between the appearance of the aid and its practicality.

- Aids should be safe to use.

Help available

More and more consumer research is being done on aids for living. Comparative information is available from the Disabled Living Foundation and local groups such as Help the Aged and Disablement Information and Advice (DIAL) schemes. *Which?* reports are appearing on subjects such as special equipment for the arthritic. The Research Institute for Consumer Affairs (RICA) has surveyed emergency alarm systems and consumer programmes on television have looked at wheelchairs. Your local social services should be able to provide useful advice.

What would help Mrs Pearson?

Mrs Pearson, who is 54, has suffered from rheumatoid arthritis for some years. She is getting

Two simple and effective aids for making tea

rather stiff, and her grip is a bit weak, but she is determined to remain independent in her ground-floor flat. If you were her, what aids might make things easier for you? Read through the problems, and then jot down some ideas.

The problems

The bath seems very slippery and she finds it hard to get in and out. She is afraid that she is going to get stuck in there one night! The other problem is in the kitchen. She is finding it harder and harder to make a cup of tea. The electric kettle is difficult to handle, and the plug is quite stiff for her to pull in and out.

Our suggestions

You may well have come up with a variety of ideas based on your experience of people with problems like Mrs Pearson's. Our suggestions to help with her bath problem would be to look at non-slip bath mats which would give her something to stand and sit on in the bath — the kind with

suction pads underneath is best. These are available from chain stores and shops which specialise in bathroom fittings. She would also find a grab-rail fitted at the side of the bath extremely useful. The local social services department should be able to give her advice as to what would fit in her bathroom. As her condition deteriorates she might have to consider a different kind of bath that she could get into and out of more easily, or possibly a bath-hoist.

There are special electric plugs available from chain stores which have handles to make them easier to pull out. Mrs Pearson might also find it easier to fill the kettle from a lightweight plastic jug rather than unplugging the kettle every time to take it to the tap to fill it, or to use a cordless kettle. There are quite a few aids for use in the kitchen — tap-turners, which make it much easier to turn taps on and off might help Mrs Pearson. The next step would be check through these suggestions with her.

Most people operate on some form of credit. You are probably no exception.

WHAT DO YOU OWE?

If you are not sure just how much credit you have, check through this list and make a rough estimate of anything you owe against each heading.

Mortgage..............................

Loans from your bank..................

Loans from your building society.......................

Current account overdraft................................

Credit cards............................

Gold card overdraft......................

Shop account cards........................

Mail order purchases on credit...............................

Hire purchase............................

Finance company loans..................

Insurance policy loans....................

Loan from your employer...............................

Telephone bills...........................

Gas bills.................................

Electricity bills............................

Total borrowing............................

Were you surprised by the total?

The average British family may owe as much as £1500, excluding mortgages.

This money is borrowed from a bewildering array of lenders — there are more than 70,000 licensed lenders in Britain, from huge banks to street-corner moneylenders, offering many different types of credit. If you're thinking about borrowing, you'll need to consider all the options available, not simply plump for the first loan that you're offered. With this much money involved, the wrong type of borrowing could cost you dear.

NEEDS AND CHOICES FOR CREDIT

When you're thinking about different kinds of loan, you also need to be aware of your feelings about credit. Bill, for instance, hates the thought of borrowing for anything. He paid off his house mortgage as soon as possible, despite all the tax advantages of mortgage repayments. His watchword is 'Neither a lender not a borrower be'. Vince, on the other hand, feels that borrowing and living on credit is such a common feature of everyday life that he barely gives it a thought. He keeps a check on how much he owes at any one time and tries not to exceed what he reckons he can manage in the way of repayments. For Vince, credit is a way of life. Where do you come between these two extremes? And how much do you really know about the different kinds of credit?

You will probably need credit at some time, if not now perhaps in the future. It might be for something relatively small, like a new vacuum cleaner, or something bigger, like a home extension. Whatever you want to buy there will be lots of different possible sources of credit.

Besides paying for the actual goods or services you are considering buying, you will probably have other requirements of the credit facility – such as arranging the loan quickly and easily, or being able to pay back early if you want to.

A very important consideration is how much the credit will cost you. The usual way of comparing the cost of various forms of credit is by means of the APR, or Annual Percentage Rate of charge. This is a way of expressing the rate of interest you are paying. It makes it easy to compare different credit deals because it's calculated in exactly the same way for all types of credit. It takes into account the size, number and frequency of repayments, together with any inescapable costs like arrangement fees or life insurance. On most loans lenders have to quote the APR. But lenders offering credit cards or overdrafts aren't *obliged* to quote the APR – and often don't. You need to make a careful check of APR, which is different for all forms of credit and may change very quickly. Go back to the list of what you owe which you made at the beginning of this topic. Do you know what the APR is for each of these debts? Check to find out what rate of charge you are paying for each of the sums owed. Doing this might mean that you decide not to use a particular form of credit again.

WHICH FORM OF CREDIT FOR YOU?

The next section lists the various possibilities for obtaining credit, although not all of them may be available to you. Decide what you might want to borrow money for, and check against each of the sources of credit to see which would be your cheapest and most convenient option.

Once you have decided which the right forms of credit are for you, and your particular purchase, you can find out who will offer this kind of credit deal in a way which will be convenient for you.

Sources of credit

Bank ordinary loan —this is a good form of flexible, longer-term borrowing (maybe for as long as 10 years) — but it is not always available. Such loans are arranged individually, so you may be able to negotiate them to suit your needs exactly. Banks tend not to advertise ordinary loans, and try to persuade you to get a personal loan instead; security for the loan might be needed (your home or an insurance policy, for example) and you might have to pay arrangement fees.

Bank overdraft — going 'into the red' on your current account. Overdrafts are convenient, but can work out expensive in the long term. Quick to arrange; can be fairly cheap if authorised; security is not usually needed; available for any purpose *but* you'll have to pay bank charges. You might have to pay an arrangement fee. The bank

can insist you pay off the loan at any time. An **unauthorised overdraft** will be very expensive. You'll almost certainly have to pay bank charges. You're likely to have cheques bounced — which you will be charged for too — and this will make you very unpopular with your bank as well as with your debtors.

Bank personal loan — this is less flexible than a bank ordinary loan. It is quick and easy to arrange, but can be expensive. There is no arrangement fee *but* there will be restrictions on repayment time and the amount of the loan.

Budget account — these are organised through banks and some finance houses. The idea is that you add up your expected outgoings, and put one-twelfth of the total into the account every month to pay household bills. This is an expensive way to budget and it would be better to pay a regular sum into an interest-bearing account or take advantage of the free schemes offered by gas and electricity boards and local authorities for rates. A scheme like this may help with budgeting *but* the interest rate when you're overdrawn is higher than that on an ordinary overdraft. You'll also

be liable for charges if you're overdrawn. On most accounts there is no interest when in credit.

Credit cards — e.g. Visa, Access. The interest rate is variable. They are quick and convenient. You can get interest-free credit for up to eight weeks, depending on when you buy and when you pay your bill. There are no arrangement fees or set repayment schedule. Cash advances and personal loans may be available. No security is required *but* you can't use them everywhere. There's no tax relief on interest, unless the loan is for a business purpose . Credit of this kind can be expensive if you don't regularly pay off what you owe.

Credit Union — a savings and loan co-operative, usually operating over a relatively small area. Members' savings form a fund from which any of them can borrow. Such schemes are cheap and profits are distributed to members, but these schemes are for members only.

Charge cards — e.g. American Express, Diners Club. These aren't really sources of credit, because you have to pay off what you owe each month. However, you may be able to use your charge card to borrow money in some circumstances. You usually have to pay a membership/subscription fee.

Employer — some employers offer cheap or free credit as a perk — usually to buy a specific item, like a season ticket. This is a cheap and easy form of credit, if you can get it. Schemes like this are often less expensive than most other types of credit *but* you have to pay off the loan as a lump sum if you leave the job.

Finance houses — many advertise in newspapers; some have High Street branches. Some retailers have arrangements with finance houses to supply credit to their customers. They are particularly worth considering if you're having difficulty getting a loan elsewhere as they will consider requests for which other lenders are not anxious to lend money. Different companies offer very different terms, so it's important to shop around. They generally offer two main types of loan

■ unsecured loans — APRs vary very widely, depending on your circumstances, the company and the reason you want the loan. You may be able to borrow more than with other types of unsecured loan. Usually quick and easy to arrange *but* can be expensive

■ secured loans — offering your home as security may get you a large amount of money on loan. This should be easy to arrange *but* you may be able to get a secured loan cheaper elsewhere. If you fall on hard times, of course, there is always the possibility that you could lose your home.

Gold card overdraft — this includes overdrafts available with upmarket charge cards such as Master-Card and American Express Gold. A cheap form of overdraft — but it's only for the better-off. Schemes like this are convenient, and are available for any purpose. No security is required. You can repay when you like *but* you can get a gold card only if you earn more than a certain (high) amount. You have to pay a subscription fee — which increases the true cost of borrowing.

Home improvement loan — available from some banks, building societies and finance companies, *but* only for home improvements. The cost varies widely and you may need security. You may not be able to borrow 100% of the cost of the improvements. You could also consider increasing your mortgage.

Increasing your mortgage — this is a further loan from the lender that gave you your original mortgage, and would be a cheap way of borrowing money to improve your home. The APR is usually at the same rate as your original mortgage. It is cheaper than most other loans. *But* it may not be as cheap as the original loan. Arrangement fees may be high and it's secured against your home.

Insurance policy loans — you borrow money against the surrender value of some life insurance policies, to be repaid when the policy matures. This can be a cheap, long-term loan. You can leave the loan outstanding until the policy pays out. There is built-in insurance *but* the maximum loan is a percentage of the policy surrender value, so you may not be able to borrow much if the policy is being used for something else, such as a policy which is being used to repay an endowment mortgage. You still have to pay insurance premiums as well as repayments on the loan.

Interest-free credit — often offered by mail-order catalogues and some shops. This can be a useful way of spreading the cost of purchases. Usually no security is necessary *but* check that the goods aren't cheaper elsewhere.

Moneylenders — make unsecured and sometimes secured loans and usually collect repayments door-to-door. They may lend to you, even if you can't borrow elsewhere *but* because they specialise in high-risk lending, they can be extremely expensive.

'Save and Borrow' account — from banks and some finance houses. With this you pay in a set amount each month, and can borrow up to 30 times the monthly payment. They are fairly convenient, but expensive. You may get interest when the account's in credit (but you could probably get more by investing elsewhere); no security is required. They are available for any purpose *but* interest rates are high when the account is overdrawn. There may be other charges.

Shop credit — many shops offer one or more different types of credit to encourage you to buy from them. Shop credit may be a good idea but it pays to compare what is available. There are several types.

■ Shop card — most are like credit cards but usually a bit more expensive. The interest rate is variable. Some forms of shop credit are like bank 'Save and Borrow' accounts. They may be worthwhile if the APR is lower than a credit card or you buy a lot from the same shop.

■ Hire purchase, credit sale, conditional sale tied to the purchase of particular goods. You pay instalments at a fixed interest rate. With credit sale, the goods belong to you immediately; with the other two, the goods aren't yours until you've finished paying. The shop will arrange the loan for you, which is convenient *but* these schemes can work out very expensive — check that you can't borrow more cheaply elsewhere.

Trading checks — you buy a check from a trading check company and pay for it in instalments. It is valid at any one of a list of shops. These schemes are usually very expensive. The shops on the list may not sell goods at the cheapest prices.

Best buys

The above list is based on *Which?* reports. Of these different possible sources of credit, *Which?* recommended the following as 'best buys' if they are suitable for what you need.

■ Bank ordinary loan
■ Bank overdraft
■ Credit cards

- Charge cards
- Employer
- Gold card overdraft
- Increasing your mortgage
- Insurance policy loan
- Interest-free credit.

They also had a 'best avoided' list.

- Unauthorised overdraft
- Trading checks
- Moneylenders.

If you want to know what your consumer rights on credit are, you need to look at the Consumer Credit Act 1974. This should be available in the reference section of your local public library, or at your Citizens' Advice Bureau. Remember to come back to your notes on this activity whenever you need credit. APRs will change, and so will the various forms of credit and their conditions.

Have you got too much credit?

If you lost your job, got divorced or were ill for a long time, could you manage to keep up the payments on all your debts? More and more people who've borrowed quite sensibly are facing severe problems as the result of an unforeseen event like redundancy or the death of a partner.

The chances are that you'll never find yourself in this situation. But if you do, it's sensible to follow some basic guidelines. These have been drawn up by the Birmingham Settlement, an old-established money advice centre.

- **Get in touch with your creditors** straight away and explain the difficulties. Go and see them, speak to them on the telephone or write to them.

- If the first person you speak to is unhelpful, a**sk to speak to** **somebody more senior** who may be able to discuss your particular problem with you.

- **Write down a complete budget** showing how much money is coming into and going out of your household.

- **Make sure you tackle your priority debts first** – the debts which can mean losing your home or having your gas or electricity cut off, or going to prison. **Don't panic**! You can't go to prison for ordinary debts.

- **Work out a reasonable offer to repay** the money owed. Don't worry if it appears very small if that is really all you can afford. Creditors prefer you to pay a small amount regularly than to make an offer you can't keep to.

- **Fill in the reply forms to court papers** and let the court have all the facts. You can attach a copy of your budget if you wish.

- **Try to attend court hearings**. Take a copy of your budget with you. Don't think that going to court makes you a criminal; it's not that kind of court.

- **Don't borrow money to pay off your debts** without thinking carefully. **Get advice first.** This kind of borrowing can lead to losing your home or other problems.

- **Don't ignore the problem**: it won't go away and the longer you leave it the worse it gets.

- **Don't ignore creditors' letters or telephone calls**. Always answer their letters. Don't give up trying to reach an agreement even if creditors are difficult.

When you buy some new piece of household equipment, you hope that it is going to last indefinitely, or at least until your needs change so much that you decide to replace it with something different.

How long-lasting?

But what's the reality? How long *do* household appliances last? It may be a very long time. In a feature which was linked to the 30th birthday of *Which?*, readers were asked to send details of appliances they'd owned since the magazine started and which were still going strong. Hundreds of people replied and the magazine

featured such veterans as a 40-year-old Hotpoint washing-machine, a 1930 Siemens toaster, a 1934 CWS Dudley vacuum cleaner and a 50-year-old Frigidaire Household Unit refrigerator. However, these are the exceptions rather than the rule. *Which?* has a panel of 16,000 readers who record the reliability of various basic household appliances. Details of each repair and its cost are recorded and compared over the first four years of ownership.

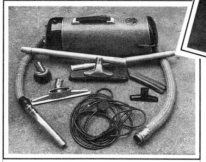

Proud owner with five 30+ year old possessions

This Electrolux has cleaned up after four children and various furred and feathery pets

A Frigidaire, bought second-hand in 1947, has an oak refrigeration chamber and double doors

A 1930 toaster which pivots out to turn the slices to toast on the other side

YOUR EXPECTATIONS

Based on your experience, how would you rank these common household appliances for reliability, that is, not needing repair? Put them in order according to which you would think was *most* reliable.

Tumble-dryers

Fridge-freezers

Colour televisions

Automatic washing-machines

Dishwashers

Upright freezers

Chest freezers

Vacuum cleaners

Answers

Results according to the *Which?* panel, starting with the most reliable and ending with the least reliable were

Upright freezers (five out of six needed no repairs over four years)

Chest freezers

Colour televisions

Tumble-dryers

Fridge-freezers

Vacuum cleaners

Dishwashers

Automatic washing-machines (overall six out of ten needed a repair in the first four years of their life).

For information on which brands are more reliable than others you will have to read the latest *Which?* reports. It is useful to consider this information in conjunction with price. It is not necessarily the most expensive brand which lasts the longest.

If having an appliance which runs for a very long time with no repairs is important to you, then you need to be sure to buy one of those brands which did well in the *Which?* readers' survey. If, on the other hand, you are not particularly concerned about having a machine which lasts for a very long time —you see major changes and improvements ahead, for example, so will not be buying for the long term — then you need not spend too much time on checking this point.

Knowing which type of appliance lasts a long time and which doesn't also helps when you're considering whether to buy second-hand. An older second-hand upright freezer is obviously a better buy than, for instance, an elderly washing-machine.

Planning for the next few years

Do you see changes in your circumstances ahead? These may well affect the household equipment you are going to need over the next few years. While it's inadvisable (and impossible) to predict exactly what you will need or to make plans which will cover every eventuality, it would be a good idea to think about conceivable changes and consider those which might affect you and in what way. You should then try to allow for them in your household equipment buying plans.

What difference would it make, for instance, if something were to change in your neighbourhood?

Gas might be laid on, giving you an extra choice of fuel, or the introduction of mains drainage might make plumbing-in a washing-machine possible. A launderette might open, or a laundry service or freezer centre start up. And what about neighbours? Will the people who lend you tools always be there? Might you be having more visitors in the future, making extra demands on your food storage and cooking capacity?

Many changes relate to children. Starting a family, with one partner giving up full-time work, is probably going to be the most demanding (in every possible sense!) change in most people's lives, and the change when two incomes are reduced to one, and new washing and drying resources are necessary, cannot be underestimated. Spend a few minutes thinking about possible changes whenever you are working out what your equipment buying needs are. This might just prevent you from buying something that turns out to be too big or too small in a very short time.

RENOVATING AN OLDER HOUSE

Jo is on her own with two grown-up sons. Having lived in council property nearly all her life, she recently became a property owner. First of all, she raised a mortgage and bought her council flat. When she had been there a few years, and found that owning, rather than renting, was manageable for her, she decided to look for an older house. She was delighted to find an old semi she could afford in a road near where she used to live as a child. The house was extremely dilapidated and very little modernising work had been done. Undeterred, Jo bought the semi, retaining some of the mortgage money for essential work. Although she is of a practical disposition, Jo had no experience of house renovation. She decided to set about getting the necessary work done by

■ making a conscious decision that some jobs (decorating, tiling) she could learn to do herself (from books, friends, relatives) but that major jobs would have to be done professionally

■ getting things done gradually, as she could afford them: she decided early on which jobs were essential, which less so

■ asking questions of everyone she came across — asking for ideas about likely costs, names of likely suppliers of services, sources of replacement period doors and windows etc.; she recorded all the answers in a notebook

■ keeping detailed records of absolutely everything she has spent on the house so that she knows where all the money has gone, and how much regular services should cost in the future.

Now that Jo has been in the 'new' house for a year or so much of the major work has been done. Two of the four bedrooms have been set up as student accommodation, so Jo will be able to finance the final stages of restoration. Jo's pleasure in her home is undiminished: despite all the hard work and problems, she has managed to achieve her dream home more or less single-handed.

Jo and her dream home: 'As soon as I set eyes on it, I fell in love with it.'

The original features which Jo especially liked included the stained glass in the front door, the balustrade and the carving on the side of the stairs.

The living room particularly attracted Jo because of its size and the original tiling in the fireplace.

One skill which Jo has taught herself and applied very successfully is rag rolling.

Another kind of skill Jo has had to learn is that of replanning and organising her kitchen to make it as convenient as possible for her needs.

CHANGING THE USE OF YOUR HOME

Ian and Anne's family home 'Wheelwrights' in the Lake District has been used in many different ways over the years.

The main house has long been the basis for a business — originally, Anne's family worked there as wheelwrights, joiners and undertakers. More recently, Anne and Ian adapted one of the buildings as a restaurant. Now the house serves as the centre for a self-catering holiday home business with houses and cottages in several neighbouring villages. Anne and Ian also serve evening meals to visitors in their own living room a couple of times a week. Other parts of the original site — the woodshed and other outhouses — have been rebuilt as holiday cottages.

Anne and Ian sum up the particular advantages and opportunities given by this latest arrangement as follows

■ they can capitalise on the situation and size of their home to earn a living for themselves.

■ they are both very sociable and enjoy the chance to meet a wide range of people in their own home

■ independence — they are their own masters and can make the decisions they feel are best for their family.

Disadvantages are

■ lack of privacy — Ian and Anne are always ' on call'

■ disruption of family life, which also affects their young son Ben.

While not everyone is able to work from home in the same way as Ian and Anne there are pointers here in the way they organise their business which other homeworkers could copy.

Ian and Anne outside 'Wheelwrights' as it is today. The painting shows it in former times.

As the house is the base for a business, Ian and Anne have had to arrange it to cope with constant calls and visits from current and potential clients.

Most of the week Ian and Anne use the living room as any other family would. On two evenings a week, however, it is prepared for evening guests and Ian acts as waiter.

Different parts of the house have been adapted to support Ian and Anne's business. One room is fully equipped as an office; the kitchen has had special equipment added to help Anne and Ian to prepare extra large quantities of food.

CHANGING YOUR HOME ABOUT

Rob and Cathy are the parents of a step-family: two older children from Rob's first marriage visit at weekends and Rob and Cathy also have three-year-old twins of their own. They both work full time. The family live in a large semi-detached house built in 1911 which has been chosen carefully to give them plenty of space for family and visitors, and can be changed around as needed. The house also gives them access to useful facilities such as the park where the children can play.

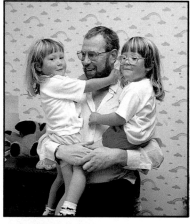

Rob and Cathy's main problems as far as the house is concerned are

■ being flexible about the way they use their home and keeping up with the changing needs of both sets of children

■ balancing their various priorities — work, family and social life

■ coping with maintenance, redecoration and other household jobs.

Rob and Cathy have chosen a capacious home and setting to suit the needs of their family.

The playroom is big enough to house toys and equipment which will suit the needs of children of different ages.

They have made a conscious decision about priorities that they try to stick to.

Rob says: 'There are a great many demands on my time, because I work full time. The priority has been the children. Socially, I think we enjoy friends coming down, and that's quite a high priority. And that leaves very little time and money for jobs on the house. So I'm afraid the house, certainly the outside, is last on the list.'

Rob and Cathy's home reflects the thought and effort they've put into making it fit their needs.

The old-fashioned
cupboards in what was
originally part of the kitchen (now the dining-room) have
been taken out and replaced by more modern fitments.

What was formerly a workroom has now
been transformed into a bedroom for the twins who need
more space as they get older.

ORGANISING YOUR HOME TO WORK FOR YOU

Sue and Dave are a couple who have organised their chalet bungalow to work for them and their lifestyle, rather than their working to maintain it. They've done this by extending their living space upwards — building two more rooms under the roof, adding extra storage elsewhere — and by choosing their domestic appliances, equipment and fittings very carefully. In detail, some of the various features of their home which give them the scope to pursue their chosen hobbies and operate efficiently are

■ Dave's hobbies room where he keeps aeroplane models in progress of construction, tools, supplies etc.

■ the home office upstairs which is used by both Dave and Sue

■ extra storage space under the stairs where Sue keeps all her wine-making equipment

■ the size, position, capacity and features of the domestic appliances they have chosen for their kitchen.

Sue and Dave's solutions to their problems will probably not be the same as yours — but you may find them interesting and even useful for your own circumstances.

Sue and Dave's weekend leisure priorities include gardening and getting away with their power boat. They have organised their home successfully to give them time for those hobbies.

Dave is able to pursue his hobby of aero modelling in the newly created hobbies room in the attic without having to worry about putting tools, equipment or work away. Both Dave and Sue make good use of the small office which has been built under the eaves next to the hobbies room. Although tiny, there is enough space for desk, chair and bookshelves.

Sue and Dave have put time and effort into equipping and laying out their kitchen so that they spend as little time as possible on household chores. Space under the stairs is used for wine-making equipment.

CHAPTER FOUR

RUNNING YOUR HOME

Very few of us have unlimited resources, time and energy to devote to our homes. We need to make choices about how to make the best use of what we have. This chapter is about running homes and deciding what to concentrate on. To start you thinking about what aspects of running your home and living in it are most important to you, consider for a few moments what makes your home feel comfortable. What makes you feel good about your home and what would give you more pleasure if it were improved? Is it

- sufficient warmth in winter
- plenty of light and air
- knowledge that it is as burglar-proof as possible
- convenient organisation of equipment so that it can be run easily
- tip-top decorative condition
- confidence that it is being run as economically as possible
- maximum insulation
- fittings and furnishings that look good
- reassurance that it is as safe as possible for those who live there
- something else?

Maybe you think that all these things are necessary to make you feel that your home is being run to your satisfaction. Or perhaps you are conscious that different points are more important to some members of the family than others.

Perhaps you feel that one aspect of comfort (plenty of warmth and hot water, for instance) partly cancels out another (economic running of the home in this case).

This chapter should help you to think through what you would like and how you're going to achieve it. Work through the following topics which deal with different aspects of running your home. They look at making savings on your energy consumption, improving insulation, making your home safer and more secure and maintaining your home to a reasonable standard. This is followed by a couple of topics to help you think about how much work in the home you can and want to do yourself. As you go through the chapter, think about what you consider most important for making your home better to live in. This may not be what glossy advertisements recommend as ways of improving your home — fitting an expensive kitchen, for instance, or installing double glazing everywhere. But it may well be something which makes your home a more comfortable and convenient place for you and your family in your day-to-day life.

Dream home

While it's unlikely that you could afford the time, money and energy to make your home comfortable in every possible way, this dream did seem to come true for one family, the Flellos.

The Flello family (mother, father and three children) bought the showpiece of the Milton Keynes Home World exhibition — known as the BBC Money Programme House or Futurehome — and have been living in it for over six years.

The house is a large, timber-frame construction built round a roof-to-ground conservatory, which nearly all the rooms open into. It is full of innovative, energy-conserving features which, initially, proved almost overpoweringly complex and difficult to manage. The Flellos weren't helped by the huge amount of initial media coverage and public curiosity — thousands wanted to see the Futurehome with a family actually living in it. Now, however, the Flellos can't imagine living anywhere else. They are totally at home with the house's many unusual features and have changed remarkably few of them, although they found some had advantages and some disadvantages.

Any changes?

The main difference in the house now from the way it was built is that the Flellos have added an extra room which doesn't open into the central conservatory like all the others. This is a quiet room at one side of the house where family members sit and read or work or entertain their friends. One of the house's three central heating systems has been taken out — the propane gas-fired Fiat Totem engine system, which produced electricity for the home with the surplus to be fed back

into the grid, took up too much space and wasn't really needed. They still have the gas and solid-fuel systems in use during the winter months. From March to October the house is so well insulated that it doesn't need to be heated and the solar panels in the roof produce hot water.

Most popular features

The Flellos are particularly impressed by the success of the system of ventilation — the house is very airy and not stuffy, and there are no draughts at all. The house does not suffer from condensation — all the double-glazed windows have triple vents.

Because the upstairs and downstairs parts of the house are programmed separately, the bedrooms can be kept perceptibly cooler than the living room. The Flellos are pleased about the heating bills, which they think are considerably lower than for other houses of a similar size. This they believe is because of the huge amount and variety of insulation (insulation in the walls, thermal blinds, double glazing) and the fact that there is only one north-facing window and few outside doors.

To sum up, the Flellos like their house immensely. It has no draughts, it's cheap to run and there's plenty of space. Would it be your ideal? Would you incorporate some of these innovative comfort features into your dream home? Or would it be quite different?

One way of saving energy is to use as little energy as possible — by controlling your space and water heating as economically as you can. There are a whole range of methods you can use to do this, ranging from very simple ideas for changing the way you do things up to special equipment — thermostats and programmers — you can get for your central heating system. What you decide to do depends, of course, on how you heat space and water and what your needs are. If you are at home all day with a small baby, there is no point in deciding to heat the house only in the evenings to save fuel. And if your water is heated in a geyser and you depend on paraffin stoves or electric fires to provide you with warmth, then you won't be considering ultra-sophisticated devices for cutting energy usage. How much time and effort are you prepared to put into making energy savings? If you have very little time available, you might prefer to devote it to something else, rather than putting effort into the energy-saving measures suggested here. It is up to you to weigh up economy and convenience.

CUT ENERGY GUZZLING

First of all, what do you think you spend most money on in your home? Is it

- cooking
- lighting
- heating space and water
- television, food processor, iron etc?

Hazard a guess at which operation you think takes most energy, and about what percentage of your bills it makes up.

You probably thought that heating space and water takes most energy, and you would be right. Did you realise, though, that it accounts for over half of the energy consumed, about 65%, in the average home which is not particularly well insulated? Television, lights, kitchen appliances and so on take up about 25% and cooking about 10%. The remainder of your bill will be made up by standing charges. When houses are very well insulated, less energy is used for heating and the proportions change. So it makes sense to put most effort into cutting down on the energy used to heat space and water, but to take a look at cooking and the use of other appliances as well.

WHAT DO YOU DO NOW?

Go through this list, checking which suggestions for energy saving you already carry out, and considering how useful the ones you haven't tried might be to you. The list is based on reports from *Which?* magazine.

☐ Read your meters at least once a month to keep you aware of spending so that you can cut back if necessary.

☐ Experiment with your central heating timer. Try setting it to come on later and go off earlier. It is a myth that it is cheaper to leave the heating on. In summer, set the boiler to come on just long enough to heat sufficient water for your needs.

☐ Use cheaper electricity. It may be worth changing to Economy 7 if an immersion heater is your only means of water heating — you'll need to fit a timer to the immersion heater to do this. If you can run your washing-machine, dishwasher or cooker overnight as well, so much the better. Using cheaper electricity at night might also cut the cost of running other appliances such as freezers, although not by a great amount, as the day rate on Economy 7 is currently (1988) higher than the standard tariff. So if you have a great many other appliances which you run during the day, it won't be worth making a change. You should be able to get advice from your local electricity board.

☐ Turn down room thermostats (although older people and young children generally need higher temperatures). Each degree centigrade less can save 7% or more of your fuel.

☐ Consider how essential it is to have hot water constantly available and whether it needs to be very hot.

☐ Don't leave doors open, especially outside and hall doors.

☐ Turn off radiators in rooms you're not using and keep the doors shut.

☐ Keep windows shut — if you're too hot, turn the heating down.

Make your central heating run more efficiently

If you have a central heating system, there may be ways in which you can make it work more economically — by changing the timer, or installing thermostats of some kind.

Heating controls

Most systems already have a timer or programmer to turn the system on and off, but older ones are not likely to be very accurate or flexible. A modern electronic programmer might be worth considering simply so that you can be sure the heating will come on exactly when you want it. Check how much an up-to-date programmer would cost for your system, so that you can decide whether or not it would be a good investment for you.

Thermostats

A reduction of one degree in average room temperature will quickly repay the cost of a room thermostat. If you have a single

thermostat for the whole house, the heating in every room is controlled by the temperature in the room where the thermostat is placed. Thermostatically controlled radiator valves will make it possible to control the temperature of rooms individually by allowing you to adjust the heat output from each radiator, but you should still have a room thermostat to give overall control.

A hot-water cylinder thermostat plus a motorised valve prevents the water in the cylinder getting too hot and using unnecessary energy (it doesn't need to be as hot as the water for radiators). The boiler can switch itself on for short periods, even when the rooms and hot water in the cylinder are up to temperature, because the water in the boiler itself has cooled. This 'short cycling' wastes fuel: a correctly wired thermostat will stop it. Fitting and wiring these thermostats is a professional job.

Cooking with less energy

There are a number of ways of reducing the amount of energy used for cooking. In some cases you might need to trade off one thing against another: grilling may use more energy than frying, but

you may prefer a lower-fat diet and therefore want to avoid frying. Have you considered any of the following?

☐ Grilling uses more energy than boiling, frying or roasting, because most of the heat does not go into the food.

☐ A gas flame licking around the edge of the pan uses a lot more gas but cooks only a little faster than a flame which remains under the pan.

☐ Pans with lids on use much less heat for cooking.

☐ Pressure cookers save time and energy.

☐ Boiling water in a kettle over a gas flame is slightly cheaper than boiling it in an electric kettle, but a lot slower.

☐ Electric kettles are much cheaper to use than kettles on electric rings. In any kettle, heating just the amount of water you need is both cheaper and faster than heating a lot of extra water. This is easier with kettles which have measures marked on them. If you regularly want only one or two cups of water boiled in an electric kettle, buy a small one or one of the tall, narrower kettles so that you are not tempted to overfill it. You can also fill a flask with boiling water to use later.

☐ A descaled kettle keeps boiling time down.

☐ A toaster is cheaper to run than a grill.

☐ A microwave oven cooks food much more quickly and cheaply than either gas or conventional electric ovens.

Around the house

Refrigerators

While the cost of running a fridge is not particularly high, freezers use more energy than most appliances because they are left on all the time. Try not to put them near stoves or boilers. Load and unload them as quickly as possible so that the cold air doesn't escape. Defrost them regularly and avoid putting food in while it is still warm. It is wasteful to run a fridge or freezer which is too large — keep them at least three-quarters full for maximum operating efficiency.

Washing-machines

Automatic washing-machines are more convenient and, now, much more popular than twin tubs, but twin tubs do have their advantages. They are cheaper to buy and run, and some can re-use the hot water for a second load. Most spin clothes reasonably dry. Effective spin-drying is especially important if you use a tumble-dryer as well. The drier clothes are spun, the less time they will need in the tumble-dryer, which, because it includes a heater, uses a large amount of electricity.

Water heating is a major part of the cost of running a washing-machine. To keep costs down, wash full loads whenever possible and partial loads only if your machine has a half-load setting. A washing-machine heats water using full-rate electricity if you use it during the day. You can use a timer to run your machine during the night, if you are on Economy 7.

If you have hot water available in the system, which has been heated more cheaply, for example by a gas boiler, you will be better off with a washing-machine that will take both hot and cold water from the taps.

Baths, showers and taps

A shower uses a lot less hot water than a bath and the water is heated to a lower temperature. Don't let hot taps drip — in only one day, a fast-dripping hot tap could waste enough hot water to fill a bath.

Irons

An iron is a heating appliance, and if used correctly an iron with an efficient thermostat will not use very much energy unless it is left on when not in use. There are some models available which cut out automatically if left unused for more than three minutes. Steam irons use slightly more electricity than dry ones.

Lights

Only a small amount of the electricity used by an ordinary electric light bulb appears as light. Most is converted directly into heat. Fluorescent bulbs give about three times as much light for the same wattage. They are more expensive, but also last longer.

Lights consume such a small proportion of most people's fuel bills, that there isn't much point in switching them off if you leave a room for only a few minutes. Turning lights off in unused rooms is sufficient.

Electronic equipment

Television sets, radios, hi-fi equipment, home computers and so on also use little electricity individually, but a significant amount in total. So if you have a lot of equipment of this kind, you could make savings by turning it off when it is not really needed.

Action

This list of suggestions should have given you some ideas about possible steps you could take if energy saving is important to you. Some of these won't cost you any money — just time and effort until they become second nature to you. Others, such as installing a new programmer or thermostat for your central heating system or buying an electric kettle or new iron, will actually cost money. If you are seriously considering buying something to save energy, do some market research now and note down details of at least three alternatives, with prices and installation details. The next step is to weigh up possible savings of energy, and, perhaps, added convenience, against the cost of the programmer or new appliance. Try and include any possible disadvantages in this decision. Will the new thermostat be very complicated to use? Is the new iron convenient as well as needing less energy to run it? It is only too easy to become so interested in one aspect of a new purchase that you forget that it may have other, less attractive features. These may outweigh the benefits for you in the long run.

There are two reasons why we insulate our homes. The first is to make them more comfortable. This involves forms of insulation from which we can actually feel the results, such as draught-proofing, double glazing, thick curtains and porches. The other reason is to save ourselves money by preventing heat from escaping. This kind of insulation is the one which doesn't affect us so directly — loft insulation, insulating jackets on hot-water tanks and wall insulation. It doesn't really make sense to install insulation for any reasons apart from these two. Claims that you should carry out improvements like double glazing to increase the value of your home need to be looked at very carefully. Even if they are true, they are less important than your present comfort and the actual savings you may be able to make.

WHICH KINDS OF INSULATION?

Most people have some form of insulation in their homes to keep warmth in and cold out. Here is a summary of the most popular types. Go through it and tick those forms of insulation you already have. It will be useful for you to consider the other possibilities available as well, as the next stage will be for you to decide whether or not it would be worthwhile installing or extending insulation in your home.

Draught-proofing

- [ ] doors to outside
- [ ] internal doors
- [ ] windows
- [ ] sausage-type removable draught excluders

Loft insulation

- [ ] loft space between joists
- [ ] cold-water tank and pipes
- [ ] rafters from inside or out (if you are renewing your roof)
- [ ] flat roof from inside or out (if you are renewing it)

Insulating jacket and lagging

- [ ] hot-water tank
- [ ] hot-water pipes

Insulating foil

- [ ] behind radiators

Double/triple glazing

- [ ] windows (may also be plastic)
- [ ] glass doors

Wall insulation

- [ ] cavity walls
- [ ] solid walls

Internal/external shutters

- [ ] windows

Extension/extra layer

- [ ] extra door
- [ ] porch
- [ ] conservatory

Thick, insulating curtains

- [ ] windows
- [ ] doors

Working through this list might have confirmed that your home is pretty well insulated. It might, however, have made you realise that quite a lot could be improved.

Before you consider whether or not it would be worthwhile improving the insulation for your home, you need to weigh up the pros and cons in terms of cost and comfort.

How much will it cost?

Some insulation measures are so cheap and easy to install that there is no doubt about getting good value. Draught-proofing, loft insulation and jackets for hot-water tanks fall into this category.

Other measures, like double glazing and cavity-wall insulation are much more expensive. There is a tremendous variation in cost and the most expensive is not necessarily the best. Be sure you consider more than one type and, if you are using a contractor, get several estimates. Beware of sales people who make exaggerated or unsupported claims. What you need to do is to be sure that the product on offer is the right one for your home.

Insulation on the outside of solid walls, or on flat roofs, or on the roof of an attic room, is generally the most expensive of all and requires a specialist contractor. It is not often worth doing unless, for instance, you have to do major repairs. Besides buying comfort, buying insulation is also like an investment. You can consider the savings in your fuel bill as the return on that investment. It is especially important to know how good your return will be if you have to borrow money to pay for insulation.

There is a simple way to judge insulation as an investment, called the 'pay back time'. For this you need to know what your fuel bills are now, and what the saving is likely to be if the form of insulation you are considering is installed. To find this out you can ask neighbours in similar houses and check objective sources such as Which? reports, as well as taking a careful look at any evidence provided by salesmen. The 'pay back time' can be calculated by dividing the installation cost by the annual savings in fuel costs. Suppose, for example, that it would cost £250 to install cavity-wall insulation. You

enquire of neighbours whose home energy usage is much the same as yours but who have installed cavity-wall insulation, and find that they reckon that is saves them about £50 a year on their bills. Dividing 250 by 50 gives an answer of 5 — so you could say that the pay back time for this insulation would be five years. If you plan to stay in this home for more than five years installing the insulation will be a good idea. Knowing the pay back time for different forms of insulation means you can compare their value for money to you.

If you need to borrow money to pay for the insulation, compare the annual repayments on your loan with the likely savings in fuel bills. On a long-term loan, like an extension to a mortgage, the savings may be greater than the repayments, so the insulation is effectively free and gives the benefit of increased comfort straight away. Moreover, the cost of fuel is likely to rise faster than the general rate of inflation. So insulation may be an especially good investment in the long term.

Here, in brief, are some conclusions on the economy of different insulation measures based on Which? reports. Some other practical points you should consider are included as well. Obviously, you can ignore the insulation types you've already got.

If saving money is your chief reason for insulating, these assessments should enable you to work out value for money to you.

The insulation measures listed below have been rated by Which? on the following scale.

★★★★★ Will pay for itself in a year or less

★★★★ Will pay for itself in one to two years

★★★ Will pay for itself in two to four years

★★ Will pay for itself in about five years

★ Not worth doing on cost grounds alone

R Worth doing only during renovation work.

★★★★★ **Hot-water cylinder jacket**
This will pay for itself within weeks. Even with a properly fitted jacket, the cylinder will still provide enough heat to air clothes. The jacket should have a label with the Kitemark symbol and the British Standard number BS 5615. If your existing jacket is old, thin or in poor condition, add a new one on top.

★ ★ ★ ★ ★ Radiator foil

Fitting foil behind radiators on external walls reflects back heat which would otherwise escape. It won't save you a great deal, but you'll soon recover the modest cost of the foil. The worse your wall insulation is the more worthwhile this will be (and therefore it's particularly useful on solid walls). Ordinary kitchen foil will do, although specially made radiator foil which has peel-off paper over adhesive on one side may be easier to stick in place.

★ ★ ★ ★ ★ Loft insulation

You should have the equivalent of at least 100 mm of mineral fibre blanket (the thickness required in new housing to meet the Building Regulations). It would be worthwhile putting in 150 mm if your ceiling joists are deep enough to take it. Many people find it's possible to install loft insulation themselves. Alternatively, the job can be done by a contractor. If you

decide to do the job yourself, you need to buy special protective clothing, and a protective face mask and gloves are essential. If you have no loft insulation at all, and are on a low income, you might be able to get a grant from your local council — it's worth checking.

★ ★ ★ Draught proofing

Cheap, and well worth installing on poorly fitting doors and windows. You should also seal cracks around pipes, skirtings and so on. A minimum level of ventilation must be provided, though, to prevent condensation and to remove smells; in a well draught-proofed house, a mechanical extractor fan in the kitchen and bathroom may be needed. Heating appliances, except room-sealed gas heaters and boilers, and electric fires, need a supply of air to burn safely — with insufficient air they can produce toxic gases. You can fit draught excluders yourself or get a professional to do it.

★ ★ Cavity-wall insulation

Most houses built since the 1930s have walls with a 50 to 75 mm cavity. You can have these filled with urea-formaldehyde foam, mineral fibre or expanded polystyrene beads. Make sure the installer is approved by the British Standards Institution (BSI) or British Board of Agrément (BBA).

With urea-formaldehyde foam, there has been the problem of vapour escaping into the house rather than outwards as the foam dries. Although the problem is extremely rare, a very small

number of people may risk suffering an allergic reaction to the vapour. If you're worried about this, choose one of the dry-fill types of insulation — mineral fibre or expanded polystyrene beads — to be on the safe side.

Ask the contractor for a written statement that your walls are suitable for being filled. With urea-formaldehyde foam, the contractor should give you a statement that the work will comply with British Standard BS 5618. Modern timber-frame houses mostly have a high standard of insulation built in and shouldn't have their cavities filled.

★ Double glazing

Double glazing isn't usually cost-effective unless you're replacing the window frames anyway, so it would be worth considering only for comfort's sake. Installing secondary double glazing (a separate pane of glass or plastic sheet attached to the inside of your

existing window frame) is a fairly simple DIY job, and is cheaper than purpose-made sealed units or replacement windows. A particularly cheap version is the plastic film you can stick over the frame and then make fast by blowing a hair dryer over it. If you install an extra pane, make sure you would be able to open or remove it quickly in the event of a fire.

Interlined curtains can be almost as effective as double glazing, particularly if they reach down as far as a radiator shelf, so trapping cold air behind them. But don't let them hang over the top of the radiator. Heat-reflecting curtain linings and roller blinds are also worth considering. Curtains and roller blinds can't of course be kept drawn in daylight, but can make a big difference when it's dark outside.

★ **Porches or draught lobbies**
These help stop cold air getting into the house when someone comes in from the outside. A lobby should be big enough to enable you to shut the outer door before you open the inner one. It is not worth adding a draught lobby to an existing house purely as a fuel-saving measure but porches can be useful for other things as well such as storing wellington boots and growing plants.

R **Floor insulation**
There's not much you can do to floors unless you're doing major renovation work or you can get access from below — from a cellar, for example. Fitted carpet with thick underlay will cut down draughts and provide some

CONDENSATION

Most of us are familiar with the signs of condensation — water lying on window sills, cloudy windows, damp patches on the wall. In severe cases, it can ruin the decoration, make walls crumble and even affect your health. You can't prevent condensation entirely – an average household can easily produce 15 litres of water vapour a day; more if steaming is used as a cooking method. The vapour produced can't escape through walls, insulated windows or draught-proofed doors and so percolates through the rooms, condensing on to cold surfaces and eventually forming mould growth as well as spoiling decoration and floors. If unchecked, condensation can cause serious damage in the roof space or within external walls. There are a number of ways of dealing with it, according to how bad it is.

Mild condensation (i.e. small pools of water, some misting up of windows and mirrors)

If your problems are mild, all you need to do is wipe up the pools of condensation from time to time and make sure you don't make matters worse by leaving bathroom and kitchen doors open when there is a lot of steam about. You can remove water vapour in a steamy atmosphere simply by opening the window for a while.

Medium condensation (some mould growth, musty smell)

If your problem is medium condensation, then you need to consider whether you are using enough of the right kind of heating and whether you need to improve insulation and ventilation. You could consider glazed-in drainage channels at the bottoms of windows which will conduct condensation moisture outside safely.

Severe condensation (large amount of mould growth, bad smell, health of family affected)

If the problem is classed as severe, then you must consider adding insulation and probably some other aid such as an extractor fan or a cooker hood. Some extractor fans have integral humidistats, which switch on when humidity reaches a certain level.

insulation. Insulating suspended or solid floors will not be a DIY job except for the very expert handyman or woman.

R **Solid-wall insulation**
Solid walls, found in older houses, are more difficult to insulate. Insulating externally, followed by rendering, is expensive, but may be worthwhile if your house needs renovating externally or re-rendering. This is another job best left to experts.

How much insulation will cost you, and whether you can afford it, will often depend on how much work you are able and willing to do yourself. There is a topic later in this chapter which looks at this.

We've devoted a fair amount of space to the value for money that insulation offers, since it's important to be realistic about possible savings. But what about the other major consideration, comfort?

How comfortable will it be?

At the beginning of this topic we picked out those forms of insulation from which you can immediately feel the effect — draught-proofing, double glazing, thick curtains and porches. These all make your home more comfortable than before. Only you will be able to decide whether it is worth installing them. You need to ask yourself questions such as who would benefit, and for how much of the time? How much extra comfort would you be buying? What are the other benefits these forms of insulation might give you, and how much do you value them?

One of the effects of double glazing is that it blocks noise. For best noise reduction the gap between the panes should be much larger than is usual for double glazing: at least 100 mm. This is easiest to achieve using secondary glazing. If you live in a particularly noisy spot, near a busy road or an airport, for example, you may be eligible for a grant for double glazing to reduce the noise. Contact your local council for more information.

Other possible advantages of porches have already been mentioned.

If you are considering insulation from the comfort point of view, look through the questions just above and work out the answers which would apply in your home. Once you've done that, you can look back to the costing exercise mentioned earlier, and weigh up whether the extra comfort is worth the extra cost.

A Department of Trade and Industry report called *Think Safety First*, which was published in November 1987, tells us that each year in Britain accidents at home kill about five and a half thousand people and injure many more. Whilst this figure may be one of the lowest in Europe, many of these deaths could have been avoided. Three million other people seek medical attention after a home accident. Even more probably just treat themselves. So the home can be a very dangerous place. Making it safe should be something you always make a priority.

Those over about 65 or under about five are most at risk. For both these age groups the most common type of injury was a fall (over 65% of the accidents to the over-65s and over 45% of the accidents to the under-fives).

So how safe is your home? There are probably quite a few things you can do to improve safety, both outdoors and inside. Work through the following checklists to see whether there are safety points here that hadn't occurred to you that you'd like to put into practice.

PREVENTING ACCIDENTS OUTDOORS

1 Is the *external fabric* of your house in good condition? Can you be sure the cladding, roof tiles or slates, chimney-stack, television aerial, guttering and drain-pipes are all safe and secure?

2 Is *access* to your home safe? Are steps and paths level and non-slip? Is there adequate, well-sited outdoor lighting?

3 If you have *glazed doors,* are they made of toughened or laminated glass, to reduce injury if broken?

4 If you have to store *fuel* (oil, coal, wood) outside, is there enough safe and weatherproof storage space and does the place of this storage accord with local regulations?

5 If you have an *outside store* (wooden shed etc.) for tools, paints, weedkillers and so on is this kept locked and secure?

6 Do you have *secondary double glazing*? How easy is it to remove the inner pane if you need to escape from a fire for instance? And if you have sealed units, is there some handy means of breaking them if necessary?

7 Do you use *electrical tools* outside? If so, are your plugs and extension leads well insulated and in good condition? Do you use a power-breaker – a residual current device to disconnect the electricity supply if the flex is damaged?

8 If you have children, do you cover *ponds and pools* with netting? And do you keep garden gates closed so that they can't get out?

PREVENTING ACCIDENTS INDOORS

1 Is your *electricity supply* modern(ised) and properly earthed?

2 Have you checked, or had checked, your *electrical wiring* within the last 10 years?

3 Have you enough *socket outlets* in every room so that you don't have flexes to trip over? And if you have children, or they visit, do you use safety plugs in sockets?

4 If you use electricity in your *bathroom*, do you have a special socket?

5 Are all your *socket outlets, flexes* and *appliances* in good condition? In particular are flexes joined with a proper flex connector?

6 If you have a *gas* boiler, heater or water heater do you have a balanced flue to take toxic fumes away?

7 If you have *gas* appliances, do you have them all regularly serviced (i.e. once a year) by a recognised service agency?

8 If you have children, do you have a *cooker guard*? And do you keep all saucepan handles turned to the back of the cooker?

9 Do you have level, non-slip *floor covering* in good condition, especially near stairs?

10 If you have an open fire, or smoke, are your furniture and curtains made of *fire-resistant materials*, or given a fire-resistant finish?

11 Are the places where you keep *medicines and drugs* locked and secure?

12 Are household cleaners, bleach, detergents, matches and other *potentially dangerous products* kept securely out of the reach of small children?

13 If you have small children, do you have a *safety gate* to use on the stairs?

14 If you have small children, is all the *paintwork* accessible to them lead-free?

15 If you have a baby, does he or she sleep on a *safety mattress* with no pillow?

16 Do you have *electric blankets* checked regularly? And do you make sure they are never left on after you've gone to bed (unless they are the extra-low-voltage type or overblankets designed to be left on)?

17 If you use *adaptors*, do you make sure that you use the kind with fuses and that you never use more than one in the same socket?

18 If you have *curtains* in your kitchen, can you be sure that they are far enough away from the cooker not to catch fire? Blinds are safer.

19 Do you have *open fires*? If so, do you use a spark guard, which should be fixed if you have small children?

20 How bright is your *lighting*? Are all entrances, steps and stairs illuminated properly?

DO YOU KNOW YOUR LABELS?

Over 10,000 people are admitted to hospital each year suspected of swallowing or inhaling household chemicals such as bleach, disinfectant or paint stripper. Almost 90% of such accidents involve children under five years old.

Some products are hazardous and carry a hazard warning label. Below are a few examples of these. For how many of them can you correctly identify the associated hazard?

1

4

2

5

3

6

The answers are

1 *Corrosive.* That is, if the substance comes into contact with any part of your body it will destroy the tissue it touches. Battery acid and caustic soda are two examples of corrosive substances.

2 *Irritant or Harmful. Irritant* means that it is not corrosive but if it touches any part of your body it should be rinsed off immediately. *Harmful* means that if you breathe in the fumes, or drink or eat the substance you are risking your health. There is also a health risk if the substance penetrates the skin (perhaps through a cut). Bleaches and dry-cleaning fluids are usually classed as harmful. The cross symbol is used for both irritant and harmful products, but they should be labelled underneath the cross to say which applies.

3 *Toxic.* These are substances which affect you in the same way as 'harmful' ones (that is, through breathing in, drinking, eating or penetrating the skin), but are more dangerous in that they are a serious risk to health and could kill. Well-known examples are rat poison and weed killer. Another example of a toxic substance is car de-icing fluid which contains the chemical methanol.

4 *Oxidising.* These are substances which, when they come into contact with others (particularly flammable ones) cause violent reactions that give off heat, and could lead to fire.

5 *Explosive.* These are substances which may explode if they come into contact with very hot surfaces or a flame, or get knocked or hit.

6 *Flammable or Highly Flammable. Flammable* is applied to substances which catch fire if they reach a temperature of less than 61°C. *Highly flammable* are those which catch fire at less than 21°C. Substances in this category (petrol, paint thinners, lighter fuel, for example) should be kept well away from lighted cigarettes, pilot lights or from anything likely to produce a spark, such as an electric drill.

How many did you get right? How informative do you think these labels are to non-experts?

Great care should be taken with mixing household chemicals. Some should never be mixed. For instance, bleach should not be mixed with acid or other cleaners. Toxic chlorine gas could be released. Cases of exploding lavatories have been recorded where different cleaners were mixed.

EMERGENCY ALARM SYSTEMS

These are particularly useful for frail people living on their own and are, of course, of benefit in all emergencies, including fire. The way they work is that when someone needs help, they push a button, usually on a gadget which is worn round the neck, which sends a message through the telephone or radio to call for assistance. Some new models are even more sophisticated — they will go off automatically if they detect smoke, an intruder or if the user hasn't been moving around

for a while. The units can be set to dial an emergency centre or friends and relatives.

Is there is someone you know who would benefit from one of these alarm systems? If so, how could you get one?

How to get an alarm

There are five main ways

- from your local authority housing department
- direct from the manufacturer or commercial firm
- through a charity such as Help the Aged
- from a housing association
- from a shop.

Most people get their alarms via their local authority, 200 or so of whom operate an alarm service with an emergency centre permanently on call.

The Research Institute for Consumer Affairs has produced a useful guide to emergency alarm systems called *Calling for Help*. It suggests the following guidelines on features to look for when choosing an alarm system.

The alarm unit

- Does it have an alarm button?
- Does it have a cancel button?
- Would these buttons be easy to use in an emergency?
- Does it make more than five attempts to call for help?
- If it doesn't get through, can you restart it by using the portable trigger?

■ Does it have battery back-up power that lasts at least eight hours?

■ Does it warn the emergency centre if mains power fails or if back-up battery power runs low?

■ Does it give clear signals to show that an alarm call is getting through?

■ Does it warn you if the telephone line is faulty or disconnected?

The portable trigger

■ Is it comfortable to wear?

■ Is it easy to use?

■ Is the range long enough for your home and garden?

If you are choosing an alarm, or helping someone else to, use this checklist to make sure you get an alarm which will work as well as possible for you.

DEALING WITH FIRES

Even when you've done everything in your power to make your home safe from accidents, they still happen. Fires are particularly dangerous, and it's worth taking time to consider what you could do to detect, escape from and fight fires in the home.

Smoke detectors

No doubt you've seen advertisements extolling the advantages of detectors. Is it worth buying them? *Which?* recommends installing a smoke detector — they are fairly cheap, easy to install and (most important) could give you

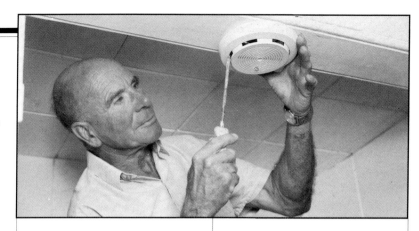

precious extra time should a fire break out. How do they work? The *Which?* report for September 1986 said

'Detectors come in two basic types: ionisation and photoelectric. In the first type a tiny (and harmless) radioactive source ionises air inside the detector producing electrically charged particles (ions) and allowing a small current to flow from a battery. When smoke enters the detector, it reduces the current flow and triggers the alarm. A photoelectric detector depends on smoke scattering a light beam to trigger the alarm.'

Which? concluded that there is little difference between the various types and brands of detector in use. As to where to fit detectors, and how many are needed, they said

'The instructions should give guidance, but in a smallish house, on the hall ceiling is likely to be a good place. If a fire breaks out at night in the living room or kitchen the smoke should then be detected before it reaches upstairs. A detector too near the kitchen may give false alarms from cooking fumes. A second detector on the

landing ceiling should sense bedroom fires. Detectors shouldn't be difficult to reach, or you won't be able to test them regularly.

'In a large house you'll definitely need more than one detector for satisfactory protection. You'll need to be sure that any detector can be heard (even if you're asleep). Some types can be interconnected so that if one detector is triggered by smoke, all the units will sound (this is an easy DIY job).

'One snag is that closing all doors last thing at night (strongly recommended to slow the spread of fire) may delay a detector's operation. The only real solution is to fit a detector in every room where there's a potential source of fire.'

Would it be worth your while installing one of these gadgets? And how about emergency alarm systems, which are heavily advertised these days?

Escaping from fires

Would you and everyone in your household know exactly what to do if a fire were to break out in your home? Most of us prefer not to think about what might happen, but lives could be saved if you follow some simple suggestions from *Which*? Go through these, and make sure that everyone is prepared.

Fire drill

■ *Shut the door* of the room where the fire is (and *don't open* a closed door if it feels hot to touch: the fire inside would be dangerous for you to deal with)

■ *raise the alarm* and get everyone out of the house

■ *telephone the fire brigade* — from a neighbour's house or public telephone if necessary. Dial 999 and ask for *fire*. When the fire department answers, give your address clearly (and in full: the control point may not be local). Giving a nearby landmark may help. Say whether people are trapped (and on which floor)

■ only if it's a *small* fire should you consider staying in the room to try to extinguish it. If it looks like getting out of control, *get out of the house yourself*, shutting doors where it's safe to do so

■ *never return to a burning property* until the fire brigade say it's safe

■ *if you're trapped on an upper floor*, try to get to a window at the front of the house so that you can be seen by rescuers. If you can close the door on a fire, you should be safe for several minutes. On the first floor, as a last resort, throw out anything which would break your fall, lower yourself from the window and let go

■ *never use a lift to leave a block of flats*

■ it is a good idea to have a *regular fire practice* with all members of the family to ensure they know how to get out of the house if, for example, a normal exit route is cut off. If a fire has taken hold and there is a lot of smoke about, you will see and breathe more clearly by crawling along the ground.

FIGHTING FIRES

Do you need any special equipment to keep in your home to fight fires? What's available, and how useful could it be to you? The cheapest kind of equipment is fire blankets, the more expensive, fire extinguishers.

Fire extinguishers

When *Which*? reported on fire extinguishers in September 1986, they stated that in a recent survey about one in five *Which*? subscibers had a fire extinguisher at home. Some fire safety experts point out the following limitations

■ an inexperienced and maybe panic-stricken user may let off an extinguisher at the wrong part of a fire or waste the contents in some other way. You could lose crucial seconds when you should be getting people out of the house and calling the fire brigade

■ domestic types may be too small to be effective, and larger ones are heavy

■ unless regularly maintained, they may let you down — and 80% of the extinguisher owners in the *Which*? survey had never had them serviced

■ extinguishers aren't suitable for the most common domestic fire — the oil in a chip-pan or frying-pan catching alight

■ one study showed that where fires had been put out or were under control by the time the brigade arrived, buckets of water, hose pipes or smothering (with a fire blanket for example) had proved more effective than extinguishers.

On the other hand, an extinguisher may be suitable for some small fires — perhaps quicker than fetching water (which anyway isn't suitable in some cases). Extinguishers may also be worth considering if you live in an area where the fire services couldn't reach you fairly quickly. But *only tackle a fire if it's in its early stages*. Don't delay getting people out and calling the fire brigade.

Fire blankets

Which? recommended buying a fire blanket to keep in the kitchen. Fire blankets are non-flammable cloths which can be used to smother flames. They are usually made of glass-fibre cloth, treated wool and non-melt polyamide. Most have handles on one side, so your fingers can be kept away from the flames. They normally come in a wall-mounting holder, to make them easy to grab in an emergency. There is a British Standard for fire blankets — BS 6575.

A free service

If you are still in doubt as to how to make your home more fireproof, you can ask for advice from your local firestation.

Burglaries have shown a steady increase over the past few years, although there was a slight fall in 1985. However, government figures show that burglary in dwellings now accounts for up to 13% of all reported crime. It is thought that a large proportion of burglaries — perhaps as many as 50% — are never even reported to the police.

HOW LIKELY ARE YOU TO BE BURGLED?

This all depends on a number of factors, such as where you live, the kind of home you live in and the precautions you take to prevent burglars getting in.

The high-risk areas

Do you live in a high-risk area? The highest and lowest numbers of recorded burglaries per head of the population in 1985 were in the following police force areas.

Highest risk

- Merseyside
- Northumbria
- Greater Manchester

Lowest risk

- Surrey
- Hertfordshire
- Dyfed — Powys.

If your home is broken into, there's less than a one in three chance that the burglar will be caught. And you're very unlikely to get your property back. When Which? surveyed two and a half thousand readers in 1987, they found that only 5% of those who'd been burgled during the previous 12 months recovered everything, and 86% got nothing at all back.

It is unlikely that the police will catch a greater proportion of burglars in the near future: with resources becoming overstretched, they are putting more emphasis on burglary prevention and self-help by the public. Neighbourhood Watch and Home Watch schemes are examples of this.

Which homes are most at risk?

In the Which? survey they found that people living in city centres or on the outskirts of cities were burgled more than those living in other areas. Flats or maisonettes on the ground floor or at basement level were more likely to be burgled than other types of dwelling. One study of convicted professional burglars has shown that detached houses, particularly if well shielded or set back from the road, also make popular targets.

Short of moving, there's not much you can do about the sort of house you live in, other than make it look uninviting to burglars. Read on to check how you might improve your door and window locks, install security lighting and perhaps an alarm.

When do burglars strike?

Of *Which?* readers who'd been burgled in the past year, two-thirds were burgled on a weekday. Break-ins were split almost equally between daytime and night-time, although about one in five people didn't know at what time they'd been burgled. Night-time burglaries appear to have increased since the last time *Which?* asked readers about this (two years previously). Two-thirds of people who were burgled were out when it happened.

How do they break in?

The most common entry point was a rear window. Doors and french windows, at the front or back of the house, were also vulnerable. The burglar usually forced or manipulated the window catch or lock, or forced the door open. But in nearly a quarter of the cases readers told *Which?* about, window glass was broken.

HOW VULNERABLE IS YOUR HOME?

Work your way through the following list of questions. As you do so, make notes about points you want to check and safety precautions you'd like to consider.

1 Do you have outside lights — front and back — and do you put them on and off with a time switch?

2 Is your front door fitted with a spy hole so that you can see who is outside?

3 Have you a chain or bar fitted to the front door, to prevent unwanted access?

4 If you live in a flat, do you have an Entryphone so that you know who's coming, and do you use it?

5 When you're away do you make sure that either you cancel all milk and newspapers, or a trusted neighbour takes them in and removes mail from the door, cuts the grass etc?

6 Do you make sure ladders and tools are locked away so that they cannot be used to break in?

7 Do you keep your garage and garden shed locked at all times?

8 Do you keep hedges and trees and shrubs cut so that they don't provide cover for burglars?

9 Do you make absolutely sure external doors and windows are closed and locked when you go out?

10 Do you try to position televisions, videos, stereos and other goods popular with burglars so that they're not visible from outside?

11 Do you make the house look occupied when you're out by leaving lights on, or putting them on a time switch, turning a radio on etc?

12 Do you make a special effort to keep keys safe, never leaving them under a flowerpot or on a string inside the letterbox?

13 Do you deter access from the back of your home with, for instance, a high, locked gate?

14 Are your external doors stout and well-fitted?

15 Have you got a dead-lock on all outside doors?

16 Do you have window locks on all your downstairs (and basement) windows?

17 Do you keep a watchdog?

If you find that you are answering 'no' to a lot of these questions, it looks as though your home might be rather vulnerable to burglars, especially if you live in one of the high-risk areas or types of home described at the beginning of this topic. Incidentally, before you start feeling guilty about the lack of security precautions in your home, you may be slightly relieved to hear that a survey among the members of the National Federation of Consumer Groups showed that 41% had no safety precautions for answering their front doors and 34% had front doors which were not adequately secured when they were out. Back doors were generally well secured but 90% of respondents had no security device to use when answering them.

A significant 40% had no window security fittings and 55% no secure place for valuables. Many people said they had doors (42%) and windows (27%) that were difficult to make secure.

So what might you do to make things more secure?

The questions that you've worked through above suggest their own solutions. In addition, you could consider some of the following measures.

Keeping burglars at bay

Fitting a burglar alarm

Burglars may well be deterred by the sight of an alarm (or even a dummy alarm box) or stopped from venturing further if an alarm goes off as they break in. The use of alarms is on the increase — the *Which?* survey showed an increase during 1985 and 1986 from 13 to 18%. Would it be a good idea to add to the statistics? Weigh up the pros and cons of burglar alarms before you decide.

Alongside is what *Which?* mentioned in their November 1987 report.

Pros

Outward visible signs of an alarm — bell-box, say — may deter burglars (but a 'dummy' bell-box may be just as effective)

The alarm going off may stop burglars getting in, or cut down the time they stay if they do get in

A system with a panic button could be useful for raising the alarm in an emergency — if someone tries to push their way in through the front door for example

It may be safer to protect a window that you depend on as a fire escape route with an alarm rather than with locks

Cons

The cost will be about half as much if you install it yourself as it would be for a professionally installed alarm, which may have maintenance or service charges in addition

False alarms can be a problem — over a third of the respondents with *Which?* burgular alarms had had problems with these in the past year

The necessary routine of activating and deactivating the alarm can be inconvenient and restrictive

If you live miles from anywhere, there may be nobody to hear an audible alarm — an alternative might be to have the alarm linked to a central monitoring station or the police

Other security measures — good door and window locks and outdoor lighting, say — may be cheaper and as effective in deterring at least opportunistic burglars

If you have decided that the pros outweigh the cons for you, you can go on to consider whether you will choose a DIY model or have your burglar alarm installed professionally.

DIY or professional installation?
DIY is cheaper, but you may not want to be bothered with fitting an alarm yourself — or you may not be that confident about your ability to install the system. You need to be fairly competent at DIY to install some kits. You could get a professional electrician to wire a kit in for you (get several estimates if you choose not to do it yourself), or select one of the types which requires less wiring. Your insurance company may insist that you have an alarm installed and maintained by a professional alarm company. A professionally installed system is also more likely to be tailor-made for your home, but you could tailor-make your own DIY system by buying individual parts.

There are two main types of alarm system

■ Wired-in alarms with magnetic door and window contacts, pressure pads and panic buttons, linked to a control panel and a bell or siren.

■ Alarms which detect movement and/or body heat, or sound.

Mark your property

Marking valuables to make them easily identifiable is designed to

■ deter a burglar from breaking in (you can get window stickers to advertise the fact that your property is marked)

■ increase the chance of your property being returned to you if it's recovered by the police

■ make it harder for burglars to 'fence' stolen goods.

You can mark valuables by engraving them or by writing on them with an ultraviolet marker pen. The marking is invisible under ordinary light and only becomes visible under ultraviolet light. You may need to re-mark your valuables every two years or so (more frequently if they've been exposed to strong sunlight), and you should renew the markings after polishing silver or cleaning china.

Make a list of your possessions

Make an inventory, at least of all your valuable things. Include any details of serial numbers and distinguishing marks. This will make it easier to check what's been stolen after a break-in (you may not notice some things have gone for some time); and claiming on your insurance is easier if you have a list of what's gone, together with their values (although your insurance company may want to carry out its own evaluation). Keep receipts since these may be needed if you claim.

Photograph your valuables

Some items — jewellery, for example — may be too small to be marked, or you may not want to mark goods such as antiques. Take colour photographs of these against a plain background, with a ruler alongside to give an idea of the size. Take several 'views', and make sure you include details of

any distinctive points or hallmarks which could help to identify the items. Keep the photographs and any inventory you make in a safe place – not in the same place as your valuables!

Put valuables in a safe deposit

If you're worried about leaving valuables in the house, think about hiring a safe deposit box at the bank. This does mean, however, that you can only retrieve the valuables when the banks are open and there will almost always be a charge for this service. It also means that you can't really enjoy having the valuables, since you are not likely to see them very often.

Check carefully on callers

If someone asks to come into your house, to read the meter or inspect your telephone for example, don't let them in until they've shown you their official card. If you're in doubt, telephone whichever company the caller says they're from, to check. The company will be able to tell you whether anyone is scheduled to visit your home. If you do need to telephone, look up the number in the telephone directory, and don't use a number given to you by the caller.

Check your house insurance

Money may not be able to replace lost goods which have sentimental value. But make sure you're adequately insured anyway — new videos and television sets are expensive.

Join Neighbourhood Watch

Since they were first introduced into the United Kingdom in 1982, Neighbourhood Watch (or Home Watch) schemes have mushroomed. There are now (1987) more than 30,000 in England and Wales alone. The schemes are intended to beat crime in two ways. First, they encourage people to look out for anything unusual in their neighbourhood. The risk of being seen is a powerful deterrent to burglars, and information given to the police by Watch members can help them in their efforts to prevent and solve crime. Secondly, Neighbourhood Watch increases people's awareness of security, encouraging them to check their homes, 'security-mark' their property and arrange visits by Crime Prevention Officers (CPOs).

There's a good deal of controversy about whether Neighbourhood Watch schemes result in a sustained, reduced level of crime in the areas where they operate. Individual schemes have reported good results, but a recent study commissioned by the Home Office suggested that, overall, there was no effect on the level of crime. Where the schemes did appear to score was in reducing people's fear of crime, and in improving community relations.

If you'd like to join, or start up, a Neighbourhood Watch scheme in your area, contact your local CPO. He or she will put you in touch with an existing scheme where you live, or help you to set one up, provided there's sufficient support from other residents in the area.

Help available

The best person to advise you on home security is the Crime Prevention Officer from your local police station. He or she will visit your home, free of charge, and make recommendations on what you should fit, where the weak and vulnerable areas are and whether you need an alarm. You could also consult the company which handles your household contents insurance policy, or the Association of British Insurers.

There may also be a community advice scheme for senior citizens and those on low incomes, such as the one operated by Keep Newcastle Warm. In addition to advice about how to operate your heating most efficiently and how to draught-proof your home, Keep Newcastle Warm gives advice on the supply and positioning of window and door locks, or burglar alarms, and will carry out work if required.

ACTION PLAN

Working through this topic should have helped you to decide what needs to be done to make your home more secure against burglars.

Draw up a list of those security measures you have decided on and work out your next step. Some measures — like listing or marking your possessions or checking insurance — will take time but not a lot of money. Others, such as installing a burglar alarm or window locks will involve some expense. So you will need to check prices and availability. Give yourself a deadline to have the work done by — the end of the month, for example, or before you go on holiday. Draw up a timetable to make sure that you can get the work, whatever it is, done by your deadline and get moving.

How do you feel about maintenance? Are you one of those people who enjoys nothing more than a weekend spent pottering around their home, checking, repairing, making good and generally ensuring that everything is in the best possible condition? Or are you at the other end of the spectrum? Does your heart sink as you notice that yet another thing has gone wrong? Do you need to steel yourself before you can change a fuse? Most of us would probably describe ourselves as somewhere between the two — with occasional bursts of wild enthusiasm and bouts of depression when even changing a light bulb is beyond us. If you really don't want to or can't carry out routine maintenance jobs on your own, then you will have to find ways of getting someone else to do the work for you or reconcile yourself to more and more things deteriorating and not working. Some maintenance jobs such as servicing a gas boiler can only be carried out by professionals anyway.

WHAT NEEDS DOING?

First of all in this topic we list suggestions for identifying and dealing with maintenance jobs in your home. Nobody is going to have every one of these things go wrong, so don't be put off by the length of the list. But you will save money and trouble in the long run if you can check problems before they get too bad. Many of these jobs are better done in the spring and summer when you can see what damage winter has done and the weather is better, too.

CHECK YOUR HOME

This checklist starts at the top of your home, on the roof, and works down to the bottom. Go round and look at each possible danger point. For each problem you may encounter a possible solution is suggested. Check whether work needs doing and consider whether you can do it, or whether you need to call in professional help of some kind. Make a list of things that require action. Once you have drawn up your list, you may find that you need to reconsider whether or not you have given yourself too many jobs to do and, if so, what you can do about it.

Outside jobs	Possible repairs	Outside jobs	Possible repairs
Chimneys		**Gutters, drains and drain-pipes**	
Are they wobbly, or is the mortar in bad condition?	Remortar chimney pots and replace if necessary	Gutters/drains blocked with debris, birds' nests, balls etc?	Clean out — possibly prevent further blockage by putting mesh or drain cover over the top
Are the chimney-stacks cracked or crooked?	Stacks may need rebuilding	If you have cast-iron guttering, is there corrosion at the joints?	Small leaks can be sealed with special paint, flexible sealant, waterproof tape or bitumen flashing
Is the flashing between chimney and roof leaking or in bad condition?	Replace flashing		
Does the chimney smoke?	Have chimney cleaned	If you have plastic guttering, is it wobbly?	Fix brackets and supports if necessary
Anything else wrong?		Are the connections in the downpipe leaking?	Fill with mastic
Roof		Anything else wrong?	
Are there any missing, chipped or cracked tiles or slates?	Replace slates or tiles, check whether nails holding them are rusted and replace if necessary	**Doors, windows and window frames**	
		Are there gaps between the windows frames and the walls?	Fill with mastic
Is the roof sagging?	May need rebuilding; get professional advice	Are there any signs of rot in the doors, windows and frames?	Use wood repair system for minor damage, replace all or part if major
Are the flashings at roof junctions in bad condition?	Replace flashings		
Are the ridge tiles firmly fixed in place?	Remortar	Is the paintwork in poor condition?	Strip down and repaint
Are the valleys (i.e. the low points) between roof sections blocked or leaking?	Clean out/fit new valley(s)	Any cracked panes? Is the putty round the windows cracked or coming out?	Reglaze Replace before it falls out
If you have a flat roof, are there splits or tears in the roofing felt?	Repair/replace felt, or apply roof sealer or mastic	Are door and window joints loose?	Glue or replace
Are there damp patches on the roof timbers or insulation in your attic?	Repair leaks in roof	Anything else wrong?	
If you have any aerials on the roof, are they loose or wobbly?	Fix securely or replace if necessary		
Anything else wrong?			

Outside jobs	Possible repairs	Inside jobs	Possible repairs
Walls		**_Plumbing_**	
Is the damp-proof course blocked with earth and debris?	Clear obstructions	Are all your pipes, tanks and cylinders sufficiently insulated?	Add more insulation wherever possible
Are there minor cracks?	Fill with external filler	If you have a metal cold-water cistern is it rusty?	Consider replacing it with a plastic one
Are there major cracks?	Monitor to try to decide cause and whether cracks will get worse — seek professional advice if they look serious	Are the cold-water cistern ball valve and float working properly?	Make sure they are not jammed open or shut; change washer, clean, adjust or replace
Finish in bad condition?	Repaint	Are any taps dripping?	Change washers valve-seating; replace worn bits of tap
Bricks crumbling?	Render, clad or replace	Anything else wrong?	
Mortar in bad condition?	Repoint	**_Electricity_**	
Ventilating bricks blocked?	Clear holes	Is it more than 10 years since your wiring was inspected?	Book inspection (by local electricity board or properly qualified independent contractor)
Anything else wrong?		Do any of the light sockets or light fittings get hot in use, or show independent discolouration? Are any insecure?	Book inspection (by local electricity board or properly qualified contractor)
Steps, paths, balconies and patios		**_Heating_**	
Are they covered with algae and moss?	Clean up with domestic or special-purpose cleaner	If you have radiators are any leaking? Are there radiators which don't heat through properly?	Repair leak or replace radiator 'Bleed' radiators to allow air to escape
Minor cracks in paths, steps or patio?	Fill with external quality filler	If you have an oil or gas central heating boiler, has it been serviced recently? Anything else wrong?	Book service
Major cracks in paths, steps or patio?	Consider replacement	**_Decorating_**	
		Inner walls and paintwork in poor condition? Anything else wrong?	Review decorating plans

DO IT YOURSELF?

Which jobs in the home would you prefer someone else to do, and which are you happy to do yourself? You may want to do a particular job yourself because you expect to get some satisfaction out of doing it. On the other hand, if the job is particularly messy or risky, or if you're not interested in using or acquiring the skill, knowledge and equipment needed for it, you may decide to pay someone to do the work because of the low level of satisfaction involved in doing it yourself.

However, just because you find one choice clearly more satisfactory doesn't mean you will automatically follow your preference. Ability to do a job, money and time come into it. Although you might prefer someone else to do the job, you may be unable to afford it, or you may have too much on hand already to take on some job that you'd really like to do yourself. But at least your preference can be used as a starting-point when weighing up which jobs to tackle yourself and which to pay someone else to do.

Work your way through your list, asking yourself the following questions for each job.

- Can I do it myself?

- What is the cost of doing it myself?

- Am I equipped to do it myself?

- Am I clear what's involved?

Can I do it myself?

The first requirement for doing it yourself is the knowledge and skill you will need to carry out a particular job. Some DIY jobs are relatively easy to tackle without knowledge or skill. For example, if you're thinking of erecting packaged kit furniture, enthusiasm and some strength is all you need to start. You can virtually wade straight in with a screwdriver and the instructions. You can quickly pick up the basic facts about how to decorate or lay cork tiles on floors from television programmes, magazines or a DIY book from your local library. In the longer run you'll get better results and find the work much easier, as you learn more. But you don't need a lot of knowledge to start.

If you're interested in doing a job but you don't have the necessary skill and knowledge, you'll have to work out what you need to know in order to start, and what is the

best way of finding this out. Can you learn all you need to know from books, or do you need advice from someone who knows how to do the job? For many jobs you could acquire the skill and knowledge you need by attending classes such as carpentry or upholstery at a local adult education centre. Another possibility might be a 'skills swop' scheme of some kind. Sometimes these are organised formally, with advertisements and even a points system. Sometimes they are just an informal exchange 'I'll mend all your socks, if you'll paint my ceiling.'

What's the cost of doing it myself?

Practically anything you do for yourself will work out cheaper than getting someone to do the job for you, unless things go so badly wrong that you have to call in an expert to put them right.

You save money doing work yourself for a number of reasons.

■ You don't have to pay for someone else's time — and time can be expensive. The hourly rate charged for some jobs is high. If you go to a firm to get a job done for you, their charge has to cover rates, lighting, equipment, administrative staff and so forth, as well as wages to the person actually doing the work.

■ If someone comes to your home to do work for you, you might well have to pay for time spent travelling. This may be covered by the firm charging a very high rate for the first hour, or a call-out charge of a fixed amount. This is not unreasonable, since they may have to come some distance, or it may take some time to work out · what needs doing.

■ You may be able to buy the materials and equipment you need for the job (like wallpaper and paint for decorating, or tiles for the bathroom) for less than you'd be charged by a firm or individual doing the work for you. By shopping around you can often find materials and equipment at bargain discount prices.

■ You may be able to buy second-hand materials or equipment — or you may find that you can use scraps and odds and ends that have been lying around, for example, for shelves that you're thinking of putting up.

The main virtue of doing it yourself is that you don't have to pay for someone else to provide their time, knowledge, skills and equipment. You could look on the savings you make by doing it yourself as wages you pay yourself. Obviously the most profitable jobs for you to do are those for which the professional rates for the job are high. However, if you spend far longer doing the job than a professional would spend you may find that you're paying yourself relatively low 'wages' per hour. If you have to learn new skills to do some job, then you might have to include learning time, which would make the 'wages' even lower. Still, you might then be able to make use of your newly acquired skills to save money in the future.

Am I equipped to do it myself?

You'll also need equipment to do the work. You probably already have some basic DIY equipment lying around the house — for example, hammers, pliers and a couple of screwdrivers. You may need to get extra tools to do some of the things in our job list — but remember that a lot of tools can be used for several different jobs. For example, an electric drill or a stepladder would come in handy again and again.

So the cost of tools for DIY jobs that you haven't done before might be quite low. If you don't have the necessary equipment and tools, you will have to decide whether to buy or hire them. Buying is a consumer decision to consider in detail, because the quality of tools is specially important. The tools available on hire should also be in good condition. You could list the places that will hire equipment, and

choose one that is convenient and gives a good service. The local paper or *Yellow Pages* will help you to find names. If you do need some expensive and bulky pieces of equipment — like a cement-mixer — it's probably best to hire. It would also be better to hire equipment that you are unlikely to need again, so you don't have to store it.

Am I clear what's involved?

Most jobs don't consist of a single task, but are made up of a series of 'small' ones, some more difficult and time-consuming than others. In this list we've broken down decorating a room into a number of 'small' tasks. Choose a room in your home that you're likely to decorate, then go through the list with that room in mind. Think about the work you'll have to do to decorate the particular room you've chosen — for example, making good the walls and paintwork before you start decorating. If you're unlikely to do any decorating in the next few months, but will be undertaking something else, like plumbing-in a washing-machine or installing a heating system, you could substitute that. If you are doing something major, you will also need to check on legal requirements, regulations and permissions. It is useful to make a plan like this since it helps you to be more realistic about what you can achieve, as well as ensuring that you don't leave out some vital stage.

Decorating a room

Stage 1 Preparatory work

- Move furniture
- Remove curtains, pictures and lampshades
- Remove carpets
- Protect vulnerable fixtures, such as polished doors or the fireplace

Stage 2 Doing the job

- Remove old wallpaper
- Remove old paint or rub down well
- Wash down paintwork, radiators etc.
- Sand down and prepare existing paintwork
- Make good walls and woodwork — fill in holes, cracks etc.
- Clean ceiling
- Paint ceiling
- Paint walls
- Paint doors, windows and radiators
- Paper ceiling/walls

Stage 3 Clearing up

- Remove paint stains
- Clean floors etc.
- Clean brushes, rollers, etc. thoroughly
- Relay carpets etc.

We've divided the job into three main stages — preparatory work, doing the job and clearing up. If a professional were to do the main part of the job he'd probably expect you to do things like removing the furniture and carpets from the room. If you were to do the whole job yourself you'd probably take longer than a professional for a number of reasons — for example

- if it's the first time you have attempted a job, you'll need to spend time checking what to do before you tackle each task — and as you've had little or no practice the job itself will take longer. If you make mistakes you'll have to correct them

- you may be doing the work to a very high standard — a common reason for doing it yourself is disappointment with the standard of work provided by the professionals; usually the higher the standard of work you aim to achieve, the longer the job will take you.

Coming to a decision

You should now know which household jobs need doing in your home, and have noted for each whether you can do them yourself. If you decide not, the last topic in this chapter is about choosing services.

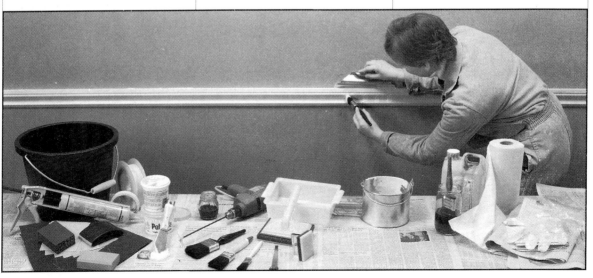

You are almost certainly going to need to use services to do jobs in your home — either because you can't do the work yourself, or because you haven't the time or energy.

The first step is to find the names and addresses of firms and individuals in your area providing the service you want.

Here is a summary of different sources of information.

Circulars through the letterbox

Some firms advertise their service by circulars to homes in the area. These may describe special deals such as introductory offers on window replacement.

Advertisements

Many firms advertise in local papers and magazines — but most advertisements give little hard information about things like price. Individuals or small firms may advertise in newsagents' windows, sometimes including charges.

Yellow Pages

No information about the quality of the firm — but a quick and easy way of getting a list of firms supplying a particular service in your area.

Friends, workmates and neighbours, people in DIY shops

May be able to recommend local services. May have information from experience about the people working in local firms as well as the quality of their work.

Trade associations

Should be able to give you the name of a member near you. Using an association member means that you usually have some comeback if things go wrong, although what the different trade associations offer varies a lot.

Suppose you've got a long list of different possibilities? How do you decide between them to get the right service at the right price?

MAKING THE CHOICE

The first thing you should do is to list the features which will influence you in choosing a particular service. It will be easier if you do this with one particular service in mind, such as having double glazing or some new power points fitted. You'll probably take into account a number of features — for example the following.

Reputation
Ask around locally to find out what people think of the firms and individuals on your list of possible suppliers. How important is their judgement?

Experience
How long has each firm or individual been in business — and how much experience do they have of doing the particular job? How much importance do you place on experience?

Qualifications
Is the person who will do the work properly qualified to do the job? Sometimes qualifications vary, so compare them. In the case of some services, everybody providing the service may be professionally qualified (like surveyors). In this case you may find experience and reputation a better guide.

Availability
Is one supplier easier to contact than another? Will one do the job sooner than another? Is any one nearer than the others?

Personality
When you're buying a service, you

USING THE BLACK ECONOMY

Many people choose to use services provided by people working 'out of hours' or when they are officially unemployed because this is cheaper. This is often the only way that people can afford to have a job done. While there are obviously benefits, there can be problems if the work isn't done to your satisfaction. By using the black economy you will probably forego your legal rights to correction or compensation if things go wrong. You have to weigh up the advantages of getting work done cheaply against this disadvantage.

may have to see the person providing it frequently – so it could be important to choose someone you like and get on well with.

Guarantee
Is there a guarantee to cover the work –– if so, how long does it last and what does it cover?

The next stage is to weigh up each possible supplier according to each of the features you have chosen as particularly important to you for the job you have in mind.

Cost
Prices for services vary, so shop around. Do you want the cheapest service available? What type of credit arrangement is available and with whom? How much extra will you have to pay if you use credit? Cost should never be the *only* thing you consider.

Deciding

You could just do this informally, putting a tick or cross by each

feature for the suppliers of the service and comparing the number of ticks. You could also try rating each supplier according to how well they met each requirement. You'll recall that in chapters one and three we suggested that you rated using a scale between 0 and 4, where 0 meant that an option didn't meet the requirement at all, and 4 meant it fulfilled the requirement very well. If some features are much more important to you than others — low cost, for instance, or immediate availability, then you could also weight the features for importance to you using the same scale of 0 to 4.

You can then score the suppliers by multiplying their ratings by your weighting for each feature, adding the results to get a grand total.

After you've selected your supplier and found out exactly how much it will cost to have the job done, you'll have to look at your budget and decide if you can afford it. If you've decided that you don't want to do the work yourself, but you can't find a satisfactory supplier or you can't afford to pay to have the job done, you'll have to rethink. Could you do part of the job yourself and pay someone to do the rest? Can you reduce the work to be done and make it a smaller and probably cheaper job? Can you borrow enough to pay to have the job done?

Here's an example of how Carl chose a carpenter.

Carl selects a carpenter

Carl has a number of carpentry jobs to be done — two windows need replacing and the floorboards on the landing need mending. He cannot manage the jobs himself, as he hasn't learnt carpentry and has no desire to try. He has contacted two carpenters who live near him. One, Bill, was recommended by someone at the place where Carl works. He is quite elderly, with a lifetime of experience, but rather slow. His rate for the job is on the high side. Carl saw an advertisement in the local newsagents for the other carpenter, Maureen, who is young and keen. She has recently completed a Construction Industry Training Board craft certificate in carpentry. Her rates are lower than Bill's and she will be available quite soon.

Carl finds it hard to choose between them. So he lists the features he wants. These are

Qualifications — job must be done really well

Experience — the windows are a rather tricky shape and could be difficult for someone who hadn't done this type of job before

Reputation — Carl prefers to rely on personal recommendation

FEATURES	RATINGS	
	Bill	Maureen
Qualifications	4	4
Experience	4	2
Reputation	4	2
Cost	0	4
TOTALS	12	12

FEATURES	IMPORTANCE	RATINGS	
		Bill	Maureen
Qualifications	2	4 (×2) = 8	4 (×2) = 8
	3	4 = 12	2 = 6
	4	4 = 16	2 = 8
	3	0 = 0	4 = 12
	WEIGHTED TOTALS	36	34

Cost — obviously it should be as low as possible.

Above are Carl's straight ratings for Bill and Maureen, then his weighted ones.

So Bill was the carpenter that Carl selected. He later found that Bill was a member of a trade association, while Maureen wasn't. This made him even more pleased that he had chosen Bill, as he preferred to employ someone with the backing of a trade association, in case of problems.

However carefully you plan, things may go wrong, often through no fault of your own. Here are some suggestions as to what you can do to try to improve matters.

This section is divided into two parts. The first part deals briefly with difficulties in making repayments on your mortgage or other large loans. You'll remember that other aspects of getting into debt have already been considered under **Choosing credit**, in chapter three. The second part looks at situations where someone else is at fault, and you need to complain.

WHEN THINGS GO WRONG FOR YOU FINANCIALLY

Whatever the nature of your financial problems, it's always well worth talking to a professional debt counsellor at a Citizens' Advice Bureau or Money Advice Centre, if there is one near you.

Problems with paying the mortgage

If you find that keeping up with mortgage repayments is difficult, perhaps because your circumstances have changed, the first thing to do is to talk to the manager of the mortgage company (building society, bank etc.) without delay. There are several options open to the manager, depending on the rules he or she has to operate by, your resources and your prospects. You may, for example, be allowed to pay only interest on the loan for a while. You may also be entitled to benefits from the DHSS, so it is worth checking on this. The important thing is to consult the people to whom you owe money before you get too far into debt. They should be reasonably understanding since they would really rather have your money, even if they have to wait for it, than take possession of your home. And they would rather have something than nothing at all, so may accept reduced payments.

Splitting up

How much splitting up will affect you financially depends on the size of mortgage you have, your income, maintenance payments, entitlement to social security and savings. If you are married and decide to break up, or if you are not married and your partner moves out of the house, you may find that the best solution is to move house yourself. This may well be easier than trying to find the money to pay the whole mortgage on your own. The manager of your mortgage company can often offer sound advice if you are able to discuss matters.

What happens if you just can't pay?

If things are so bad for you that you can't keep up your mortgage and/or loan repayments, what is the worst thing that can happen? If he of she can't get the money from you in any other way, the lender may take legal action. This may have different outcomes, depending on the type of loan. You'll remember from chapters one and three in this book that loans may be of two kinds — secured and unsecured. Although large loans of money may legally be secured on anything of value — insurance policies or shares, for instance — they are usually secured on a person's home. A loan secured on your home gives the lender the right, when you, the borrower, fail to keep up the repayments, to ask for the house or flat to be sold, and the money to be used to pay off the loan. All mortgages are, of course, secured loans. So what is the sequence of events when a lender takes legal action?

■ When your repayments stop, the lender will write to you asking you to pay what is owed and restart the repayments.

■ If you do nothing, the lender will write threatening to take legal action. This means that he or she will start legal proceedings for the recovery of what you owe.

■ If you still don't contact the lender, details of your loan or mortgage and what you granted the lender to secure it will be given to the lender's solicitor and the solicitor will take over the proceedings from then on.

■ You will receive a summons from the court ordering you to appear on a particular date. This will be accompanied by details of what you owe according to the lender. You should check this to see if it is accurate and return it within the specified time, saying what you propose to do about what you owe.

■ The court hearing will take place. You will have your chance to explain your circumstances and make an offer about how you propose to repay the lender and the court will decide whether or not to accept your offer. In the case of a mortgage or secured loan, if you are unable to make an offer or it does not accept your offer, the court can make out a possession order in favour of the lender, which will usually give you 28 days to pay what you owe.

■ In England, Wales and Northern Ireland (but not in Scotland) the lender may apply to the court to send in the bailiff if you don't keep to the terms of the court judgement.

■ If you are still in the house after the 28 days have passed, you are liable to eviction by the bailiff. However, the bailiff will notify you of the date of eviction.

If you do have financial problems and cannot keep up repayments on a mortgage or secured loan, you might ultimately lose your home, unless you can make arrangements with your lender. So it is very important to consult him or her as soon as problems arise or your circumstances change, before the situation gets serious.

WHEN SOMEONE ELSE HAS GOT IT WRONG

Virtually everyone has cause to complain about goods or services at some time, and many people emerge from their battle so exhausted, out of pocket and enraged that they never summon the energy to complain again. They thus encourage more shoddy goods and substandard service.

This may sound unfair to those manufacturers, retailers and service organisations who genuinely care about their customers and take time and trouble dealing with complaints.

It is also worth observing that often the complainant has misused a product, or not complained correctly. But in many cases people have genuine cause for complaint. If you are one of them, how do you set about making the complaint?

First, ensure that your complaint is genuine. You cannot complain about a dress with dry-clean-only label that shrank in the wash or a damaged food-processor bowl in which your children mixed plaster of Paris.

You will also have difficulty complaining about poor work if you have employed a shoddy workman. Always look at examples of a person's work — be it loose covers or a loft conversion — before hiring them. You should, however, be wary of people who have been paid by firms, or offered special deals, to praise work done for them.

What *are* your legal rights as far as goods and services are concerned?

Your legal rights when complaining

When complaining about goods and services, you can use your rights under the Sale of Goods Act 1979 and the Supply of Goods and Services Act 1982.

If you buy things on credit, you may have additional rights under the Consumer Credit Act 1974.

The Sale of Goods Act
Whenever you buy new or second-hand goods from a business — whether from a shop, a catalogue or via mail order — you enter into a contract with the seller. In return for your paying the asking price, the seller is obliged to provide goods which

■ are of *merchantable quality* — free of faults and able to do the job you would reasonably expect of them (taking into account their price, age and so on)

■ are *fit for their purpose* — if the seller sold them as suitable for a particular purpose

■ *correspond to the description* you were given (whether on the label or otherwise) — for example, in colour or size.

If any of these three obligations is not met, you have two options: to reject the goods and get a full refund of the price you paid (if you act quickly); or to claim compensation (which is usually the cost of a repair). Whichever you choose, you'll also be entitled to compensation if the failure of the goods causes you any additional loss (for example, if a faulty cleaning fluid damages your carpet).

To get a full refund, you must reject the goods within a 'reasonable time' of when you bought them — the length of time depends on the type of goods and the nature of the fault. But you must reject the goods as soon as you find that they aren't up to scratch. You should do this in writing — a verbal rejection is open to dispute. Even then, you might not be entitled to a refund, since a 'reasonable time' can be quite short. And if you accept a repair, you may lose your right to reject the goods. You wouldn't, however, lose your rights if you accepted a repair on condition that, should it not cure the problem, you could then have a refund on the faulty goods.

If the seller offers you an alternative to money — an exchange , a repair or a credit note, for example — you don't have to accept it. But you're only entitled to compensation if the seller has broken the contractual rights outlined above. Some shops will let you return things which are perfectly all right if you've changed your mind or don't like the colour — but they don't have to.

The Supply of Goods and Services Act

When you buy services like having your mower serviced or curtains dry cleaned, or call in someone such as a plumber to do work for you, you have similar rights to those you have when buying goods. There's a contract between you and the person providing the service, and any goods supplied with the service (e.g. spare parts and materials) must meet the standards required under the Sale of Goods Act. This is, of course, always provided that the person selling you the service is acting in the course of business.

Additionally, the work must be done

- to a reasonable *standard* — i.e. using the skill and care you could expect from an experienced firm
- at a reasonable *price* — for example, compared with what others might charge in the same area (unless you've agreed to a higher price to start with)
- in the time agreed (or in a reasonable time if none was agreed).

Legal rights in Scotland and Northern Ireland
The Supply of Goods and Services Act applies in Northern Ireland but not to Scotland. In practice consumers in Scotland enjoy much the same rights as those in England and Wales under the common law.

The Consumer Credit Act

If you have bought something on credit then Section 75 of this Act could help you.

Where a loan is separate from the sale, but linked with it, such as in credit card sales, the supplier of credit is held to be equally liable with the trader for defects in the goods. This means that you not only have a right of redress against the trader but also, if you choose, against the creditor; so if the trader refused to do anything or has gone bankrupt, you can claim redress from the creditor. This applies if

- the cash price of the goods is between £100 and £30,000 (including VAT)
- the amount of credit does not exceed £15,000.

If you obtained your credit card before July 1988 (when Section 75 of the Consumer Credit Act was implemented) you cannot rely on the rights conferred by Section 75. However, although the credit card company may be prepared to abide by this right, legally it does not have to; so you should check with your company.

If goods are defective you should complain to the trader just as you would in a cash sale. You should continue to pay the instalments while you pursue your complaint as you might otherwise be branded as a defaulter. If you do not get anywhere, you should then stop making the payments and tell the finance company in writing what you are doing and why. The finance company will probably then put pressure on the trader to put matters right. Alternatively, you can have the defect put right elsewhere and claim the cost of repair from the trader or the finance company.

So those are your basic legal rights.

Should you complain?

Knowing your rights helps you decide whether you have grounds on which to complain or not. But how can you work out if it's worth

COMPLAINING

Advantages

Might get the cost of new curtains

Might get refund of cleaning charge

Would feel better about the loss

Disadvantages

Might have row with manageress

Will worry about taking them back

Will have to make special visit

NOT COMPLAINING

Advantages

No row

Disadvantages

Loss of good-quality living room curtains

Can't afford to replace them myself

Continuing feeling of dissatisfaction as it wasn't my fault

DOES COMPLAINING WORRY YOU?

Most people don't enjoy complaining. What are your particular worries about the prospect of complaining about something? Is your main feeling one of annoyance with the person you think is to blame for whatever's gone wrong? Do you feel nervous at the prospect?

Think back to the last two or three times you had to make a complaint, and consider each occasion against each of these possible reactions.

Did you feel

■ upset that it's happened

■ angry that it's happened

■ nervous of the reaction you might get

■ worried that your complaint will fail

■ afraid that you might make a fool of yourself

■ frustrated that things have gone wrong

■ worried that you'll be thought stupid

■ afraid that you will be made to look foolish in front of other customers

■ other worries?

Now think back — how many of those worries actually led to a major problem? Was there a scene? Did you make a fool of yourself? Did anyone show that they thought you were stupid? When you complain, you need

complaining? Complaining has its advantages and disadvantages — you have to balance one against the other. Not complaining also has advantages and disadvantages. You can summarise the alternatives on a chart, by writing down the advantages and disadvantages of complaining and not complaining.

This is what Dave did when he was deciding whether or not to complain about the way in which his living room curtains had been dry cleaned. They had been done very badly, and had such strange marks on them that he was reluctant to hang them up again.

Dave's chance of success was reasonably high, so, as the advantages outweighed the disadvantages, he decided to go ahead with his complaint.

confidence. First, you need to be confident that your complaint is justified. If you have checked carefully that you are within your rights, then this should not be a problem. But you also need confidence that you can carry your complaint through and counter any attempts by the shopkeeper or the supplier of a service to deter you from your purpose. Here are some hints based on suggestions from *Which?* to help you to 'fight off the fob-off'.

It's no excuse—five fob-offs you should never accept

1 'You'll have to take that up with the manufacturer'
If you've bought something faulty, it's up to the person who sold it to you to deal with it — not the manufacturer. But all too often, the seller will try to pass you on to the manufacturer on the grounds that 'we only sell them'. If this is the answer you get, don't accept it — tell the seller that it may not be his fault, but it is his legal responsibility. It is reasonable for the seller to want the manufacturer's representative to see the fault, to make sure he is credited for it, but he shouldn't keep you waiting for his decision.

Note that this also applies to complaints about things you buy through someone doing work for you — for example, if the bath your plumber supplies you is chipped.

2 'It's not covered by the guarantee'
Any guarantees are offered in addition to your rights — they give you the extra choice of using the guarantee procedure to settle your complaint. Having a guarantee doesn't affect or remove your legal rights against the seller — but the delay caused by taking up a complaint under the guarantee procedure may mean you lose your right to 'reject' the goods. And you might do better with your basic legal rights if the guarantee doesn't cover your complaint — or if you're expected to pay the labour or parts.

3 'You didn't complain within 30 days (or three months or six months'
Your legal rights last for six years from the date of purchase — so don't let people tell you otherwise. If you want to get all your money back, you must reject faulty goods very quickly. But even after it's too late for a full refund, you should still be entitled to a repair or compensation — so don't accept arbitrary time limits like this.

4 'The fault was yours — it was the way you used it'
If the school shoes you've bought your child fall apart after a few days' wear, don't be fobbed off by being told that they weren't made to play in. School shoes are meant to be played in unless you're told otherwise when you buy them (for example, if the shop assistant says they're only fashion shoes). The same principle also applies to other goods that you buy.

If you can't agree with a trader whether the goods were faulty or not, ask if he belongs to a trade association. This may offer a free conciliation service to try and settle the dispute — and even an independent testing procedure.

5 'It's not our policy to give refunds'
If you buy goods which aren't of merchantable quality, fit for their purpose, or what you were told they were, you're entitled to a refund if you act quickly. This applies even to goods in the sales, unless a defect was pointed out to you when you bought them (or the defect was so obvious that you should have noticed it). *Displaying a notice which says 'No refunds given' is an offence.* It should be reported to your nearest Trading Standards Department.

A step-by-step guide to complaining

1 Visit the shop
Go back to the shop or supplier who sold the product or service to you. *You should do this as soon as possible* — if you delay, you might lose some of your rights.

Save your complaint for the right person. A shop assistant doesn't usually have the power to deal with complaints or give refunds, so explain that you have a complaint and ask to speak to the manager. In some firms, an individual shop manager does not have authority to resolve a complaint by giving a refund and he may have to contact his head office. However, it's always best to start with the shop where you bought the goods. If you start by complaining to the head office, they will very often refer you to the shop.

When you visit the shop, take the faulty goods with you if this is possible. You should also take the bill or receipt for the goods or service, as this will usually prove that you bought them. But do not give a bill or receipt back to the seller until your complaint has been satisfactorily dealt with. You may need it later on if you decide to take further action against the seller — for example, if you decide to sue to recover your money. You don't have to have the receipt — but it's useful.

If you are unable to visit the shop, then telephone. Explain the problem. Try to get the name of the person you speak to. Follow this up with a letter if necessary. If you are asked to return the goods and the receipt, take a photocopy of the receipt and any letters (most libraries have machines) and send them by recorded delivery.

2 Write a letter

If the seller still refuses to do anything about your complaint, then write to the shop (again using recorded delivery) and send a copy of the letter to the firm's head office. Make the letter as short as possible and stick to the facts. A long letter full of righteous anger usually has little effect.

Your letter should contain

■ the *name and address* of the person or shop which sold the goods or service

■ the *date the goods were bought* or the date the service was supplied

■ the *model number or name* of the goods

■ the *receipt number* — never send the receipt, send a photocopy

■ a *description of your problem*. You do not have to use technical terms, just explain what happened

■ a *statement of your demands.*

If you have to reply to a letter from the firm or head office you should also give their reference, if a reference number, initial or name is given.

Always keep copies of your letters — you may need to refer to them later.

3 Ask for advice

If you are getting nowhere with your complaint, it is time to get help and advice. Ask your local Consumer Advice Centre, Trading Standards Department or Citizens' Advice Bureau to help. They will be able to give an opinion on the merits of your case. They might be able to suggest an argument or approach that you have not thought of and, if all else fails, they may be able to approach the shop or supplier on your behalf. It is always worth trying one of these agencies before consulting a solicitor. Their advice and help is free, whereas you will normally have to pay a solicitor.

4 Final steps

If your complaint has not been dealt with satisfactorily after getting help, there are still other things you can try.

The next stage

What can you do if you've gone back to the firm with your complaint and they've refused to do anything about it, or you're not satisfied with the offer they've made?

You've asked for advice from your local Citizens' Advice Bureau, Trading Standards Department or

Consumer Advice Centre to no avail, and you're still not satisfied. There are more possibilities. First, you can check whether the trader belongs to a trade association. Those who do normally display its symbol on their promotional literature and letterheads and at their premises. You can also enquire of the trade association direct.

Trade associations

If the firm you want to complain about belongs to a trade association, you should check whether that trade association has a Code of Practice. Codes of Practice are rules drawn up by some trade associations and other organisations for their members to follow. They aim to improve standards and provide customers with a better deal. They can mean that you have protection over and above that given by your normal legal rights. For example, they lay down proper procedures for dealing with complaints about goods or services. If the trade association in question has such a Code, send for a copy and see what it says about the handling of complaints.

Usually it will be suggested that if their member hasn't settled the complaint to your satisfaction, you can send it to their Customer Advisory Service. This Advisory Service will look into the matter and advise you what to do. This might be to have laboratory or independent tests if appropriate. Advice should be given free of charge.

Arbitration under a Code of Practice

As a last resort, most trade associations offer an independent arbitration service. You will usually have to pay for this, although you may well get your money back if the arbitrator rules in your favour. If he or she doesn't, you may have to pay the trader's fee, but you will never have to pay more than that. An advantage with using this kind of arbitration is that it is almost always decided on the evidence of documents only, so there's no need for you to appear in person. If you want to use this kind of arbitration, contact the trade association for a copy of the necessary form.

The arbitrator is usually one of a selected panel from the Chartered Institute of Arbitrators — and so has no connections with the company involved. Some of these schemes are quite frequently used — the holiday scheme operated by the Association of British Travel Agents (ABTA), for example — and others are hardly used at all. But because these schemes are set up under Codes of Practice, they can help to ensure that the trader agrees to arbitration, and that you get your money if you win — and so can offer an effective (and relatively cheap) way to settle disputes.

However, not every retailer or manufacturer belongs to a trade association. What else can you do if you are not satisfied with the way your complaint has been dealt with?

PROBLEMS WITH LANDLORDS

A specialised kind of service is that provided by someone who lets their property to you — your landlord. His services are not covered in the Supply of Goods and Services Act. They come under various landlord and tenant acts, in particular the Rent Act of 1977 and the Housing Act of 1961.

Repairs

Provided that you are what the Rent Act calls a regulated tenant, the landlord has to take responsibility for repairs and some decoration, according to what is laid down in the lease. You have to tell your landlord what needs repairing — this is best done in writing, sending the letter by recorded delivery and keeping a copy. If nothing gets done, you can ask for help from the local authority's environmental health inspector, who can serve an order on your landlord telling him what repairs he must do.

Eviction and harassment

Tenants of furnished or unfurnished houses or flats cannot be evicted by their landlord unless he can prove to a court that he has a legal right to get the accommodation back. If he tries to evict you illegally, get legal advice immediately, as illegal eviction is a criminal act. It is also a criminal offence for him to try and get you to move out by harassing you in some way calculated to interfere with your peace or comfort. This can be hard to prove, but if you think you can prove it, contact an advice centre which deals with housing problems or ask at the town hall for the tenancy relations (or harassment) officer.

Tell someone else

If you've reached this stage in your complaint, you are probably feeling quite angry and fed up. You might feel that you'd like to tell someone else about your problem and enlist their support and sympathy and maybe even get publicity for your cause. So who might be interested? This depends, of course, on what your problem is and how badly you've been affected by it. But the sorts of people you could consider contacting are

■ specialist consumer organisations including local consumer groups in your area

■ the press, either local or national

■ radio and television, either local or national.

Which of these you choose will depend on who you think will get you the best results. The most important thing is that when you contact them you give as clear and well-documented an account of your complaint as possible, with all the supporting evidence. Never send original documents. It is probably best if you're writing to send a short letter first, with a summary of your problem, which you can offer to supplement with evidence if possible. You could also join the *Which?* Personal Service, whose lawyers deal with over 8000 cases a year.

Let somebody else decide

If you still can't come to some agreement it's time to let somebody else decide on the rights and wrongs of your complaint. In almost all cases you'll have the option of going to court. But this can be expensive. The 'small claims' procedure in the County Court offers a cheap and relatively informal way of dealing with fairly straightforward cases. But at the moment (1988) it will only deal with claims up to £500 although recommendations have been published for the limit to increase to £1000. There is no 'small claims' procedure in Scotland yet. In Northern Ireland the limit is lower, and the courts have different names.

There may be another option open to you, too: having the case decided by an arbitrator, but not under a Code of Practice. This can offer a cheaper, and quicker, alternative to going to court. You still have the option of going to court after using a trade association conciliation service. Yet another alternative could be using an Ombudsman scheme.

USEFUL ORGANISATIONS

Trade associations

Trade associations which you might want to contact in connection with enquiries about goods and services you'd like to buy or have already bought for your home are

Aluminium Windows Association 102 Great Russell Street, London WC1B 3LA   Tel: 01-637-3572

Architects Registration Council 73 Hallam Street, London W1N 6EE Tel: 01-580-5861

Association of Manufacturers of Domestic Electrical Appliances (AMDEA), Leicester House, 8 Leicester Street, London WC2H 7BN Tel: 01-437-0678

Association of Master Upholsterers 564 North Circular Road, Neasden, London NW2 7QB   Tel: 01-205-0465, 01-452-4469

Association of Noise Consultants Spectrum House, 20-26 Cursitor Street, London EC4A 1HY   Tel: 01-405-2088

Bituminous Roofing Council P.O. Box 125, Haywards Heath, West Sussex RH16 3TJ   Tel: 0444-416681

Brick Development Association Woodside House, Winkfield, Windsor, Berks SL4 2DX   Tel: 0344-885651

British Association of Removers 277 Grays Inn Road, London WC1X 8SY   Tel: 01-837-3088/9

British Bathroom Council, Federation House, Station Road, Stoke-on-Trent, Staffs ST4 2RT   Tel: 0782-747123

British Board of Agrément P.O. Box 195, Bucknalls Lane, Garston, Watford, Herts WD2 7NG   Tel: 0923-670844

The Draught Proofing Advisory Association Ltd, The External Wall Insulation Association and **The National Cavity Insulation Association** are also at this address

British Chemical Dampcourse Association, 16a Whitchurch Road, Pangbourne, Reading, Berks RG8 7BP Tel: 07357-3799

British Decorators Association 6 Haywra Street, Harrogate, North Yorks HG1 5BL   Tel: 0423-67292

British Plastics Federation, 5 Belgrave Square, London SW1X 8PH   Tel: 01-235-9483   (incorporates British Plastic Windows Group)

British Wood Preserving Association 6 The Office Village, 4 Romford Road, Stratford, London E15 4EA   Tel: 01-519-2588

Builders Merchants Federation 15 Soho Square, London W1V 5FB Tel: 01-439-1753

Building Employers Confederation 82 New Cavendish Street, London W1M 8AD   Tel: 01-580-5588

Building Research Advisory Service DoE Building Research Establishment, Bucknalls Lane, Garston, Watford, Herts WD2 7JR   Tel: 0923-676612

Carpet Cleaners Association 126 New Walk, de Montfort Street, Leicester LE1 7JA   Tel: 0533-554352

Electrical Contractors' Association 34 Palace Court, London W2 4HY Tel: 01-229-1266

Electrical Contractors' Association of Scotland, 23 Heriot Row, Edinburgh EH3 6EW   Tel: 031-225-7221/3

Faculty of Architects and Surveyors 15 St Mary Street, Chippenham, Wilts SN15 3JN   Tel: 0249-655398

Federation of Building and Civil Engineering Contractors, 143 Malone Road, Belfast 9   Tel: 0232-245501

Federation of Master Builders 33 John Street, London WC1N 2BB Tel: 01-242-7583

Fencing Contractors' Association 23 St Johns Road, Watford, Herts WD1 1PY   Tel: 0923-227236

Flat Roofing Contractors' Advisory Board, Maxwelton House, Boltro Road, Haywards Heath, West Sussex RH16 1BJ   Tel: 0444-440027

Glass and Glazing Federation 44-48 Borough High Street, London SE1 1XB   Tel: 01-403-7177

Guaranteed Protection Trust Ltd P.O. Box 7727, London Road, High Wycombe, Bucks HP11 1BW Tel: 0494-447049

Heating and Ventilating Contractors Association, Esca House, 34 Palace Court, London W2 4HY Tel: 01-229-2488

Incorporated Association of Architects and Surveyors, Jubilee House, Billing Brook Road, Weston Favell, Northampton NN3 4NW Tel: 0604-404121

Institute of Plumbing
64 Station Lane, Hornchurch, Essex RM12 6NB Tel: 04024-72791

Law Society, 113 Chancery Lane, London WC2 AIPL Tel: 01-242-1222

Law Society of Scotland
26 Drumsleigh Gardens, Edinburgh EH3 7YR Tel: 031-226-7411

Metal Roofing Contractors Association, 55 Waverley Road, Sale, Cheshire M33 1AY Tel: 061-973-8398

National Association of Plumbing, Heating and Mechanical Services Contractors, 6 Gate Street, London WC2A 3NX Tel: 01-405-2678

National Association of Retail Furnishers, 17-21 George Street, Croydon, Surrey CR9 1TQ Tel: 01-680-8444

National Bedding Federation
251 Brompton Road, London SW3 2EZ Tel: 01-589-4888

National Federation of Roofing Contractors, 24 Weymouth Street, London W1N 3FA Tel: 01-436-0387

National Fireplace Council
P.O. Box 35 (Stoke), Stoke-on-Trent, Staffs ST4 7NU Tel: 0782-744311

The Wood and Solid Fuel Association of Retailers and Manufacturers, The National Association of Chimney Sweeps and **The National Association of Chimney Lining Engineers** are also at this address

National House Building Council
Head Office, 58 Portland Place, London W1N 4BU Tel: 01-637-1248

National House Building Council
Bedford House, Bedford Street, Belfast 2 Tel: 0323-245501

National Inspection Council for Electrical Installation Contracting
Vintage House, 36-37 Albert Embankment, London SE1 7UJ Tel: 01-582-7746

Radio, Electrical and Television Retailers' Association, RETRA House, 57-61 Newington Causeway, London SE1 6BE Tel: 01-403-1463

Royal Incorporation of Architects in Scotland, 15 Rutland Square, Edinburgh EH1 2BE Tel: 031-229-7205

Royal Institute of British Architects
66 Portland Place, London W1N 4AD Tel: 01-580-5533

Royal Institution of Chartered Surveyors, 12 Great George Street, Parliament Square, London SW1P 3AD Tel: 01-222-7000

Royal Society of Ulster Architects
2 Mount Charles, Belfast BT7 1NZ Tel: 0232-323760

Scottish Decorators Association
249 West George Street, Glasgow G2 4RB Tel: 041-221-7090

Scottish House Furnishers' Association, 1 Royal Exchange Court, Glasgow G1 3DR Tel: 041-248-2824

Scottish and Northern Ireland Plumbing Employers' Federation
2 Walker Street, Edinburgh EH3 7LP Tel: 031-225-2255

Society of Architects in Wales
75a Llandennis Road, Cardiff CF2 6EE Tel: 0222-762215

Solicitors' Complaints Bureau
Portland House, Stag Place, London SW1E 5BL Tel: 01-834-2288

Thermal Insulation Contractors' Association, Kensway House, 388 High Road, Ilford, Essex IGI ITL Tel: 01-514-2120

Timber Research and Development Association, Hughenden Valley, High Wycombe, Bucks HP14 4ND Tel: 024024-2771

Trade associations whose members are concerned with insurance and financial matters are

Association of British Insurers
Aldermary House, 10-15 Queen Street, London EC4N 1TT Tel: 01-248-4477

British Insurance Brokers' Association, Biba House, 14 Bevis Marks, London EC3A 7NT Tel: 01-623-9043

Building Societies Association
3 Savile Row, London W1X 1AF Tel: 01-437-0655

Corporation of Insurance and Financial Advisors, 6-7 Leapale Road, Guildford, Surrey GU1 4JX Tel: 0483-35786/39121

Finance Houses' Association
18 Upper Grosvenor Street, London W1X 9PB Tel: 01-491-2783

Industrial Assurance Commission
15-17 Great Marlborough Street, London W1V 2AX Tel: 01-437-9992

Lloyds Advisory Department
Lloyds, 1 Lime Street, London EC3M 7DQ Tel: 01-623-7100

National Bank Users' Association
39 Rooks Lane, Thame, Oxon OX9 2EA Tel: 084-421-6986

Ombudsmen

If you want to contact one of the Ombudsmen, here are their addresses

Building Societies Ombudsman
Grosvenor Gardens House, 35-37 Grosvenor Gardens, London SW1X 7AW Tel: 01-931-0044

Insurance Ombudsman Bureau
31 Southampton Row, London WC1B 5HJ Tel: 01-242-8613

The Local Ombudsman England
21 Queen Anne's Gate, London SW1H 9BU Tel: 01-222-5622

The Local Ombudsman Wales
Derwen House Court Road, Bridgend, Mid-Glamorgan CF31 1BN   Tel: 0656-61325

The Local Ombudsman Scotland
5 Shandwick Place, Edinburgh EH2 4RG   Tel: 031-229-4472

The Local Ombudsman Northern Ireland, Progressive House, 33 Wellington Place, Belfast BT1 6HN   Tel: 0232-233821

N.B. You may only submit a complaint to your local Ombudsman by getting your local councillor to countersign it or submit it on your behalf

Office of the Banking Ombudsman
Citadel House, 5-11 Fetter Lane, London EC4A 1BR   Tel: 01-583-1395

Housing and consumer affairs

Other useful bodies to do with housing and consumer affairs are

The Advertising Standards Authority
Brook House, Torrington Place, London WC1E 7HN   Tel: 01-580-0801

British Standards Institution
2 Park Street, London W1A 2BS   Tel: 01-629-9000

Consumers' Association
2 Marylebone Road, London NW1 4DX   Tel: 01-486-5544

General Consumer Council for Northern Ireland, Elizabeth House, 116 Holywood Road, Belfast BAT4 1NY   Tel: 0232-672488

Housing Advice Centre, 1 May Street, Belfast 1   Tel: 0232-240588

Housing Corporation, 149 Tottenham Court Road, London W1P OBN   Tel: 01-387-9466

Money Advice Association
c/o National Consumer Council, 20 Grosvenor Gardens, London SW1W 0DH   Tel: 01-730-3469

Money Advice Centre, Birmingham Settlement, 318 Summer Lane, Birmingham B19 3RL

Money Management Council
18 Doughty Street, London WC1N 2PL   Tel: 01-405-1985

National Consumer Council
20 Grosvenor Gardens, London SW1W 0DH   Tel: 01-730-3469

National Federation of Consumer Groups (NFCG), 12 Mosley Street, Newcastle-upon-Tyne NE1 1DE   Tel: 091-261-8259

National Federation of Housing Associations, 175 Grays Inn Road, London WC1X 8UP   Tel: 01-278-6571

Northern Ireland Housing Executive Property: refer first to your local district office — see telephone book — and second to the regional office — Belfast Regional Office, 2 Adelaide Street, Belfast BT2 8PB   Tel: 0232-240588   There are also regional offices for the North East, North West, South East, South and West

Office of Fair Trading, Field House, 15-25 Bream's Buildings, London EC4A 1PR   Tel: 01-242-2858

Scottish Federation of Housing Associations, 40 Castle Street North, Edinburgh EH2 3BN   Tel: 031-226-6777 and 180 West Regent Street, Glasgow G1 4RW   Tel: 041-221-8113

INDEX